What is Critical Environmental Justice?

Dedication

To Sun-Hee and Jin-Young – thank you for giving me hope
and sharing your love

To Y.I.M.J.R.S.I. – thank you for guiding and connecting
all of us

What is Critical Environmental Justice?

David Naguib Pellow

polity

First published in 2018 by Polity Press

Polity Press
65 Bridge Street
Cambridge CB2 1UR, UK

Polity Press
101 Station Landing, Suite 300
Medford, MA 02155, USA

ISBN-13: 978-0-7456-7937-2
ISBN-13: 978-0-7456-7938-9 (pb)

A catalogue record for this book is available from the British Library.

Typeset in 11/13 Sabon by
Servis Filmsetting Limited, Stockport, Cheshire
Printed and bound in the UK by Clays Ltd, St Ives PLC

The publisher has used its best endeavours to ensure that the URLs for external websites referred to in this book are correct and active at the time of going to press. However, the publisher has no responsibility for the websites and can make no guarantee that a site will remain live or that the content is or will remain appropriate.

Every effort has been made to trace all copyright holders, but if any have been inadvertently overlooked the publisher will be pleased to include any necessary credits in any subsequent reprint or edition.

For further information on Polity, visit our website: www.politybooks.com

Contents

Acknowledgments

As much as I would like to take full credit for this project, it turns out that researching, writing, and publishing a book is always a collective effort. I am indebted to a great number of people for sharing their ideas, criticisms, guidance, and labors to make this work possible. Students who provided me with critical assistance along the way include: Marjan Abubo, Mark Avalos, Reid Bongard, Martha Escobar, Sheila Estrada, Denise Garcia, Erin Hoekstra, Sanna King, Rebecca Kinney, Annie Milburn, Ivan Rodriguez, Alison Thompson, Ashkaun Shaterian, Yue (Rachel) Shen, and Amy Tam.

I want to thank my colleagues, students, and friends at UCSB who have warmly welcomed me into the Santa Barbara community with open arms and so much support. They include: Peter Alagona, Celia Alario, Javiera Barandiaran, Vilna Bashi-Treitler, Joe Blankholm, Eileen Boris, Angela Boyd, Oliver Chadwick, Alenda Chang, Grace Chang, Maria Charles, Jia-Ching Chen, Jordan Clark, Mariah Brennan Clegg, David Cleveland, Carla D'Antonio, Mona Damluji, Hilal Elver, Richard Falk (who gave me really helpful feedback on chapter 4), Ingrid Feeney, Richard Flacks, John Foran, Diane Fujino, Helene Gardner, Hunter Gelbach, Avery Gordon, Corrie Grosse, Hahrie Han, Robert Heilmayr, Cami Helmuth, Ken Hiltner, Cheryl Hutton, Melody Jue, Terence Keel, Ed Keller, Zachary King, Renan LaRue, Theo LeQuesne, Mel Manalis, Matto Mildenberger, Dena Montague, Erinn O'Shea, Michelle Oyewole, Sameer Pandya,

Acknowledgments

Tristan Partridge, Simone Pulver, Martin Rodriguez, Josh Schimel, Daniela Soleri, Jeffrey Stewart, Leah Stokes, Susan Stonich, Ra Thea, Jennifer Tyburczy, Richard Widick, Bob Wilkinson, Emily Williams, and Eric Zimmerman.

A big thanks to friends and colleagues at the University of Minnesota (Cawo Abdi, Ron Aminzade, Liz Boyle, Bruce Braun, Vinay Gidwani, Michael Goldman, Teresa Gowan, George Henderson, and Rachel Schurman), the University of California at Davis (Thomas Beamish, Vicky Smith, Julie Sze, Jonathan London, Lindsey Dillon, Jacque Leaver, and Ingrid Behrsin), Vanderbilt University (David Hess, Zdravka Tzankova, Holly McCammon, André Christie-Mizell, Rachel McKane, Anna Jacobs, Magdalena Sudibjo, Lacee Satcher, Larry Isaac, Kate Pride Brown, Lijun Song, and Anne Wall), and the University of Michigan (Dorceta Taylor, Rebecca Hardin, Sonia Joshi, Ivette Perfecto, and Paul Mohai) for offering space to share and receive feedback on many of the ideas contained in this volume.

Colleagues spread far and wide across the country who were also instrumental in this effort include Hollie Nyseth-Brehm, Joni Adamson, Kari Norgaard, Shannon Bell, Julian Agyeman, Traci Brynne Voyles, Laura Pulido, Sylvia Hood Washington, Beth Schaefer Caniglia, Manuel Vallee, Beatrice Frank, Brian Mayer, J. Timmons Roberts, David Takeuchi, Sara Bruya, Yonette Thomas, Samantha Teixeira, Mia White, Anthony Nocella II, Ryan Holifield, Panagioti Tsolkas, and Mike Ewall.

And at Polity Press, my editor Jonathan Skerrett and Editorial Assistant Amy Williams have been wonderful partners throughout this process, and I am grateful to the extraordinary anonymous reviewers of the manuscript, and Ann Klefstad for her outstanding copy editing. I also have to extend a big thank you to Emma Longstaff who, while at Polity some years back, extended a generous invitation to me and came up with the initial idea that eventually resulted in this book.

1

Critical Environmental Justice Studies

Michael Brown was an African-American teenager living in Ferguson, Missouri. On August 9, 2014, police officer Darren Wilson shot and killed him, sparking worldwide outrage at the seemingly unending series of police shootings of African-Americans. When protesters took to the streets of cities around the US and the world to declare that "Black Lives Matter," they and those who were the targets of police shootings were frequently referred to as "animals." Juana Gutiérrez is the daughter of a Mexican farmer; she immigrated to the US at age fifteen. She started an organization called Mothers of East Los Angeles (MELA), which has fought to keep prisons from being built in her city and around the state of California. Nicholas Morrissey was an inmate at a state prison in LaBelle, Pennsylvania, who suffered from a chronic illness he believes was caused by the fact that the prison is next to a coal ash dump. Foad al-Amodi is president of the fishermen's syndicate in Khan Younis, a town in the Palestinian Occupied Territories. His livelihood is threatened because the fish that he and his customers depend upon are dying from exposure to the massive volume of sewage that flows into the Mediterranean Sea – a result of the Israeli blockade of the Gaza Strip, which has prevented the purchase of much-needed equipment to upgrade Gaza's waste management system. Havah Ha-Levi was a Jewish Israeli woman who lived in a kibbutz near an old Palestinian Arab village, Sarkas, which was destroyed and converted into a garbage dump. In her memoir she writes, "Yet I remember. I testify." State-sanctioned police killings of black people. Prisons and jails. The Israel/Palestine conflict. Each of these cases reveals how human suffering and social inequality also are sites where that pain is intimately linked to the harm visited upon fragile ecosystems and other animals. And each of these cases speaks to the ways that ordinary people and, in some cases nonhumans, have worked for environmental and social justice.

Human societies have always been deeply interconnected with our nonhuman relations and with ecosystems, but today those relationships are witnessing greater frictions, tensions, and harms than ever before, prompting scholars to label this epoch the *Anthropocene* because of the dominance of the human species on planet Earth. And while that dominance has led to incalculable damage to ecosystems and to human societies as well, the opportunities for addressing these problems and challenges are within our grasp, if we only dare to break out of conventional modes of thinking and action. The harms suffered by ecosystems today are closely linked to and mirror the harms experienced by the most marginalized human beings across the planet – what many scholars call the problem of *environmental injustice*. For example, where we find rivers dammed for hydropower plants we also tend to find indigenous peoples and fisherfolk, as well as other working people, whose livelihoods and health are harmed as a result; when sea life suffers from exposure to toxins such as mercury, we find that human beings also endure the effects of mercury when they consume those animals; and the intersecting character of multiple forms of inequality is revealed when nuclear radiation or climate change affects all species and humans across all social class levels, racial/ethnic groups, genders, abilities, and ages. The power (or agency) of the more-than-human world is on display here as well when, for example, nuclear radiation or extreme climate patterns are triggered by human actions and then, in turn, exert their own force on various bodies, spaces, and ecosystems. The agency of human beings is evident when people imagine and work to bring about a different set of relationships with each other and with the more-than-human world through art, protest, music, research, planning, and other forms of action.

2

Environmental justice struggles reveal how power flows through the multi-species relationships that make up life on Earth, often resulting in violence and marginalization for the many and environmental privileges for the few. But environmental justice struggles are also evident – *if* we are paying close attention – within spaces of conflict and collaboration that are not always typically defined as "environmental." Consider, for example, the roles that land, air, water, and nonhuman species play in the Black Lives Matter movement, in the construction and maintenance of the US prison industrial complex, and in religious and ethnic conflicts in Israel and Palestine. I draw on each of these examples in this book to explore the future of environmental justice research and politics. One path toward this future is made clearer through what I call Critical Environmental Justice Studies.

In our book *Power, Justice, and the Environment*,[1] Robert Brulle and I used the term "Critical Environmental Justice Studies" to call for scholarship that builds on research in Environmental Justice (EJ) Studies by questioning assumptions and gaps in earlier work in the field, by embracing greater interdisciplinarity, and moving toward methodologies and epistemologies including and beyond the social sciences. A number of other scholars have adopted this term as well, as they work to expand the academic field and politics of environmental justice.[2] In the rest of this chapter I offer an overview of some key ideas and advances from the field of EJ studies and introduce the concept of Critical EJ Studies as a way of pushing the ideas and potential of earlier generations of EJ studies into new and productive directions. I view Critical EJ Studies not as an alternative to earlier-generation EJ studies, but as an extension of that foundational scholarship.

Environmental Justice Studies: An Overview of the Field

Why Critical Environmental Justice Studies? In order to answer that question, I must first offer an overview of the field of Environmental Justice Studies. But before one considers the scholarly research on the topic of environmental justice (EJ), we must begin with the EJ movement. The US EJ movement gained visibility and strength beginning in the late 1970s and early 1980s, as activists and movement networks confronted a range of toxic hazards that were disproportionately located in communities of color (while the closely related Anti-Toxics movement was concentrated primarily in white working-class neighborhoods). This movement fused discourses of public health, civil and human rights, anti-racism, social justice, and ecological sustainability with tactics such as civil disobedience, public protests, and legal action to prevent the construction or expansion of unwanted and controversial facilities and developments such as landfills, incinerators, mines, and chemical plants. Activists also demanded that owners of existing facilities improve their operational safety, reduce pollution levels, and provide economic benefits to and offer power sharing with local residents or face the threat of being shut down. This movement sought to openly integrate campaigns for justice on behalf of vulnerable human beings with the goal of ecological sustainability.[3] From the movement's early days, activists sought environmental justice not only through shutting down polluting facilities, but also by demanding and creating access to parks and green space and affordable, healthy foods,[4] safe neighborhoods, and for climate-related policies and practices that are socially just and ecologically sustainable.[5] Thus even during its earliest days, the EJ movement articulated a transformative vision of what an environmentally and socially just and sustainable future might look like, at the local, regional, national, and global scales. For example, during the historic Environmental Justice Summit conference in 1991, participants drafted what became known as the Principles of Environmental Justice, which not only embrace a synthesis of anti-racism and ecological sustainability but also support anti-militarist, anti-imperialist, gender-justice politics. The Principles also recognize the inherent and cultural worth of nonhuman natures.[6]

The EJ movement is largely comprised of people from communities of color, indigenous communities, and working-class communities who are focused on combating environmental injustice, racism, and gender and class inequalities that are most visibly manifested in the disproportionate burden of environmental harm facing these populations. For the EJ movement, the battle for global sustainability cannot be won without addressing the ecological violence imposed on vulnerable human populations; thus social justice (that is, justice for humans) is inseparable from environmental protection.

What Is Environmental Justice?

EJ Studies scholar Robert Bullard defines environmental justice as the principle that "all people and communities are entitled to equal protection of environmental and public health laws and regulations."[7] The US Environmental Protection Agency (USEPA) definition further elaborates on this principle by defining environmental justice as:

> The fair treatment and meaningful involvement of all people regardless of race, color, national origin, or income with respect to the development, implementation, and enforcement of environmental laws, regulations, and policies. Fair treatment means that no population, due to policy or economic disempowerment, is forced to bear a disproportionate share of the negative human health or environmental impacts of pollution or environmental consequences resulting from industrial, municipal, and commercial operations or the execution of federal, state, local and tribal programs and policies.[8]

While environmental justice is a vision of a possible future, environmental inequality (or environmental *in*justice) generally refers to a situation in which a particular social group is disproportionately affected by environmental hazards.[9] One specific form of environmental inequality is the phenomenon of environmental racism, which Benjamin Chavis first defined this way:

> Environmental racism is racial discrimination in environmental policymaking, the enforcement of regulations and laws, the deliberate targeting of communities of color for toxic waste facilities, the official sanctioning of the life-threatening presence of poisons and pollutants

in our communities, and the history of excluding people of color from leadership of the ecology movements.[10]

Thus environmental racism "refers to any policy, practice, or directive that differentially affects or disadvantages (whether intended or unintended) individuals, groups, or communities based on race or color."[11] The scholarship and social movement focused on environmental racism and inequality sought to develop a vision of its opposite – environmental justice – which often involved a call for new legislation and the fair application of existing laws. In this chapter and throughout the book, I consider both the promise and limitations of such an approach, which seeks a path to justice through the state.

What is Environmental Justice (EJ) Studies?

The field of EJ Studies has moved us toward a clear understanding that, where we find social inequalities by race and class, we tend to also find environmental inequalities in the form of marginalized groups being exposed to greater levels of pollution, toxics, "natural" disasters and the effects of climate change/disruption, as well as their exclusion from policymaking bodies that influence those outcomes.[12] Researchers have also refined and improved our ability to measure the details and granularity of spatial environmental inequalities by race, class, and space.[13] For example, in the study *Toxic Wastes and Race at Twenty*, the authors offered new evidence that *clustering* of environmental hazards – rather than just single sources of pollution – is a significant and measurable threat to communities of color.[14] In that report, the authors also challenged the "minority move-in hypothesis," which was the claim that people of color move into polluted neighborhoods rather than being targeted by polluters. To the contrary, the authors found that polluting facilities actually single out communities of color more often than not, moving into neighborhoods with high percentages of minority residents. This disturbing finding has extraordinary sociological and policy implications and was a major development in the field of EJ Studies, since up to that point there was a lively debate on this topic.

A small but growing group of researchers – including and especially environmental humanities and ecofeminist scholars – have focused on the ways that gender, sexuality, citizenship, indigeneity, and nation shape the terrain of ecological inequalities, but those areas of scholarship remain in need of further development.[15] Though EJ Studies has traditionally focused on race (and, to a lesser extent, class), scholars have explored other intersections of inequality and the environment in recent years. For example, gender and sexuality are categories receiving more attention for a number of reasons. Women are often physically and socially relegated to some of the most toxic residential and occupational spaces in communities and workplaces[16] and several studies document the ways that women experience and resist discriminatory environmental policies in workplaces, residential communities, and other gendered spaces.[17] Ironically, women activists in the EJ movement are less politically visible because they tend to work for smaller, community-based organizations that rarely make headlines and survive on volunteer labor and small grants, despite the fact that women form the overwhelming majority of the movement's leadership.[18] Moreover, scholarship in gender, feminist, and queer studies reminds us of the importance of a focus on the human body, which opens up numerous possibilities for EJ Studies to expand. For example, as Stein writes, "When . . . we view our bodies as 'homes,' 'lands,' or 'environments' that have been placed at risk, stolen from us, and even killed due to social or physical harms that may be exacerbated due to our gender and sexuality – we may understand the need for new perspectives on environmental justices that encompass such factors within our analysis."[19] The sexuality and reproductive capacities of women of color, immigrant women, and Indigenous women have long been the targets of state authorities, with varied and troubling consequences for human health, cultural integrity, and ecological resilience. Examples include: the justification for the conquest of the Americas was largely shaped by a contempt by European settlers and religious leaders for diverse sexualities and sexual practices among Indigenous peoples in the Western Hemisphere;[20] the enslavement of Africans and the legal construction of enslaved women as breeders whose children would also be chattel property whose primary value was labor that facilitated control over land and livestock; and historical and ongoing debates over "pro-environmental" policies such as population control, which directly target the reproductive capacities of women of color and have resulted in forced sterilization, among other devastating practices, thus emphasizing the fertility of global south women rather than prioritizing the overconsumption of resources by global north populations. By offering analyses of how discourses of "nature" have been deployed to enforce heteronormativity, regulate sexuality, and criminalize and marginalize persons deemed sexually transgressive, scholars have reframed "environmental studies" concerns to include an understanding of the ways that diverse sexual identities, expressions, and practices have been defined as "unnatural," thus allowing for creative ways of linking EJ Studies to gender, feminist, sexuality, and queer studies. If sexuality has been a target of oppression and environmental exploitation, it has also been used historically as a site of resistance, as persons of varied sexualities engage gender and sexuality through means that challenge the colonization of their peoples, cultures, and lands, and that confront enslavement, genocide, and heterosexism.[21] Lastly, the very material landscapes being polluted and fought over in EJ struggles are deeply imbued with meanings that are gendered, sexualized, and expressed as such in local and global imaginaries, state policies, corporate practices, and activist resistance campaigns.[22]

EJ research on the ways that immigrant communities are affected by – and respond to – environmental and climate change threats is another important area of scholarship in the field, which is now receiving more attention.[23] More recently, important work by scholars studying food justice movements reveals that, as a result of a complex matrix of policy mechanisms that tend to subsidize and support the industrial agricultural system, working-class communities and communities of color are often sites of hunger and malnutrition as a result of the dominance and control of food systems by a small group of large corporations focused on making profit rather than feeding communities.[24] Moreover, those corporations tend to produce food using large quantities of toxic herbicides, pesticides, and fossil fuels that imperil consumers, fenceline communities, ecosystems, and the climate. Thus the literature on climate justice and food justice is an integral component of EJ Studies.

The relatively recent development of EJ Studies should not be accepted as evidence that the phenomenon of environmental inequality is new. As a number of scholars demonstrate, a core component of European colonization was the production of many environmental injustices, as people and land were exploited for the benefit of colonizers in earlier eras.[25] Historians and historical social scientists have explored what one might call the "long Environmental Justice movement" – those indicators that the scourge of environmental inequality and struggles against it have been in evidence long before the oft-cited beginnings of the EJ movement in the 1980s.[26] While environmental injustice reaches back centuries, however, the recent intensification of global industrial and technological production, combined with heightened human migration patterns within and across national borders, extends this phenomenon into the present and amplifies its consequences globally. That fact, along with the growth of social justice movements among marginalized peoples, influenced the development of EJ Studies and the EJ movement. In possession of this new lens for viewing environmental injustices, grassroots activists and scholars have worked to document, study, and combat the roots of the problem. Like the EJ movement, EJ Studies has spread well beyond the borders of the US to places as diverse as Australia, Canada, Latin America, Europe, the United Kingdom, India, West Africa, South Africa, and the former Soviet Union.[27]

Recent scholarship divides EJ Studies into two phases: the "first generation," which was focused primarily on documenting the existence of environmental inequality through the lens of race and class; and "second generation" studies that extend beyond questions of distribution to incorporate a deeper consideration of theory and the ways that gender, sexuality, and other categories of difference shape EJ struggles.[28] The aim of this framing is to

push the field toward a greater embrace of methodologically creative and interdisciplinary approaches to EJ Studies. I agree with
much of that principle, but I find this framing misleading. That is,
while it describes the majority of social scientific articles published
during the early years – which were based on quantitative, positiv-
ist models that sought to measure environmental inequality – this
perspective overlooks a wealth of highly visible and important
books, edited collections, and qualitative studies published in
academic and non-academic presses and journals that offer a very
different perspective on EJ Studies. For example, during the so-
called first generation of EJ Studies, some scholars were actually
engaged in exploring the gendered dimensions of EJ conflicts,[29]
extending beyond the question of whether race versus class was
the primary driver of unequal risk distribution and asking what
the health and psychological impacts of environmental inequalities
might be in residential communities and workplaces.[30] Significant
"first generation" scholarship involved excavating the historical,
social, and political forces that produce environmental injustices
in the first place.[31] During that "first generation" period, scholars were also exploring: the complexities and contradictions of
claims-making around environmental racism/injustice in cases
where communities of color and indigenous communities declared
the right to welcome hazardous and toxic industries and wastes
in the name of environmental justice and sorely needed economic
development;[32] the historical process of social identity construction and the intersections of race, class, and gender as they relate
to environmental injustice;[33] and EJ struggles across a variety of
social spaces, including the workplace.[34]

Thus the field of EJ Studies has always been marked by a great
diversity of scholarly approaches. Having registered the above
qualifications, it would be generally accurate to say that the
second generation emphasizes a wider variety of methodological
approaches and interdisciplinarity, the extension of scholarship
into areas of greater theoretical breadth, and the expansion of
social categories under consideration, particularly a stronger attention to gender, sexuality, and, increasingly, nonhuman natures.
Scholars also are envisioning and grappling with questions of

justice and sustainability at greater depth.[35] This book is written in this spirit, building on the important work of these earlier generations of EJ scholarship.

How do we define justice?

Recent scholarship has struggled with the various ways to theorize the meaning of justice, and how this can include justice defined as distribution, inclusion, participation, recognition, fairness/procedure, and capabilities,[36] thus raising complex questions about how the scholarship and the movement have imagined both the problem and solution. Some years earlier, sociologist Stella Čapek laid the groundwork for these ideas when she introduced the "environmental justice frame,"[37] which is a lens for constructing meaning among EJ activists. Capek's EJ frame consists of six key claims, including the right to accurate information from authorities concerning environmental risks; public hearings; democratic participation in decisionmaking regarding the future of any threatened community; compensation for injured parties from those who inflict harm on them; expressions of solidarity with survivors of environmental injustices; and a call to abolish environmental racism/injustice. Environmental injustice was not just about the threats associated with disproportionate hazards facing marginalized communities, under this framing; it was about ordinary people demanding respect for their grassroots definition of the situation, while gaining access to democratic processes and exercising power. That is, EJ was ultimately focused on reordering power relations among stakeholders. These arguments were later explored by David Schlosberg and others, who concluded that much of the EJ literature's focus on justice was limited: scholars and activists tended to focus on distributional outcomes of environmental inequality when they should also emphasize the power structures and social systems that give rise to environmental inequalities to begin with.[38] When activists and scholars first issued demands for EJ, much of the movement activism and scholarship focused on *distributive* justice. In other words, they focused on issues of equity regarding the distribution of environmental harm and risk. Recent scholarship has called for a move beyond the "distributive paradigm" because it seemingly fails to challenge the underlying power structures that facilitate environmental injustice.[39] Some of these scholars have also argued for expanding EJ to include a focus on *procedural justice*.[40] Arising from the idea of participatory democracy, procedural justice shifts the lens from distributive outcomes to decisionmaking processes and the importance of recognition of excluded and/or aggrieved groups. That is, proponents of procedural justice maintain that a focus on mere distribution is incomplete; they argue for a closer examination of group recognition – those political and cultural practices involving the acknowledgement and inclusion of marginalized groups and their unique experiences with oppression. These issues have particular salience in communities of color and Indigenous communities globally, where dominant state forces and elites have denied residents the opportunity to participate in decisions regarding environmental impacts that shape their lives.

David Schlosberg points out that "recognition" efforts can but do not always include the state.[41] However, much of the literature on theories of justice – whether distributive, procedural, or recognitional – *does* center on the state. That is problematic because the state is one of the primary forces contributing to environmental injustice and related institutionalized violence. That is, these ideas of justice are important in principle, but *in practice*, they have often meant the inclusion and recognition of EJ community leaders by the state, followed by co-optation and siphoning of grassroots energy away from other key goals, and ultimately achieving relatively little by way of policy changes. Consider, for example, how poorly the enforcement of environmental laws in communities of color has proceeded via the President's Executive Order 12898 on Environmental Justice, and how poorly communities of color have fared in seeking environmental justice through the courts and the legal system, years after these communities and the issue of environmental racism enjoyed state "recognition" at the highest levels in the US.[42] "Justice" as defined above is primarily a quest for inclusion in the political process under the assumption or hope that such a move will be more likely to lead to substantive changes in that system. Political theorist Iris Marion Young refers to this tension as the disagreement between "deliberative democrats" who seek to work inside the system and "activists" who seek to pressure the system from the outside. Critics (myself included) have argued that the dream of deliberative democracy is made difficult by the realities of structural inequality that shape and limit ordinary people's access to the deliberative table, as well as the terms of debate and questions considered for discussion, and ultimately reinforce existing institutional arrangements.[43] Iris Young writes that "advocates of deliberative democracy who believe that deliberative processes are the best way to conduct policies even under the conditions of structural inequality that characterize democracies today have no satisfactory response to this criticism."[44] Going further than the "insider" versus "outsider" orientation – because both are really little more than different approaches that ultimately focus on making change via the state – few political theorists working on this issue seem to have considered the possibility that some people and communities might *not* want to be included in a political process that has meted out so much punishment and brutality to their groups. That is, if we take a different approach to social change we might find that many communities seek to walk *away from* the state rather than *toward* it.[45] In other words, why can't we imagine that some communities want to be left alone and enjoy their autonomy as a means to social change?

Lisa Cacho writes that justice via inclusion of people of color and undocumented persons in a white supremacist state like the US is a seriously flawed goal, given the deep historical and ongoing exclusions of these populations and their association with criminality:

> As criminal by being, unlawful by presence, and illegal by status, they do not have the option to be law abiding, which is always the absolute prerequisite for political rights, legal recognition, and resource distribution in the United States. When subjugation is engendered, justified, and maintained by the law, legal recognition cannot be a permanent or meaningful solution to subjugation.[46]

While I agree that justice via procedural inclusion and recognition *can* be important to the future of the EJ movement and to any community's efforts to create change, the reality is that it is often a step toward a more ⌈sophisticated ⌋effort at differential inclusion,[47] co-optation, displacement of movement goals, diffusion of grassroots energy, assimilation, and a strengthening of existing power relations. The push for this limited brand of justice within EJ Studies and the EJ movement reflects a longstanding tendency that seeks to take a pragmatic approach to social change, but I believe we must take bolder steps. Critical EJ Studies offers one such approach.

Toward Critical Environmental Justice Studies

Critical EJ Studies is a perspective intended to address a number of important limitations and tensions within earlier generations of EJ Studies. These include, for example,

1. Questions concerning the degree to which scholars should place emphasis on one or more social categories of difference (e.g., race, class, gender, sexuality, species, etc.) versus a focus on multiple forms of inequality;
2. The extent to which scholars studying EJ issues should focus on single-scale versus multiscalar analyses of the causes, consequences, and possible resolutions of EJ struggles;
3. The degree to which various forms of social inequality and power – especially state power – are viewed as entrenched and embedded in society, elements that must be confronted rather than embraced;
4. The largely unexamined question of the *expendability* of human and nonhuman populations facing socioecological threats from states, industries, and other political economic forces.

On the first point, EJ scholars have a tendency to focus on only one or two forms of social inequality in studies of environmental injustice. For example, some scholars continue to debate the relative importance of race versus class as drivers of the unequal distribution of environmental hazards,[48] while only a small group of scholars have explored the role of gender and sexuality in EJ Studies. Moreover, the key social category *species* remains, at best, at the margins of the field of EJ Studies, despite the fact that, generally, when and where humans suffer from environmental inequalities, so does the more-than-human world (and vice versa), often as a result of ideological frameworks that devalue and associate marginalized humans with "nature." A small number of researchers are grappling with these ideas, primarily in the fields of ecofeminism and Critical Animal Studies.[49] My point is that since multiple forms of inequality drive and characterize the experience of environmental injustice, the field would do well to expand in that direction.

With respect to the second point, concerning *scale*, the EJ Studies literature tends to be characterized by research at one scale or another, rather than taking a multiscalar approach. Aside from important work by political ecologists and geographers,[50] few studies attempt to grasp how EJ struggles function at multiple scales, from the cellular and bodily level to the global level and back.[51] CEJ seeks to promote a more consistent attention to multiscalar research. Some scholars have addressed this important question by exploring cases in which pollutants produced in one part of the world travel across national borders and affect human and ecological health in another hemisphere.[52] For example, German sociologist Ulrich Beck's concept of the "risk society" underscores that, in the contemporary age, the scale and impacts of technological threats to human and ecological well-being have expanded enormously, rendering our capacity to understand, measure, and respond to them much less effective.[53] The enormity of what some scholars have called "wicked problems" (such as climate change and nuclear radiation) leaves us at a loss, and prompts many of us to withdraw and engage in denial.[54] Scale is of critical importance because it allows us to understand how environmental injustices are facilitated by decisionmakers who, for example, behave as if sites where hazards are produced "out of sight and out of mind" are somehow irrelevant to the health

15

of people and ecosystems at the original sites of decisionmaking power and consumption, when they clearly affect both spaces. For example, the deforestation of much of Indonesia to supply timber for Japan reduces carbon sinks and air quality for the entire region and world. When US-based companies dump toxic electronic wastes in China, this produces chemical poisons in the air and water in China that ultimately cycle through ecosystems and affect US residents. As Peter Newell argues, "injustices enabled through processes of globalization are rendered invisible through distance."[55]

Attention to scale also assists us in observing how social movement *responses* to environmental injustices draw on spatial frameworks, networks, and knowledge to make the connections between hazards in one place and harm in another. Scholars have demonstrated that the environmental justice and climate justice movements are examples of networks of activists from local communities who collaborate with partners at transnational and global scales, launching campaigns directed at multinational corporations and participating in United Nations–sponsored gatherings to implement a stronger global climate treaty.[56] This is essential for understanding and addressing environmental injustice: it functions at all scales in both its driving forces and its consequences. That is, environmental threats "jump" scale, crossing vast expanses of geographic space and time, by refusing to be contained by artificial boundaries such as national borders and election cycles. Finally, my conceptualization of scale includes both spatial/geographic dimensions and temporal understandings of this phenomenon, which I will address later in this chapter. A Critical EJ Studies approach embraces multiscalar analyses for producing more robust understandings of the reasons why environmental inequalities exist and for developing more effective responses to them.

Regarding the third point – the degree to which various forms of inequality and power are viewed as entrenched in society, elements that must be confronted – this concern stems from my conclusion that the vision of change articulated by many EJ Studies scholars and EJ activists generally looks to the state to accommodate demands via legislation, institutional reforms, and other policy concessions. The issue here is that such an approach may leave intact the very power structures that produced environmental injustices in the first place. Yes, it names those institutions as sources of the problems and seeks to reform them, but by working in collaboration with those entities, such efforts ultimately risk reinforcing their legitimacy. A Critical EJ Studies approach raises the question as to whether scholars and activists should look to the primary actors responsible for producing environmental injustices to offer remedies for those harms. Thus CEJ invites perspectives that ask whether we should rely on the state to facilitate social change, or whether there may be other paths that can lead us to those goals.

Regarding the fourth point, EJ Studies suggests that various marginalized human populations are treated and viewed as inferior and less valuable to society than others. This topic is largely undertheorized in the EJ Studies literature because it is often reserved for discussion of specific places – communities that are highly contaminated and frequently referred to as "sacrifice zones" – while a CEJ perspective argues that entire *populations* are viewed as expendable, not just particular, localized communities and spaces.[57] The implication of a "sacrifice zone" is that one could presumably move away to safety, but the implication of expendability is that there is no escape. Critical EJ Studies makes this theme explicit by arguing that these populations are marked for erasure and early death, and that such ideological and institutional othering is linked to the more-than-human world as well. Moreover, CEJ counters the dominant perspective with a framework that contends that these threatened bodies, populations, and spaces are *indispensable* to building socially and environmentally just and resilient futures for us all.

Thus, what Critical EJ Studies offers earlier-generation EJ Studies is the following, which I call the Four Pillars of CEJ: 1. greater attention to how multiple social categories of difference are entangled in the production of environmental injustice, from race, gender, sexuality, ability, and class to species, which would attend to the ways that both the human and the more-than-human world are affected by and respond to environmental injustice and related forms of state-corporate violence; 2. an embrace of multiscalar methodological and theoretical approaches to studying EJ issues in order to better comprehend the complex spatial and temporal causes, consequences, and possible resolutions of EJ struggles (and by "multiscalar" I mean that we should be paying attention to how EJ struggles may simultaneously function through many spatial *and temporal* scales); 3. a deeper grasp of the entrenched and embedded character of social inequality – reinforced by the power of the state – in society and therefore a reckoning with the need for transformative (rather than exclusively reformist) approaches to realize environmental justice. In other words, Critical EJ Studies seeks to push our analyses and actions beyond the human, the state, and capital via a broad antiauthoritarian perspective; and 4. an intensified focus on the ways that humans and more-than-human actors are *indispensable* to the present, and necessary for building sustainable, just, and resilient futures. As EJ Studies has had difficulty promoting a productive and transformative vision of change,[58] indispensability is a key ingredient in that effort. In the following sections I elaborate on the four pillars noted above.

What Does Critical Environmental Justice Studies Look Like?

Building on the work of scholars across numerous fields that only periodically intersect (such as Environmental Justice Studies, Critical Race Theory, Critical Race Feminism, Ethnic Studies, Gender and Sexuality Studies, Political Ecology, Anti-Statist/ Anarchist Theory, and Ecological Feminism), I propose *Critical Environmental Justice Studies* as a framework built on the following four pillars.

First Pillar — *In tersectionality*

The first pillar of Critical EJ Studies involves the recognition that social inequality and oppression in all forms intersect, and that actors in the more-than-human world are subjects of oppression and frequently agents of social change. The fields of critical race theory, critical race feminism, gender and sexuality studies, queer theory, ecological feminism, disability studies, and critical animal studies all speak to the ways in which various social categories of difference work to place particular bodies at risk of exclusion, marginalization, erasure, discrimination, violence, destruction, and othering. These insights are important for building an understanding of the ways that intra-human inequality and oppressions function and how they intersect with human-nonhuman oppression. As David Nibert and Michael Fox put it, "The oppression of various devalued groups in human societies is not independent and unrelated; rather, the arrangements that lead to various forms of oppression are integrated in such a way that the exploitation of one group frequently augments and compounds the mistreatment of others."[59] Some of those "various devalued groups in human societies" include women, immigrants, LGBTQ persons, people of color, indigenous peoples, disabled persons, the elderly, children, low-income people, and nonhuman species. And while the *experiences* of these various groups are qualitatively distinct (they are not equivalent), the *logic of domination and othering* as practiced by more powerful groups against them provides a thread of intersectionality through each of their oppressions.

Thus CEJ views racism, heteropatriarchy, classism, nativism, ableism, ageism, speciesism (the belief that one species is superior to another), and other forms of inequality as intersecting axes of domination and control. That is, these inequalities are mutually reinforcing in that they tend to act together to produce and maintain systems of individual and collective power, privilege, and subordination. With respect to speciesism, CEJ extends beyond the category of the human to include the more-than-human world (from nonhuman animals and ecosystems to the built environment) as subjects of oppression and as agents of social change. Worms, viruses, ants, water, rocks, mountains, fish, elephants, krill, air/wind, and trees are just some of the infinite nonhuman beings and things that are affected by environmental injustice but that also exert their own influence on the character of those conflicts in particular and on the course and trajectory of human society and ecology more generally. The built environment, and in particular the urban environment, is a vast assemblage of what urban political ecologists call "socionatures" or nature/culture hybrids[60] that reflect the entangled and inseparable character of buildings, roads, communication technologies and residential, commercial, and public spaces with respect to the ecosystems that make them possible. The urban built environment is a "socionature" because it is impossible to delineate where its human imprint ends and its non-human imprint begins, or vice versa, and that environment shapes how humans think and behave. And since most of the human beings on this planet are living in cities and other urban spaces, much of the future of environmental justice studies, EJ struggles, and efforts to create resilience and sustainability will pay considerable attention to cities and the built environment.

Second Pillar

The second pillar of Critical EJ Studies is a focus on the role of scale in the production and possible resolution of environmental injustices. While much of the EJ literature does include the use of scalar analyses, attention to and use of multiple scales in the literature has been inconsistent. Julie Sze writes, "thinking globally and acting locally also demands that people more fully comprehend the relationship between the local and the global or, in other words, to consider scale."[61] And by scale, environmental studies scholars mean both spatial and temporal dimensions of how objects, ideas, bodies, beings, things, and environmental harms and resilient practices are linked, how they are connected ecologically. While much of the EJ literature pays attention to only one scale of analysis (a neighborhood, census tracts, and so on), some scholars use multiple scales, pointing to the ways that, for example, persistent organic pollutants produced thousands of miles away from the Arctic end up in high concentrations in the breast milk of indigenous Nunavik women[62] and how EJ activists in Louisiana collaborate with and stand in solidarity with activists in Nigeria, the Philippines, and other parts of the world because they are fighting the same global oil corporation (Shell).[63] A Critical EJ Studies framework embraces multiscalar spatial and temporal analyses as a productive direction for this body of scholarship. This approach allows us to examine how, for example, pollution generated by a coal-fired power plant in the Bronx can emit carbon, particulate matter, and other substances that contribute to respiratory disorders such as asthma in children who live in New York City, but also how that pollution exacerbates the broader challenge of global climate change/disruption.

But scale is about much more than size and space. Attention to the *temporal dimensions* of scale allows us to explore, for instance, how the emergence and use of coal-fired power plants and petroleum-based economies developed and changed over historical periods, thus unveiling some of the social causes of our ecological crises and perhaps revealing clues as to how things might have unfolded differently and therefore inviting interventions for the future. The production of a molecule of carbon dioxide or nitrous oxide can occur in an instant, but it remains in the atmosphere for more than a century, so the decisions we make at one point in time can have dramatic ramifications for generations to come.[64] The decisions by European colonizers to enslave peoples of African descent and conquer the indigenous peoples and lands of what became the United States of America had dramatic consequences for human and environmental health that are evident today. Native American and African-American communities today face some of the most intense impacts of climate change, because Native peoples often live on lands that are targeted for fossil fuel drilling (which pollutes their water tables and endangers the lives of flora and fauna they depend on) and African-Americans are more likely than most populations to live near health-impairing coal-fired power plants. These examples of environmental racism reveal the ongoing violence associated with the reservation system and residential segregation as well as legacies of conquest and enslavement. This approach helps us to locate the multiple scales at which environmental injustice functions, from the cells in the bodies of individual humans and more-than-humans affected by these forms of violence, to how the damage *generational equity*

crosses populations and generations. As Sze writes, "At the core of the term *environmental justice* is a redefinition of 'the environment' to mean not only 'wild' places, but the environment of human bodies, especially in racialized communities."[65] But if we are to take the temporal scale seriously, we might consider the fact that EJ struggles are also about the *future*, something scholars of the Anthropocene are engaging with respect to how climate change will affect humanity and ecosystems for millennia to come.[66] What our futures might look like is a topic that novelists – and especially science fiction writers – have long considered. As Walidah Imarisha puts it, "Whenever we try to envision a world without war, without violence, without prisons, without capitalism, we are engaging in speculative fiction. Organizers and activists dedicate their lives to creating and envisioning another world, or many other worlds – so what better venue for organizers to explore their work than science fiction stories?"[67] An embrace of multiscalar methodological and theoretical approaches to studying EJ issues is important for developing a stronger comprehension of the complex spatial and temporal causes, consequences, and possible future resolutions of EJ struggles.

Third Pillar

The third pillar of Critical EJ Studies is the view that social inequalities – from racism to speciesism – are deeply embedded in society (rather than aberrations) and reinforced by state power, and that therefore the current social order stands as a fundamental obstacle to social and environmental justice. The logical conclusion of that observation is that social change movements may be better off thinking and acting beyond human supremacy and beyond the state as targets of reform and reliable partners – although in this project I focus primarily on the state.[68]

As far as a vision of change is concerned, the general thrust of earlier-generation EJ Studies and the EJ movement is that scholars and activists are *not* asking how we might build environmentally just and resilient communities that can exist *beyond* the state, but rather how we might do so with a *different* model of state intervention. While perhaps generative and seemingly firmly on the political cutting edge, that view is also limited and perhaps contradictory, if we consider the work of scholars who conclude that modern nation states are both inherently racially exclusionary and ecologically unsustainable.[69] EJ scholars and activists tend to argue for the dedication and expansion of state resources away from anti-ecological and anti-humanist purposes to the causes of ecological protection, environmental justice, civil and human rights – in some ways part of a classic progressive-Left platform. The problem with this approach is that it assumes that states can and do perform such functions separately (say, the anti-socioecological and pro-socioecological), when in fact they tend to be integrally linked in a fashion that serves to reinforce state power and various forms of inequality (including institutional racism and speciesism). In the view of many scholars, the *purpose* of a state is to exert control over populations, ecosystems, and territory, among other things.[70]

The EJ movement and EJ scholarship generally share a consensus that they are looking to the state and its legal systems to deliver justice, to police itself, and to regulate industry. Thus far, as studies have demonstrated consistently and conclusively, the track record of state-based regulation and enforcement of environmental and civil rights legislation in communities of color has not been promising,[71] and yet, as Robert Benford argues, the EJ movement continues to seek justice through a system that was never intended to provide justice for marginalized peoples and nonhuman natures.[72]

Most of human history has been marked by the absence of states, suggesting that the modern condition of state dominance is anything but natural or inevitable. My view, and the view of a growing number of scholars, is that states are social institutions that tend to lean toward practices and relationships that are authoritarian, coercive, racist, patriarchal, exclusionary, militaristic, and anti-ecological. Given that view, my argument is that environmental justice movements would be better off seeking social change through institutions and practices that rely less on the state in order to achieve their goals. As James Scott points out, however, we are likely stuck with states for the time being, and when grassroots social change movements engage in massive disruption, progressive and positive developments do sometimes materialize[73] (although one could raise the question as to why we should exert so much energy in making largely undemocratic institutions more democratic rather than just practicing direct democracy ourselves). My argument, therefore, is that EJ and other social movements would be best off articulating, developing, and supporting practices, relationships, and institutions that *deepen direct democracy* – without strict concern over whether the location of such practices and relationships is inside or outside of state institutions – because such processes are more likely to be supportive of environmental and social justice. This is a twenty-first-century framework that is nuanced and non-fundamentalist, that is always wary of state power but concedes that there are moments and spaces where states can be pushed to do work that is supportive of social and environmental justice. This is a framework that also urges social movements to ask first to what extent we can meet our goals without a default reliance on the state, and if not, whether we can minimize that reliance. In that vein, my goal and vision is not to seek the abolition of the state but rather to seek the abolition of socioecologically violent, hierarchical relationships that tend to support state institutions and flow from them. When I invoke the third pillar of CEJ studies, then, I mean that EJ scholars and activists would be well served by always considering the pros and cons of embracing the state, and asking how their conceptual and tactical choices could instead be focused on the most robustly democratic options. My point is that by building and supporting strongly democratic practices, relationships, and institutions, movements for social change will become less dependent upon the state, while any elements of the state they do work through may become more robustly democratic.[74]

I offer two examples as illustrations of this vision in practice. First, activist scott crow co-founded the anarchist-inspired Common Ground Collective to provide basic services for survivors of Hurricane Katrina on the Gulf Coast in 2005. He was proud of that organization, and told me:

We did service work, but it was a revolutionary analysis and practice. We created a horizontal organization that defied the state and did our work in spite of the state . . . not only did we feed people and give them aid and hygiene kits and things like that, but we also stopped housing from being bulldozed, we cut the locks on schools when they said schools couldn't be opened, and we cleaned the schools out because the students and the teachers wanted that to happen. And we didn't do a one size fits all like the Red Cross would do – we asked the communities, every community we went into, we asked multiple people, the street sex workers, the gangsters, the church leaders, everybody, we talked to them: what can we do to help your neighborhood, to help your community, to help you? And that made us different because for me, it's the overlay of anarchism. Instead of having one franchise thing, you just have concepts, and you just pick the components that match the needs of the people there.[75]

In a second example, Isabelle Anguelovski's study of environmental justice organizing in low-income neighborhoods in Barcelona, Boston, and Havana reveals how residents and activists successfully cleaned up illegal dumping sites and created space for new parks, green space, and community gardens, initially through an autonomous process that had no support from state officials. Eventually the project received some government support as a result of their success and persistence.[76] In the absence of a state presence (or state oversight), these activists took it upon themselves to act autonomously to make change happen in terms of reclaiming space, and once state officials took notice, activists gladly accepted their support.

These cases reflect my caution about being wary of the role of the state in responding to environmental justice threats and the importance of devising ways that ordinary people can meet their needs through deepening direct democracy via cooperation, mutual assistance, and grassroots organizing. In the case of the Common Ground Collective, they were explicitly anarchist and worked entirely outside the ambit of the state, while the cases that Anguelovski details reveal that activists were less ideologically driven and more practical, so they organized anarchically when necessary but also sought and welcomed state support when it made strategic sense for their democratic goals.

25

Fourth Pillar

The fourth pillar of the Critical EJ Studies framework centers on a concept I call *indispensability*. In the book *Black and Brown Solidarity,* Critical Race and Ethnic Studies scholar John Márquez introduces the concept "racial expendability" to argue that black and brown bodies are, in the eyes of the state and its constituent legal system, generally viewed as criminal, deficient, threatening, and deserving of violent discipline and even obliteration.[77] Márquez and other Ethnic Studies scholars and activists contend that, in a white-dominated society, people of color are constructed as and rendered expendable.[78] Philosopher and critical race theorist Charles Mills argues that people of African descent, for example, are considered "black trash" by policymakers and institutions that perpetrate environmental racism because these populations are frequently associated with filth, waste, and uncleanliness in the popular imagination, so locating pollution in their communities actually makes cultural common sense.[79]

A Critical EJ Studies perspective builds on this work by countering the ideology of white supremacy and human dominionism, and articulating the perspective that excluded, marginalized, and othered populations, beings, and things – both human and more-than-human – must be viewed not as expendable but rather as *indispensable* to our collective futures. This is what I term *racial indispensability* (when referring to people of color) and *socioecological indispensability* (when referring to broader communities within and across the human / more-than-human spectrum). Racial indispensability is intended to challenge the logic of racial expendability; it advances the idea that institutions, policies, and practices that support and perpetuate racism suffer from the illogical assumption that the future of people of color is delinked from the future of white communities. In fact, white communities have always been dependent upon communities of color, for labor, for consumers, for political support, and for the existence of the idea of whiteness itself, which provides what W.E.B. DuBois called a "psychological wage" so that even the poorest white Americans could feel the pride of knowing that at least they were, at the end of the day, "not black."[80] In other words, whiteness has no meaning without people of color. Those are troubling reasons why people of color are indispensable to this society. More positively, people of color are members of our society, are core participants in our social systems, are members of our socioecological systems, and are therefore key to ensuring the continued functioning, sustainability, and resilience of our society and planet. Hence, people of color are indispensable to our collective futures.

The idea of indispensability is distinct from an assimilationist perspective, which seeks to (often involuntarily and violently) incorporate "others" into one's own vision of a society.[81] Rather, indispensability honors key EJ and ecological principles by seeing all communities (more-than-human and human) as interconnected, interdependent, but also sovereign and requiring the solidarity of others. Indispensability should also not be confused with a Functionalist view of society and socioecological relations, as it recognizes that social roles, positions, and behaviors among various populations can and do conflict and change over time, and that the character of inequality and state and market power in most societies is highly unjust and must be confronted. Functionalism, on the other hand, posits that whatever the character of inequality, social roles, and behaviors may be, it must be positive for that society and therefore is in no need of change.[82] Indispensability argues against that logic because CEJ is fundamentally focused on securing justice and sustainability in a highly unjust and unsustainable system. Thus indispensability demands dramatic change but does so from the perspective that all members of society and socioecological systems have something to contribute to that process and to our collective futures.

Socially, politically, philosophically, and ecologically, what this means is that we are all linked in webs of interdependence, so that what happens to one group affects, in some way, all others. As Dr. Martin Luther King, Jr. famously wrote in his landmark "Letter from a Birmingham Jail" with regard to racism and the future of the US:

Injustice anywhere is injustice everywhere. . . . In a real sense all life is inter-related. All men are caught in an inescapable network of mutuality, tied in a single garment of destiny. Whatever affects one directly, affects all indirectly. Never again can we afford to live with the narrow, provincial "outside agitator" idea.[83]

King demonstrated a profound understanding of indispensability.[84] The impacts of climate change offer a telling example of environmental racism and injustice in the face of indispensability. While the findings and conclusions of climate scientists are remarkably clear that anthropogenic climate change is occurring at a dramatic pace and with increasing intensity, this is also happening unevenly, with people of color, the poor, indigenous peoples, peoples of the global south, and women suffering the most.[85] Climate change is also contributing enormously to the disruption of daily life and health (including extinction) of countless nonhuman species. This is a clear case of environmental racism/inequality and human dominionism/speciesism, but the fossil fuel industries, national governments, and religious conservatives have invested enormous sums of energy, time, and money into denying these facts; the climate change deniers believe it to be in their interests to ignore or actively work against the recognition of the problem.[86] A Critical EJ Studies framework suggests that, regardless of perceptions and politics, this approach is not only harmful to marginalized communities, species, and ecosystems around the globe, it is also self-defeating for those who appear to be operating in their own short-term self-interest. The problem of climate change reveals in stark terms the fact of racial indispensability and socioecological indispensability – the fourth pillar of Critical EJ Studies.

Environmental justice and climate justice movement activists have recently issued a number of statements and declarations of indispensability, reflecting a critical shift in language and politics among social movements in the early twenty-first century. In 2002, at the Second People of Color Environmental Leadership Summit, activists penned and endorsed a document: The People of Color Environmental Justice "Principles of Working Together." One of those principles reads, "The Principles of Working Together recognize that we need each other and we are stronger with each other. This Principle requires participation at every level without barriers and that the power of the movement is shared at every level."[87] This statement reflects the view that all people are needed to offer their ideas, labor, and participation in order to address our common socioecological crises, and that such a principle is in direct confrontation with historical and ongoing practices of segregation, exclusion, othering, and state-sanctioned and market violence.

A slogan that became a rallying cry at the 2014 People's Climate March in New York City, where 400,000 people marched to demonstrate their support for progressive climate change policy, was "to change everything we need everyone." When Naomi Klein's 2014 book was published and titled *This Changes Everything: Capitalism vs. the Climate*, this language was reinforced. In the fall of 2014 and 2015, climate activist groups led actions targeting corporations and financial institutions that contribute to climate change and climate injustice. One of those groups released a statement that read, in part,

> Like Naomi Klein said – "To change everything, we need everyone." That still holds true. We've been working with an array of economic justice, racial justice and climate justice groups for Flood Wall Street West. If we truly want to hold the banks and oil companies accountable than we need truly need everyone.[88]

This slogan is a key aspect of indispensability because it sees everyone not just as beings in a broad ecological sense, but also as *agents* in the political sense. Everyone is linked to everyone else and we all have some degree of agency to change the course of history. After all, like it or not, we are all in this together. Article 3 of the Bolivian Law of Mother Earth, passed in 2012, defines the Earth as "the dynamic living system formed by the indivisible community of all life systems and living beings, who are interrelated, interdependent, and complementary, which share a common destiny."

CEJ extends the work of Ethnic Studies scholars and activists who argue that, in this society, people of color are constructed as and rendered expendable.[89] Building on those ideas and challenging the ideology of white supremacy and human dominionism, CEJ articulates the perspective that excluded, marginalized, and othered populations, beings, and things – both human and more-than-human – must be viewed as *indispensable* to our collective futures. Indispensability might be described as a public declaration to this effect, because this idea is only implied in earlier-generation EJ Studies, largely because environmental racism has been framed primarily in terms of civil rights violations rather than genocide, extermination, and annihilation, to which both Ethnic Studies and CEJ studies speak more directly.

Discussion and Conclusion

A growing group of scholars working to expand EJ Studies beyond its earlier emphasis on questions concerning the racial and class dimensions of environmental inequality (using either quantitative or small-case study methods) use the term "Critical Environmental Justice Studies."[90] This concept is meant to build on that earlier scholarship in EJ Studies and expand on its important conceptual, theoretical, disciplinary, and methodological foundations. Since the path toward Critical EJ Studies is still very much in formation, this book is an effort to chart one course in that direction with greater specificity.

Critical EJ studies draws from numerous fields of scholarship in order to produce more robust and richer accounts for why environmental injustices occur and persist, for how human and nonhuman forces shape and are shaped by them, and for what environmental justice could look like. That is, the promise of Critical EJ Studies lies in its capacity to more fully explain the sources and consequences of our socioecological crises and develop more generative analyses of how social change efforts within and across species may meet those challenges.

In addition to building on Environmental Justice Studies, Critical

EJ Studies draws inspiration from a number of other important fields, such as Critical Race Theory and Ethnic Studies,[91] Critical Race Feminism and Gender and Sexuality Studies,[92] and Anti-Statist/Anarchist Theory,[93] which have done an enormous service by producing rigorous conceptual and grounded understandings of how social inequality, oppression, privilege, hierarchy, and authoritarian institutions and practices shape the lives of human beings. These scholars have explored and revealed myriad ways in which gender, race, sexuality, citizenship, social class, and ability reflect and are reflective of how social structures function in society. They have also elucidated the ways that courts, legal systems, policing, educational institutions, militaries, and other arms of the state and corporations *produce* race, gender, sexuality, social class, and ability. They show how the domination of those persons without privilege is accomplished through practices, policymaking, and discourses on a daily basis. Thus these fields are invaluable to strengthening Environmental Justice Studies, which is, at its root, an area of inquiry concerned with inequality, domination, and liberation. Specifically, EJ Studies might benefit from taking more seriously the ways in which multiple categories of difference, authoritarianism, and hierarchy structure the formation of environmental injustices, the way these injustices are experienced across different populations, and what this means for intersectional organizing and resistance against and beyond the state and capital. In turn, what the above areas of scholarship generally pay less attention to are the means through which these social categories and social practices are always shaped by their relationship to nonhuman species and ideas about the broader more-than-human world. Critical EJ Studies thus can expand those boundaries in these fields.

Critical EJ Studies draws inspiration from another group of academic fields of study as well, including the Environmental Humanities,[94] Political Ecology,[95] and Ecofeminism,[96] which have performed an admirable job of exploring the many ways in which humans and the more-than-human world are entangled, inseparable, and bound up in collaboration, cooperation, conflict, and violence, producing socioecological crises as well as responses to them in practices of co-existence, sustainability, solidarity, and justice. Scholars in these fields have also done excellent work at linking various forms of social inequality within human societies to forms of inequality and oppression across the human/nonhuman species divide. Thus these fields are helpful for strengthening Environmental Justice Studies – which is, at its core, focused on the links between social inequality and ecological politics – in the broadest possible terms. Specifically, these fields offer the possibility for deepening EJ Studies' capacity for considering the ways that environmental inequalities are structured within and across species and space and how those processes are interconnected. For their part, these fields have paid less serious attention to the centrality of race and racism in shaping human and-more-than human life; Critical EJ Studies can thus suggest direction and depth on those matters. Furthermore, since these fields – Environmental Humanities and Ecofeminism in particular – tend to approach research questions with nonsocial scientific research methods, Critical EJ Studies' orientation to multiple research methods can offer a productive conversation across these fields.

CEJ Studies is interdisciplinary and multi-methodological. It is activist-scholar inspired in that it seeks to bridge and blur the boundaries and borders between the academy and community, theory and practice, analysis and action. I also want to emphasize that Critical EJ Studies is intended to be only *one* of many possible approaches to EJ scholarship and action. It is not prescriptive, nor is it a declaration of where the field should be headed; it is simply one of a number of ways to think about and work toward environmental justice.

The rest of this book allows the reader to consider how the CEJ framework might be applied to actual cases where humans and nonhuman natures are bound up in the struggle for environmental justice against myriad threats at multiple scales. Chapter 2 is a consideration of how a CEJ perspective might be productive for thinking through the limits and possibilities of the Black Lives Matter movement and racist state violence. Chapter 3 brings together concerns over mass incarceration with efforts to secure environmental justice by zeroing in on the intersections between the prison industrial complex and environmental inequality in the US. Chapter 4 applies a CEJ analysis to the seemingly intractable Israel/Palestine conflict, with a particular eye to the sensitive and controversial character of that long-running tense relationship. In the Conclusion I present my thoughts on how these three cases intersect and what they mean for the future of EJ scholarship and activism. My data and evidence in these cases are drawn primarily from hundreds of documents, including scholarly books and articles, studies, reports, and other publications written by advocates and activists, and secondarily by some participant observation, and a small sample of interviews.

Black Lives Matter as an Environmental Justice Challenge

Black Lives Matter (BLM) is a social movement centered on the problem of state-sanctioned racist violence. The movement began as a response to the acquittal of George Zimmerman, the man who murdered Trayvon Martin, a seventeen-year-old African-American boy in Sanford, Florida in 2012. Zimmerman was an adult Neighborhood Watch volunteer who became involved in an altercation with Martin while the youth was walking through the community where Zimmerman lived. The incident ended with Martin being shot to death. Zimmerman faced no charges since he claimed "self-defense" under the state of Florida's "stand your ground" law, which allows citizens to use lethal force against others (and absolves them of the mandate to retreat) if they feel their well-being is endangered. As a result of a major national public outcry at that decision, law enforcement officials eventually and reluctantly charged Zimmerman with second-degree murder and manslaughter. He was later acquitted by a grand jury in 2013. This outcome reflected a longstanding divide in US racial politics, wherein African-Americans overwhelmingly report in survey research and opinion polls a sense that the legal system is stacked against them while white Americans see the system as much more even-handed.[1]

While the media coverage and a series of massive protests in the wake of Martin's murder and Zimmerman's acquittal were unprecedented in intensity, things were only beginning to heat up. From that moment on, social media, mainstream media, and the Black

34

Lives Matter movement would routinely intensify the national and international focus on racialized state-sanctioned violence when yet another video or testimony surfaced featuring an African-American being shot, beaten, choked, and/or killed by police or white vigilantes. To many people, it seemed like an epidemic of violence was engulfing black communities and finally some media organizations and politicians were paying attention.[2] The list of African-Americans who lost their lives to police violence, in police custody, or to white vigilantes during the period between 2012 and 2016 is massive, but includes the following persons whose murders or deaths made headlines and pushed people into the streets to protest: Sandra Bland, Rekia Boyd, Mike Brown, Philando Castile, Jamar Clark, John Crawford, Jordan Davis, Samuel DuBose, Ezell Ford, Eric Garner, Freddie Gray, Akai Gurley, Renisha McBride, Laquan McDonald, Trayvon Martin, Tamir Rice, Walter Scott, Aiyana Stanley-Jones, Alton Sterling, and many others.

BLM co-founder Alicia Garza, explained what the movement stands for:

> Black Lives Matter is an ideological and political intervention in a world where Black lives are systematically and intentionally targeted for demise. It is an affirmation of Black folks' contributions to this society, our humanity, and our resilience in the face of deadly oppression.[3]

In this chapter, I draw links between what I view as the most important insights, issues, demands, and questions that come out of the Black Lives Matter movement and the struggle against environmental racism. This is a connection that many scholars and observers might not make at first glance because police brutality and environmental politics would appear to be only tangentially related; I argue they are in fact closely intertwined, and that we must explore their myriad connections in order to excavate the roots of racist violence no matter the form it takes.[4] This exercise is a critical challenge for expanding the power and relevance of scholarship and advocacy centered on social and environmental justice movements. While Black Lives Matter and EJ movements are extremely important social formations, they could learn from one another, and separately and in combination, offer more in terms of their analysis of racist violence and inequality, and of their respective visions of social change. The questions I explore here include: How can Black Lives Matter's emphasis on police violence against African-American communities inform our understanding of the scourge of toxic chemicals, hazardous waste, pollution, climate change/disruptions, and other ecological burdens facing those same communities? Conversely, what can the violation of black bodies and spaces by ecologically destructive agents produced by states and corporations tell us about the violation of those same bodies by police and law enforcement agents? How can these seemingly disparate forms of oppression and repression inform efforts at intersectional, multi-issue movement building, coalition formation, and social change? I find that an earlier-generation Environmental Justice Studies framework can assist in this effort, but can only take us so far because it is primarily focused on the intersection between environmental risk and racial inequality, and police and state-sanctioned violence are almost entirely missing from that perspective. Therefore I propose that a Critical Environmental Justice Studies framework can more fully address these pressing concerns.

In the following sections, I apply a Critical EJ Studies framework to the Black Lives Matter movement to demonstrate the importance of CEJ for pushing scholars and activists to think through linkages across theory and social change politics that might not usually emerge from EJ Studies or from within many social change movements.

Critical EJ Studies and Black Lives Matter

In order to examine Black Lives Matter as a CEJ case study, I gathered data from the BLM website, archives, and social media, as well as major essays published in national and international media outlets. I also draw on my experiences from attending anti–police brutality protests, Black Lives Matter–led protests, and the countless conversations I have had with activists, scholars, and everyday people concerned with police violence. This selection of data is not intended to be strictly representative. As a purposeful sample it reflects and speaks to the core BLM frames and the four pillars of Critical Environmental Justice studies.

First Pillar: Intersection

The first pillar of Critical EJ Studies involves the recognition that social inequality and oppression in all forms intersect and that members of the more-than-human world are subjects of oppression and agents of social change.

Intersectionality and intersecting oppressions: Humans and more-than-humans

Black Lives Matter is a social movement organized primarily around the social category of race, but extends its analysis to multiple categories of difference, which brings us to the importance of *intersectionality*. "Intersectionality" describes how identities and social categories work together to produce advantages and disadvantages across bodies and space; the concept acknowledges that inequalities do not act independently of one another.[5] As Jodi Melamed writes, "intersectionality" comes out of the scholarly tradition known as women-of-color feminism, in which analysts "examine how procedures of race, class, gender, and sexuality and economic forces aggregate and interlock to create the lived conditions of the everyday."[6]

What struck me as I read through scores of posts and essays on the Black Lives Matter website is how different the movement's self-presentation is from its representation in the mainstream media. Specifically, the founders of BLM present a deeply intersectional, multi-issue approach to the problem of devalued black life that is inclusive of class, gender, sexuality, immigration status, citizenship, age, ability and other differences and social categories. All three founders of BLM are women of color. One of them – Alicia Garza – identifies as a queer woman of color, while another – Opal Tometi – is the daughter of Nigerian immigrants and works for an organization focused on the human rights of black immigrants. The third founder – Patrisse Cullors – who also identifies as queer, organizes support for incarcerated persons and their families, with a particular emphasis on mental health and other disabilities. Thus their political and professional work is a study in intersectional theory and practice. Their framing of the BLM movement centers around combating state-sanctioned violence against black bodies, but unlike the mainstream media representations of their message (which generally centers exclusively on race and racism), BLM has embraced an agenda that is explicitly and insistently inclusive of a range of categories that intersect with and shape race. As BLM co-founder Alicia Garza writes, "Black Lives Matter affirms the lives of Black queer and trans folks, disabled folks, Black-undocumented folks, folks with records, women and all Black lives along the gender spectrum. It centers those that have been marginalized within Black liberation movements. It is a tactic to (re)build the Black liberation movement."[7]

The BLM discourse reflects Roderick Ferguson's "queer of color critique" – a method of analysis that takes direct aim at the heterosexist, patriarchal, and racist underpinnings of the nation state and the importance of culture as a space of resistance. Ferguson uses the term "nonheteronormative racial difference"[8] when referring to people of color in the US, to underscore the ways in which intersectionality works insofar as race is gendered/sexed and gender and sexuality are raced. In other words, whiteness is associated with heteronormativity and nonwhiteness is associated with sexual deviance.[9] The state and many of its academic collaborators in fields like US Sociology have historically viewed African-American culture, bodies, and spaces/neighborhoods as nonheteronormative, since they are considered "deviant" racially and sexually, and the two are inseparable.[10]

Another essay on the Black Lives Matter website reminds us that intersectionality is not just a theoretical concern of academics, but a matter of life and death for everyday people:

Gabriella Naverez, a queer Black woman was killed at 22 years old, unarmed. 37 year old Tanisha Anderson's family dialed 911

38

for medical assistance. Instead, Cleveland police officers took her life. Anyia Parker, a Black trans woman was gunned down in East Hollywood. This brutal attack was caught on camera, yet her murder, like so many murders of Black trans women, have gone unanswered.[11]

Police departments are arms of the state, which reserves the right to use lethal force against those defined as a threat. There is no question that police officers engage in uncommon bravery every day performing a job that many people would find anxiety-inducing and unacceptably risky. But the larger and more important point is that this job entails upholding the power of the state to control, manage, subdue, contain, repress, and inflict violence on whomever it determines should be a target of such practices. This includes people of color, low-income persons, women, people with disabilities, the elderly, immigrants, indigenous persons, and many other marginalized groups. It also includes nonhuman animals when they are deemed a threat, as the New York City Police Department's *Annual Firearms Discharge Report* reveals:

> Police officers are among a select few to whom society has granted the right to use force in the course of their duty. . . . An officer's role encompasses service, crime control, and order maintenance. . . . Compliance in these matters is not optional. The vast majority of police encounters involve nothing more than words, but when words are insufficient – when people choose to ignore or actively resist police – officers have an ascending array of force options to compel others to submit to their lawful authority. . . . Police officers shall not discharge their firearms at a dog or other animal except to protect themselves or another person from physical injury and there is no other reasonable means to eliminate the threat.[12]

The above excerpt indicates the power and the prerogative of the state to employ lethal force against humans and nonhumans who are judged to be a threat. Unfortunately, police officers routinely engage in violent acts against humans and nonhumans even when no threat is evident, thus revealing how state violence produces intersecting oppressions, in the sense that this matrix of institutions practices control and brutality against multiple populations who may therefore find common ground in a common oppressor. A 2015 *Baltimore Sun* investigation of the Baltimore, Maryland, Police Department (the same town where Freddie Gray died in police custody), detailed numerous incidents in which vulnerable people and nonhumans were the subjects of brutal and sometimes lethal force at the hands of police in that city. The report notes, for example, in a series of cases, not only were young African-American males the targets of such violence, but so were elderly people, women, children, and nonhuman animals:

> A grandmother's bones were broken. A pregnant woman was violently thrown to the ground. . . . Even animals couldn't escape the brutality of the Baltimore police. . . . Officer Thomas Schmidt, a 24-year veteran assigned to the Emergency Services unit, was placed on paid administrative leave after police say he held down a Shar-Pei while a fellow officer, Jeffrey Bolger, slit the dog's throat. A month later, a Baltimore police officer pled guilty to a felony animal cruelty charge after he *fatally beat and choked his girlfriend's Jack Russell terrier*. That very same year, even one of Baltimore's good cops couldn't escape the horror show of dead animals: Four investigators from agencies outside Baltimore are working to determine who *left a dead rat on the car windshield of an officer who was cooperating with prosecutors on a police brutality case*. What about the prior year? There was a murder-suicide, with a policeman killing a firefighter, his girlfriend, and himself. There was a different officer who killed himself in jail after being charged with killing his fiancée.[13]

The *Baltimore Sun* investigation appears to reflect and support what scholarly studies have long revealed: that there is a well-documented link between the use of violence against nonhuman animals and efforts to exert control over other humans, whether in the destruction of livestock and other food sources during wartime and conquests or through domestic violence directed primarily at women, children, and nonhuman companion animals or pets. Consider, for example, the intersecting violence and oppression from the excerpt above, which includes the murder of a rat to intimidate a police officer working on a police brutality case and the murder of a dog to intimidate a girlfriend. The use of violence against nonhumans as a means of control over other humans is a time-honored tradition. Historian David Smits writes about the link between the extermination of the buffalo and the US army's efforts to starve and conquer Plains Indians:

> Scholars of Western American history have long recognized the post-Civil War frontier army's complicity in the near-extermination of the buffalo. Historian Richard White represents the scholarly consensus in stating that "various military commanders encouraged the slaughter of bison" by white hide hunters in order to cut the heart from the Plains Indians' economy. Some scholars implicate the army's high command more directly in the annihilation. Retired Brigadier General S. L. A. Marshall, for instance, claimed that Generals William T. Sherman and Philip Sheridan viewed the eradication of the buffalo as "the critical line of attack" in the struggle with the Plains tribes.[14]

The co-extermination of indigenous peoples and the buffalo is a painful reminder and example of intersecting oppressions, revealing the deep and disturbing links between genocide and ecocide.[15]

The *Baltimore Sun* investigation also reflects the scholarly research on intersecting oppressions associated with domestic violence in particular.[16] For example, in 2011, there were 1.3 million reported incidents of intimate partner violence in the US and more than 70 percent of those cases are believed to have included violence directed at a companion animal.[17] Research reveals that persons who wish to harm or control their partners or children often do so by harming a companion animal,[18] and that children in such domestic situations have a high probability of committing harm against a companion animal as a result.[19]

Intersectionality and the social discourse of animality

This brings us to what I call the *social discourse of animality*, a term meant to capture the language that people use to describe human behavior using nonhuman references and analogies, signaling a set of assumptions surrounding what we view as acceptable "human" versus nonhuman behavior and how different bodies are valued (the racial discourse of animality is a subset of this phenomenon).[20] It reveals the means through which we discuss social difference and cultural politics in more-than-human terms, as a way of defining the limits and boundaries of the human. This discourse is common in discussions of racial politics and flared up many times around BLM protests against police brutality. What is fascinating is that people on all sides of the issues – activists, lawyers, and agents of the state – use this language. In other words, people deploy the social discourse of animality in the service of white supremacy *and* in the service of racial justice. Consider the following examples:

> Lesley McSpadden, the mother of Michael Brown (an African American teenager killed by a police officer in Ferguson, Missouri) spoke to reporters at a public demonstration to call attention to the tragedy of her son's death. She spoke to the bleak outlook of young African Americans facing police brutality: "You took my son away from me! You know how hard it was for me to get him to stay in school and graduate? You know how many Black men graduate? Not many! Because you bring them down to this type of level where they feel they don't got nothing to live for anyway!" While other protesters around McSpadden peacefully raised their hands in symbolic surrender, a police officer's voice was heard and recorded yelling at them, calling them "animals."[21]

In early 2015, Freddie Gray, a twenty-five-year-old African-American man, was taken into police custody in Baltimore, Maryland and, in the process, incurred severe spinal cord and neck injuries and died shortly afterward, sparking nationwide protests. In Baltimore, the protests, led by African-Americans and many supporters of the BLM movement, were mainly peaceful but were unfortunately marred by property destruction, looting, and a number of police officers being injured. Many whites took to social media – including Baltimore County police officer Jennifer Lynne Silver – and expressed their views on the matter, referring to the people involved as "animals" and, in her words, a "disgrace to the human race."[22] An article in *The Guardian* countered by arguing that police and society often treat nonhuman animals better than African-Americans:

But "animals" is a misnomer. People – including police officers – are punished for killing or doing harm to domestic animals. Baltimore has busted dog fighting rings and sent offenders to prison for animal cruelty. In 2014, former Baltimore City police officer Alec Taylor was sentenced to a year behind bars for killing a dog. That might not seem like much, but it is longer than the sentences given to the killers of Michael Brown, Eric Garner, Trayvon Martin, Rekia Boyd or 7-year-old Aiyana Stanley-Jones.[23]

In yet another example of the social discourse of animality, a scandal rocked the San Francisco Police Department in 2015 when a series of racist and homophobic text message exchanges among police officers surfaced. In one exchange, an officer wrote the following: "I hate to tell you this but my wife friend [sic] is over with their kids and her husband is black! If [sic] is an attorney but should I be worried?" His colleague wrote back: "Get ur pocket gun. Keep it available in case the monkey returns to his roots. Its [sic] not against the law to put an animal down."[24]

The above are, of course, all examples of how the social discourse of animality is used in the service of white supremacy. Below are instances of how people have used this discourse to combat racism.

In response to the scandal among the city's police force, Jeff Adachi, the San Francisco public defender, stated, "These texts evidence a deep culture of racial hatred and animus against blacks, Latinos, gays and even South Asians" – thus revealing that anti-blackness is often part and parcel of a broader set of ideas, language, practices, and policies that target people of color and LGBTQ populations for mistreatment. Reflecting the social discourse of animality, he went on to further say, "These are people who have the power to arrest and the power to kill somebody. . . . If you're thinking 'This is a wild animal or this is a crazed black man who's going to hurt me,' that's when you might pull the trigger. That's where it becomes scary."[25]

In the spring of 2015, a police officer shot Walter Scott, an unarmed African-American man in North Charleston, South Carolina, after he fled his car during a traffic stop. Malik Shabazz, president of Black Lawyers for America and former chairman of the New Black Panther Party, appeared on *CNN Newsroom* and stated, "The community here is in pain. And the community here and all over the country is outraged that Black men are being killed and hunted down like deer and like dogs."[26] That same month, Democratic Congressman Hank Johnson of Georgia took to the floor of the House of Representatives to urge his colleagues to confront the apparent epidemic of police brutality facing the nation. Drawing on a phrase usually reserved for hunting nonhuman animals, he stated, "It feels like *open season* on Black men in America, and I'm outraged. ... In fact, all Americans are at risk when bad actors in law enforcement use their guns instead of their heads."[27]

In the above examples, references to nonhumans are used to communicate the sentiment that African-Americans – like all human beings, presumably – should not be treated like nonhuman animals. The assumption here is also problematic because it is speciesist in that it implies that it is acceptable to wantonly hunt and slaughter nonhumans, even if the aim of the narrative is to counter racist violence. My point is that we cannot understand racist violence and the way we think, talk about, and enact it, without paying attention to the relationship between humans and nonhumans.

Unfortunately but predictably, animal welfare activists stepped into the fray and made highly insensitive comments reflecting the social discourse of animality, which ultimately functioned in the service of white supremacy. First, I should note that there has been considerable tension over the use of the phrase "all lives matter" versus "black lives matter" since many white activists and politicians have chosen to emphasize the former phrase over the latter presumably to seek a more "inclusive" and less "divisive" approach to race. BLM activists have stated repeatedly that the slogan "black lives matter" is meant to underscore the qualitatively distinct experience of African-Americans with racist police violence in the US, and that while "all lives matter" sounds more pluralistic, it erases those particular experiences and realities. Enter the UK-based vegan advocacy group Vegan Revolution, who, in a social media message, insisted that if "all lives matter" then so do the lives of nonhuman animals who suffer the violence of slaughter every day. In a posting on Twitter, the group compared "black lives" to those of "chickens" and "cows," setting off a firestorm of criticism.[28] There is a long and troubling history of vegan and animal rights advocacy groups comparing the suffering of marginalized human populations to nonhuman animals, so this was no surprise.[29] More fascinating, however, was the general public outcry when, in July 2015, Walter Palmer, a trophy hunter and dentist from Minnesota, killed Cecil, a protected lion on a Zimbabwean nature preserve. Palmer allegedly lured the lion off the preserve before killing him with a crossbow, and when Cecil's murder was made public, it made global news headlines. In less than twenty-four hours, Palmer's past records of other hunting violations were made public and he had to close his dental practice and go into hiding. As one news outlet reflected, the "social media response from white Americans has never been this intense for Black Lives Matter."[30] Clearly Cecil's killing was horrific, but the differential response by white Americans to his murder versus the murder of countless unarmed African-Americans is revealing. The social discourse of animality was on full display in both the Vegan Revolution and Cecil murder cases because many whites were registering their views that some behaviors are unacceptable and that some lives matter more than others, but in neither case were those black lives.

Agency and social change

Finally, the role of *agency* – an act or intervention with the capacity to effect change – is critical to the first pillar of CEJ, since African-Americans and other marginalized populations are not just the targets of domination and oppression but also regularly engage in myriad forms of resistance. While we see traditional elements of what sociologists call "resource mobilization"[31] on full display with the Black Lives Matter movement – including the mobilization of human bodies, ideas, words, discourses, tactics, and strategies in protest – the built environment and other forms of more-than-human objects, technologies, and natures are also integral to that agency and therefore central to making this vision and practice of social change possible. Consider the following examples:

- The *urban built environment* has been a critical site for the mobilization of people around protests against police brutality in the twentieth and twenty-first centuries. These spaces are, in many ways, ideal because they are frequently sites where large densities of people – particularly people of color – reside, so they allow for rapid and often large convergences and displays of support for the BLM movement. Buildings in urban areas have served as sites of protest planning and implementation, while roads – streets, highways, and bridges – have been particularly important circuits, pathways, and targets for marches, rallies, and acts of civil disobedience when activists gather, speak out, and often disrupt traffic to symbolize the need to challenge "business as usual." And since buildings, roads, and other aspects of the built environment are produced by humans extracting materials from ecosystems and then used by other humans for a range of purposes, the built environment is what urban political ecologists call a "socionature"[32] in that it represents a human/nonhuman nature hybrid that reflects how humans and the more-than-human world interact in ways that demonstrate their inseparability and their "conjoint constitution."[33]
- *Information technology* and emerging communication networks such as cell phones with cameras, computers, the Internet, and social media sites have become immensely important to twenty-first-century social change movements like BLM. In the hands of people who are activists, these nonhuman objects facilitate the recording and dissemination of images of police brutality and aid in the recruitment of people all over the world in the campaign to educate the public about this problem and to confront it. These technologies have also been crucial for the sharing of ideas and images from the protests as well, thus revealing the widespread nature of the movement and its supporters. It should be noted that these technologies are also routinely used to control, manipulate, repress, and produce surveillance data on various populations around the globe, with a particular emphasis on consumers as well as individuals and groups involved in political dissent. Information technologies are made

possible by massive industrial-scale mineral mining and extraction (among other practices) that generally produce widespread ecological harm and co-occur in communities where corporate and state repression is frequently rampant.[34] Thus the linkages between such technologies and human politics and power struggles signal the entangled character of "socionatures" and how agency within social movements relies not only on human activists but on many more-than-human actors as well.

- Finally, the nonhuman element *air* (or oxygen) plays a key part in the Black Lives Matter movement. "I can't breathe!" were Eric Garner's last words as a police officer choked him to death on Staten Island, New York in July of 2014. Caught on a cell phone camera and shared on media and Internet networks around the globe, Garner's death sparked a major series of Black Lives Matter actions during which many activists declared "I can't breathe!" to memorialize Garner and to symbolize the choking and murderous effects of racialized state violence. Other activists made connections between Garner's words and the lack of clean air in communities facing environmental racism. Eddie Bautista is director of the New York City Environmental Justice Alliance. Making the link between the police killing of Eric Garner and environmental racism, he told a journalist, "Limiting the conversation about racism to just about how we're policed is a lost opportunity. Folks should care not only about how racism kills quickly (via the police), but how racism also kills slowly and insidiously"[35] through other means, such as environmental racism. Bautista's words reflect what environmental humanities scholar Rob Nixon has called the "slow violence" of environmental injustice.[36]

US Congressman Keith Ellison and activist and author Van Jones have both devoted years of their lives to the struggle for environmental justice, playing major roles in elevating a number of key EJ issues into the legislative and policymaking arenas and in the media. In a *Guardian* article they authored, they spoke to the relationship between EJ issues and Black Lives Matter. They point out that African-Americans are more likely than whites to live near coal-fired power plants and that African-Americans have the highest asthma rates of any racial/ethnic population in the US, due to exposure to higher levels of carbon dioxide, ozone, particulate matter, and nitrogen oxides. These exposures also contribute to higher rates of cardiovascular disease, respiratory illness, and infant mortality in Black communities. Ellison and Jones write:

> Thanks to people's movements like Black Lives Matter and the Fight For 15, the call for racial and economic justice is getting louder and stronger. But while we are out on the streets fighting for equality, *our kids are being poisoned by the air they breathe.* Environmental injustices are taking black lives – that's why our fight for equality has to include climate and environmental justice too. . . . Centuries of racial discrimination as well as bad trade deals and economic policies that favor the wealthiest have led to black Americans being almost three times more likely to live in poverty than white Americans. We can't fight this trend by believing the lies that rich fossil fuel and utility executives tell us. Black lives matter more than corporate profits – now is a chance to make sure our laws reflect that.[37]

Ellison and Jones urged readers to support legislation aimed at reducing carbon pollution and encouraging investments in clean energy technologies. Bautista, Ellison, and Jones all underscored that racism and environmental racism act as a social toxin that, as Frederick Douglass once wrote, "fills the air," both figuratively and literally. Racism and environmental racism also fill bodies of water and land literally, and contaminate human and more-than-human bodies via the chemicals and other forms of pollution that corporations and states produce and introduce into our ecosystems. What has been the state's response? In a 2015 investigative study, the Center for Public Integrity found that when communities of color that are surrounded by polluting industry decide to bring a civil rights violation claim to the USEPA, that agency denies those claims 95 percent of the time.[38] Therefore, from a police chokehold on Eric Garner's neck to the air pollution choking communities of color suffering asthma epidemics related to toxic industrial operations allowed to function with near total impunity, the nonhuman element of air is an agent that acts to

48

sustain us (when it's available), to harm people when it is polluted (facilitated, of course, by other actors), and to mobilize people in the BLM and EJ movements because they seek to clean up the air that we *do* have, which could ultimately benefit everyone.

Second Pillar: Scale, Race, and Difference

The second pillar of Critical EJ Studies applies multiscalar methodological and theoretical approaches to studying EJ issues in order to better comprehend the complex spatial and temporal causes, consequences, and possible resolutions of EJ struggles. EJ Studies scholarship is largely characterized by a focus on just one scale, so a Critical EJ Studies framework would explore how EJ struggles function at multiple spatial/geographic and temporal scales.

Race and scale are deeply linked. The impacts of climate change offer a telling example of how environmental racism reflects this fact. While the conclusions of climate scientists are remarkably clear – anthropogenic climate change is occurring at a dramatic pace and with increasing intensity – this is also happening unevenly, with people of color and indigenous peoples suffering some of the worst consequences.[39] If one only pays attention to the global scale it appears that the worst effects of climate change are not yet upon us. But if one examines what is occurring in neighborhoods, *barrios*, indigenous peoples' lands, and much of the global south, the picture is quite different. The impacts are visible and extensive. Scale matters, and when scale and social difference intersect we are able to see phenomena that were invisible or seemingly less urgent prior to that moment.

Scale is a highly racialized phenomenon. Consider the much-debated subject of "tipping points" in research on residential segregation versus integration and how this supports racial discrimination and violence against people of color. The "tipping point" is said to occur when a certain percentage of people of color move into a majority white neighborhood and triggers an exodus of whites.[40] In many cases, that point was said to be triggered when as little as 5 percent of the neighborhood residents are people of color. While the efficacy of this theory has been supported and challenged over the years, the evidence is strong that when people of color, immigrants, and other marginalized populations move into majority white neighborhoods their presence often sparks anxieties on the part of whites that are disproportionate to the number of newcomers. The phenomenon of "environmental privilege" illustrates this dynamic nicely, as in those cases when whites seek to hold onto scarce and cherished socioecological spaces in exclusive communities like Aspen, Colorado.[41] Thus race and scale intersect here to reinforce white supremacy and resist efforts by even a small group of people of color to "move on up" into more desirable neighborhoods with greater access to valued amenities and infrastructure.

Research on social cognition and interpersonal interactions has found that ~~implicit bias~~ exists with such great intensity in the US across racial groups that white research subjects tend to perceive threats to their well-being when they see black and brown people when no such threat exists.[42] While this research on implicit bias has been described as highly consequential for the kinds of everyday microsociological interactions between and among individuals across the racial spectrum (especially in the case of gun violence in the name of white "self-defense"), it has major macrosociological implications as well. Therefore I find the concept of implicit bias useful for thinking more deeply about the intersection of race and scale.

In other words, if these studies find that people of color are implicitly viewed as threatening, then the presence of nonwhite individuals and communities is perceived to be much *larger* in the cognitive terrain of whites. This (mis)perception and social inflation of the scale of people of color's presence, and the anxiety-inducing meaning of that presence, suggests that responses ranging from everyday exclusions and social slights to white vigilante violence, institutional racism, and state violence may often be, albeit perversely, reactions commensurate with that (mis)perception. As the sociological mantra known as the Thomas Dictum reminds us, "if men [sic] define situations as real, they are real in their consequences."[43] That is, if whites define people of color as threatening, then the response to that "threat" will be real in its consequences. Under these conditions, it is even more challenging to ensure that the lives of black people will matter.

Race and scale intertwine to reveal that when black people respond to racism (whether by police or via environmental racism), their actions are generally viewed as a menace and a threat that is disproportionate and outsized. We can see this, for example, in the militarized response by police departments when interacting with the Black Lives Matter movement, which was on full display in Ferguson, Missouri in 2014. In the 1990s, under the Pentagon's Excess Property (or 1033) Program, the US Department of Defense provided roughly $5 billion in military equipment to local police departments, a legacy of the surplus from two foreign wars.[44] Such equipment has included Humvees, mine-resistant and ambush-protected trucks, and M14 rifles, among other items. The 1033 Program came under fire by civil rights activists, supporters of the Black Lives Matter movement, and even military veterans, when disturbing images of police and protesters clashing in Ferguson, Missouri in response to the police killing of Michael Brown seemed to be indistinguishable from media images of civilians being repressed by an occupying military force in some faraway land. President Obama promised to scale back the worst abuses of the 1033 program, but since 2003 – long before the Black Lives Matter movement emerged – local police departments have been able to access similar equipment through the Department of Homeland Security. This fact begs for a scalar analysis that links the militarized oppression of African-American bodies and communities to the US military's oppression of people of color elsewhere in the world – in Afghanistan, Iraq, Syria, Pakistan, Yemen, Palestine, and many other nations where the US uses military force directly or by proxy to protect its interests. This is also an environmental justice issue: the US military is one of the largest sources of pollution on earth.[45] Also, militarism and masculinist politics tend to go hand in hand, and both tend to result in socially and ecologically harmful practices.

We can now connect the phenomenon of white anxieties at the micro scale (implicit bias), the neighborhood scale (collective

51

acts such as white flight and support of residential segregation), and the macro scale (the state's militarized responses to Black Lives Matter protests) to better understand how the intersection of race and scale is so consequential. Let's consider a question: Does one hundred really always equal one hundred? Imagine one hundred white protesters marching through a neighborhood in the US of any racial composition, protesting anything. Then imagine one hundred African-American or Muslim protesters marching through a white and Christian neighborhood. Consider the various likely police and security responses (to say nothing of the potential response by white residents). It will be both qualitatively and quantitatively different, because when African-Americans, Muslims, and other people outside of the racial and religious mainstream attempt to exercise political power publicly and disrupt a white community, they are seen as a threat not only to that community but to the nation and the symbols upon which it was founded. So one hundred does not always equal one hundred: the intersection of race and scale reveals how our perceptions of certain groups shapes the way we imagine their presence, their numbers, their influence, and how "we" should respond.

Race and the scales of time, history, and the future

Finally, BLM's work speaks to the myriad ways in which scale can be thought of and articulated temporally. In fact, the entire point of the BLM movement is, in some ways, an intervention to remind and challenge the US: to make the point that blatant, violent acts of anti-black violence are not a thing of the past; that they are still rampant in what some observers had hoped would be a "post-racial" era. Critical Ethnic Studies scholars such as Joy James, Ruth Gilmore, Dylan Rodriguez, Martha Escobar, and Dennis Childs have argued that the US criminal legal system is not just an institutional force that has a disproportionately negative impact on people of color. They contend that the system was designed to be, and remains, a racial punishment system that is rooted in the history and logic of chattel slavery.[46] The 1857 Dred Scott decision by the US Supreme Court (*Dred Scott v. Sandford*) declared that

African-Americans – whether free or enslaved – had no rights that white persons were bound to respect and could never be citizens of the US. And while the Emancipation Proclamation would seem to have dismantled that decision, there are at least two limitations to that assumption. The first is that we must be reminded that the Dred Scott decision applied to all African-Americans regardless of their status as free or enslaved persons. The second limitation of that view is that the Thirteenth Amendment to the US Constitution contained an exception clause that allows enslavement "as punishment for a crime." In Dred Scott and the Thirteenth Amendment, we have two major precedents that produce a continuing legal and Constitutional foundation for the devaluation of black life in the US.

More specific to the question of policing, as other scholars have pointed out, the very origins of the police in the US were to control and repress the white working classes in the North and to patrol and maintain slavery in the South. Brutality, anti-black racism, and anti–working class sentiment were thus built into the American policing system from the beginning.[47]

Black Lives Matter movement activists have been keenly aware of the history of racist violence in the US and how it reflects the intersections of race and scale. BLM co-founder Alicia Garza uses time as an indicator of the intersection of race, sexuality, and scale's intersections, but does so linking history to an imagined future:

> But what I can say to my child, just like my mom says to me, is that there was a time when it wasn't OK for people to be out [about their sexuality]. There was a time when black people were being slaughtered. And I hope that the end to that story is, "and then we organized, and we built a vibrant international movement, and we really changed conditions for black people in this country, and for everybody." And I'm hoping that the story that I'm also able to tell is that our demands went beyond "stop killing us," to ensure the quality of life for everybody. And that we won that.[48]

Third Pillar: An Anti-Statist/Anarchist Reading of BLM

The third pillar of Critical EJ Studies is the view that social inequalities – from racism to speciesism – are not aberrations, but rather are deeply embedded in society and reinforced by state power. Therefore the current social order stands as a fundamental obstacle to social and environmental justice. A logical conclusion of this observation is that social change movements may be better off being cautious about engaging the state as a target of reform and/or as a reliable partner.

Racism, for example, is a foundational component of the political, legal, economic, and cultural systems in the US. At the Constitutional Convention of 1787, it was decided that enslaved African-Americans would count as 3/5ths of a human being for the purposes of determining each state's population for legislative representation and taxation, a decision that would shape the life chances of black people for generations. While that decision was later legally dismantled in the formal sense, today, centuries after the US was founded, African-Americans de facto enjoy fewer rights and significantly lower social value than whites. African-Americans suffer from, for example, deep economic, educational, public health, and environmental inequalities; earn far less income and own far less wealth and property than whites; are more likely to attend low-quality segregated schools and to live in residentially segregated communities marked by financial disinvestment, a brutal occupying police force presence, and environmental racism. Public health disparities affect African-Americans dramatically, as homicides, infant mortality, life expectancy, asthma, and a range of other illnesses and life events reveal a much lower statistical value of black life.[49] And millions of African-Americans are either confined to prisons through the system of mass incarceration or subjected to routine surveillance and control through the system of mass probation.[50] Thus, racism is, for Black Lives Matter co-founder Alicia Garza, "a disease that this country has in our very DNA."[51]

The Black Lives Matter message is resoundingly clear: in an era during which Barack Obama – an African-American President

54

– was elected and served two terms, the United States did not move into the "post-racial" historical period that some observers had hoped for or even claimed was imminent and emergent. Rather, the realities and experiences of anti-black racism at the hands of agents of the state, corporations, and everyday people and vigilantes has continued to mar society and do extraordinary harm to African-American communities in particular and to the nation more generally. Warehousing people of color in prisons, racial profiling, warrantless searches of persons and property, and mandatory minimum sentencing for minor drug-related offenses constitute just a few examples of the "overpolicing"[52] and hypercriminalization of African-American communities that are routine.[53] After the killing of Michael Brown and the brutalizing of racial justice protesters in Ferguson, Missouri by a police force using military equipment, BLM activists Darnell Moore and Patrisse Cullors wrote, "many more of us have decided that we could not allow Ferguson to be portrayed as an aberration in America: it must remain understood as a microcosm of the effects of anti-black racism."[54] BLM sees anti-black racism today as a continuation of centuries of racist violence directed at and intended to destroy African-American communities. In other words, BLM shares the perspective of Critical EJ Studies: that racism is deeply entrenched in US society.

Debates will continue over whether social movements should seek to reform or transform the criminal legal system. BLM is an important part of that conversation because it is a movement whose participants often embrace the state, but do so in a rigorous and critical fashion. For example, much of the chanting and protest calls at BLM events include demands to "prosecute the police" and implement stronger laws against hate crimes and police brutality.[55] After white police officer Darren Wilson killed Mike Brown, a young African-American man, in Ferguson, Missouri, many protesters held signs declaring "Arrest Darren Wilson for Murder!" and members of the local Hands Up Don't Shoot Coalition issued that same demand on a routine basis.[56] Moreover, two leading BLM activists declared "We will call on the office of US attorney general Eric Holder to release the names of all officers involved in killing black people within the last five years, both while on patrol and in custody, so they can be brought to justice – if they haven't already."[57] The BLM's "National Demands" document reads, in part, "We will help develop a network of organizations and advocates to form a national policy specifically aimed at redressing the systemic pattern of anti-black law enforcement violence in the US."[58] In November 2015, after a group of white supremacists shot and wounded several activists who were protesting the police killing of an unarmed African-American man named Jamar Clark in Minneapolis, BLM released a statement declaring, "The war on black lives is escalating, and it's time for President Obama to intervene. The Black Lives Matter Network urgently calls upon the Department of Justice to investigate this shooting as a hate crime."[59] That statement continued, "This shooting of black activists by white vigilantes in Minneapolis is a symptom of a much larger problem – that while the homegrown domestic terrorism of white supremacists is alive and well in 2015, it too often lives in the shadows of media coverage dominated by the international terrorism of so-called religious extremists. But, organized white American vigilantism too, is terrorism." Finally, BLM activists have regularly called for greater oversight over police and for increased presence of black people in government decisionmaking bodies. For example, in the wake of numerous police killings of African-Americans in recent years, the Los Angeles chapter of BLM has demanded that the mayor appoint activists from the black community to key city commissions.

When BLM demands inclusion in governmental bodies and invokes the language of hate crimes and terrorism, such practices and legislation reflect the power of grassroots movements to move state actors on important progressive issues. They also, however, signal the movement's willingness to expand troubling, controlling, authoritative, and lethal state power. BLM is therefore *not* asking how we might build safe communities *beyond* the state, but rather how we might do so with *greater* state intervention of a progressive kind. BLM co-founder Patrice Cullors' vision of social change includes a plan to "divest from policing and divest from this prison system ... and reinvesting into poor communities, reinvesting into allowing us to have access to healthy food, access to jobs, access to shelter."[60] As Cullors and Darnell Moore elaborated,

> We will advocate for a decrease in law-enforcement spending at the local, state and federal levels and a reinvestment of that budgeted money into the black communities most devastated by poverty in order to create jobs, housing and schools. This money should be redirected to those federal departments charged with providing employment, housing and educational services. . . . Our group is proof that dedicated and skilled black folks can work – together – to end state violence, homelessness, joblessness, imprisonment and more inside black communities.[61]

While perhaps generative and seemingly firmly on the progressive cutting edge, these BLM statements are also limited and contradictory, in the view of scholars who believe that states are both inherently racially exclusionary and violent. Many BLM activists like Moore and Cullors hope to reassign state resources from overtly punitive, criminal legal purposes to public services, basic needs, and human rights. The problem with this approach is that it overlooks the possibility that reinforcing progressive state power may also reinforce state power more generally, including its repressive dimensions.

My point is that, while shifting state resources away from openly punitive to less openly punitive functions may appear to represent meaningful change, BLM falls short of a transformative vision of change with respect to challenging the state. Consider this quote from one BLM supporter: "In order for world powers to maintain slavery and post-slavery racist legislation, it was crucial for the people to believe that the uncivilized nature of Africans required excessive force, policing, and restraint."[62] This statement, like much of the BLM-related discourse, suggests that it is *excessive* state force, not state force itself, that is the primary problem, and that if we can reduce that excess and bring the state into alignment with BLM goals then the state's behavior will reflect a greater valuing of African-American communities. But, according to many scholars, repression and violence are not practices that states engage in on an occasional basis; they are at the core of what states do and why they exist. Modern nation states claim a "monopoly on the legitimate use of physical force."[63] They are, according to a number of scholars, inherently authoritarian and exclusionary forces. As philosopher Charles Mills writes, "To understand the long, bloody history of police brutality against blacks in the United States, for example, one has to recognize it not as excesses by individual racists but as an organic part of this political enterprise."[64] Moreover, historically, modern nation states co-emerged with and made possible the modern categories of race, gender, class, sexuality, citizenship, and species, as well as their bases for inclusion/exclusion, manipulation, and domination. So any social movement seeking to push for reforms may do so from within a statist tradition, but such visions and practices will generally be limited, since they tend to rely on and therefore reinforce state dominance rooted in the goals of control of knowledge, ideas, people, nonhuman populations, ecosystems, and territory. Thus any social movement concerned with state-sanctioned racist police brutality might do well to heed the implications of the anarchist slogan "Police existence is brutality."[65]

From a traditional pluralist perspective, states are sites where citizens and various other stakeholders and interest groups converge to elect representatives and make their voices heard in public spaces and shape public policy.[66] Departing from that view, a power elite perspective casts states as sites of power struggles, where certain interest groups tend to dominate others, setting public policy agendas and unevenly shaping life chances for members of society.[67] From a women-of-color feminist, critical race theory, and anarchist perspective, however, states are also institutions that, by definition, practice exclusion, control, and violence (in addition to their other functions), and so statecraft involves the management and manipulation of our everyday existence and mobility regardless of our consent.[68] Social change movements can be thought of, then, as efforts aimed at opposing objectionable practices or promoting others (such as reform), or as efforts aimed at either moving beyond the state or reducing social movements' reliance on the state for building community and the capacity for coalitions, mobility, and decisionmaking.

If Black Lives Matter was founded to challenge state-sanctioned violence, then it makes sense to extend the reach of this movement's analysis and action to the problem of environmental racism. Keith Ellison and Van Jones (cited earlier) make this connection, and argue that black lives should also matter in terms of environmental racism. They do not, however, explicitly make the link to state-sanctioned violence. Since environmental racism is often a form of state-sanctioned violence through the direct harm that state agencies and state-regulated companies do via polluting in communities of color, then BLM might do well to pay greater attention to this issue. Likewise, EJ scholars studying the BLM movement might be encouraged to theorize environmental racism with greater depth and linkages to the relationship between state institutions and racialized violence. BLM activists and EJ scholars might begin to think about how to make our communities sites of environmental justice *beyond the state* or at least through a major reduction in the presence of state actors. In fact, some BLM activists urge us to think about how to make our communities safe "beyond policing,"[69] which is a good start. The BLM movement, the EJ movement, and EJ scholarship generally share a consensus that they are looking to the state and its legal systems to deliver justice and to regulate industry, and that view must be questioned.

Policing, police shootings, jailings, harassment, imprisonment, surveillance, and social movement repression are all forms of state control over African-American populations. Black Lives Matter is focused on police violence and state-sanctioned violence, but few have made the link to environmental racism explicitly on those grounds. Consider that state-sanctioned violence is about social control, the control over a population's mobility and its access to various spaces and resources. It is a technology of control over bodies and the spaces they occupy, and reflects a system of differential valuation that places certain bodies, populations, and the knowledge and cultural practices they produce beneath that of dominant groups. Thus if we think of environmental racism as an extension of these practices then we can more effectively theorize

Beyond the state

it as a form of state violence, a framework that is absent from most EJ scholarship.[70] Moreover, a Critical EJ Studies perspective contends that since this kind of violence and the maintenance of a range of social inequalities are integral to the function of states, then racial, social, and environmental justice efforts will be necessarily limited if they do not seek change that limits or even goes beyond the reach of state power.

Fourth Pillar: Indispensability

The fourth pillar of the Critical EJ Studies framework centers on the concepts of *racial* and *socioecological indispensability*. In his book *Black and Brown Solidarity,* John Márquez introduces the concept "racial expendability" to argue that black and brown bodies are, in the eyes of the state and the legal system, cast as a threat that should be confronted with institutional violence.[71] Márquez and a number of other ethnic studies scholars and activists contend that, in a white supremacist society, people of color are therefore viewed as expendable.[72] Critical geographer Ruth Wilson Gilmore speaks to this point in her book *Golden Gulag*, in which she argues that the massive buildup of prisons to warehouse people of color in the state of California and the US nationally was a public policy decision to attempt to contain and control populations whose very existence is viewed as troubling to the state and its institutions, which are generally committed to upholding and defending white supremacy.[73]

A Critical EJ Studies perspective builds on these ideas by countering the ideology of white supremacy and human dominionism, and articulating the perspective that excluded, marginalized, and othered populations, beings, and things – both human and more-than-human – must be viewed not as expendable but rather as *indispensable* to our collective futures. This is what I term *racial indispensability* (when referring to people of color) and *socioecological indispensability* (when referring to broader communities within and across the human / more-than-human spectrum). Racial indispensability is intended to challenge the logic of racial expendability, and is the idea that institutions, policies, and practices that support and perpetrate anti-black racism intended to destroy African-American bodies suffer from the flawed assumption that the future of African-Americans is somehow de-linked from the future of white communities.

Thus the importance of Critical EJ Studies here is to underscore that when social systems and practices upholding white supremacy and whiteness are predicated on the annihilation of black life, they are making a self-defeating error. This is the failure to realize that white supremacy and whiteness are impossible without black bodies and the idea of blackness. That is, since race, racial categories, and racism are all *relational* social forces, the very existence of whiteness and white supremacy is predicated on the existence of people of color and the idea of non-whiteness, blackness, etc. Thus to rid the world of black people or people of color would be to destroy whiteness itself. In other words, the idea that whiteness can only triumph and survive via the annihilation of black life commits the classic ecological error of *dualism* or *separation*. In environmental studies, dualism is the idea that we see various categories of existence as separate and arranged in oppositional hierarchies, such as culture/nature, man/woman, European/non-European, human/animal, white/black, heterosexual/homosexual, and so on, when in fact these categories are constantly blurred, transgressed, and revealed to be socially constructed and highly fluid and malleable. So Critical EJ Studies facilitates an understanding that a vision of white supremacy premised on the destruction of people of color is as illogical and self-defeating as a vision of an economy and a nation state premised on the destruction of ecosystems. In a sense, this observation reflects a reality of social systems as ecosystems, and vice versa: that everything in the universe is hitched to everything else, so that what affects one member or element affects all of them. The destruction of people of color harms white people and it harms the more-than-human world, and vice versa, so Critical EJ Studies affirms that black lives, the lives of people of color, are *indispensable*. Going further, the idea of *socioecological indispensability* reflects the Critical EJ Studies affirmation that the well-being of all living things and of all species is *indispensible*. This is both a socioecological reality and an affirmation of a politics of solidarity and coalition building that firmly states "All of us or none!"

Black Lives Matter activists routinely speak to this issue as well. In 2015, BLM issued a "State of the Black Union" in which they wrote, "None of us are free until all of us are free."[74] This is a variation on a quote that has been attributed to the likes of the poet Emma Lazarus, the Reverend Dr. Martin Luther King, Jr., and many others. It is also articulated powerfully in Barry Mann's rhythm and blues song "None of Us Are Free," which includes the chorus, "None of us are free, none of us are free, if one of us is chained, none of us are free."[75]

Reflecting this view more than a century ago, African-American historian, author, and public speaker Anna Julia Cooper spoke to a group of black clergymen in 1892 and said, "Only the black woman can say 'when and where I enter, in the quiet, undisputed dignity of my womanhood, without violence and without suing or special patronage, then and there the whole . . . race enters with me'."[76] A year later, making this claim even stronger, at the 1893 World's Congress of Representative Women, Cooper stated,

Let woman's claim be as broad in the concrete as the abstract. We take our stand on the solidarity of humanity, the oneness of life, and the unnaturalness and injustice of all special favoritism, whether of sex, race, country, or condition. If one link of the chain is broken, the chain is broken. A bridge is no stronger than its weakest part, and a cause is not worthier than its weakest element. Least of all can woman's cause afford to decry the weak. We want, then, as toilers for the universal triumph of justice and human rights, to go to our homes from this Congress demanding an entrance not through a gateway for ourselves, our race, our sex, or our sect, but a grand highway for humanity.[77]

BLM co-founder Alicia Garza echoes and articulates this idea more than a century later, as follows:

Black Lives Matter doesn't mean your life isn't important – it means that Black lives, which are seen as without value within White supremacy, are important to your liberation. Given the disproportion-ate impact state violence has on Black lives, we understand that when

Black people in this country get free, *the benefits will be wide reaching and transformative for society as a whole.* When we are able to end hyper-criminalization and sexualization of Black people and end the poverty, control, and surveillance of Black people, every single person in this world has a better shot at getting and staying free. *When Black people get free, everybody gets free.* This is why we call on Black people and our allies to take up the call that Black lives matter. We're not saying Black lives are more important than other lives, or that other lives are not criminalized and oppressed in various ways. We remain in active solidarity with all oppressed people who are fighting for their liberation and we know that our destinies are intertwined. . . . And, perhaps more importantly, when Black people cry out in defense of our lives, which are uniquely, systematically, and savagely targeted by the state, we are asking you, our family, to stand with us in affirming Black lives. Not just all lives. Black lives. . . . Our collective futures depend on it.[78]

Author and environmental activist Naomi Klein draws on Garza's words and analysis in support of racial and socioecological indispensability as it relates to climate change:

According to Alicia Garza, one of the people who founded the Black Lives Matter project, the slogan is not meant to claim that black lives matter more than others. Rather, by highlighting the foundational role that anti-black racism has played in constructing a system of racial superiority, it tells everyone that black lives "are important to your liberation." . . . What climate change tells us is that this is as true at a global, species-wide scale as it is within the borders of the United States. In Copenhagen in 2009, African governments argued that if black lives mattered, then 2 degrees of warming was too high. By disregarding this basic humanist logic, the biggest polluters were making a crude cost-benefit analysis. They were calculating that the loss of life, livelihood and culture for some of the poorest people on the planet was an acceptable price to pay to protect the economies of some of the richest people on the planet.[79]

Expendability and erasure tend to be the order of the day for people of color in a white supremacist society.[80] The evidence for this claim is abundant and clear. For example, consider that in the United States, a nation where surveillance and collection of private, personal data are expanding through the use of the US PATRIOT Act, the National Security Agency, and telecommunications companies gathering "meta data" in the alleged interests of national security against "terrorist" threats, there was, as of 2015, no national database of police-involved shootings, which are engulfing black communities with no end in sight. In other words, ordinary people have to gather these data themselves because the state is uninterested in doing so, which raises particular concerns given the rampant anti-black police brutality in the US. That is a profound illustration of both the proliferation of state violence and its erasure. Indispensability is the antithesis of expendability and erasure because it is a concept and claim that challenges that violence by calling for multiracial, multi-issue solidarities and a socioecological vision that insists that our collective futures will include "all of us or none." As Alicia Garza states, "That, to us, is really the next frontier that we need to just get deeper into – a real valuation of life overall."[81]

Collective Punishment, Black Lives Matter, and Critical Environmental Justice

A fundamental tenet of criminal law is that individuals may only be punished for crimes or offenses they have committed and that such punishment must be directed at that individual person. In international law, any sanctions imposed on a community or population without regard to guilt or innocence of an offense committed is considered *collective punishment* and is therefore prohibited.[82] Zero-tolerance policing is one of the prevailing practices in US law enforcement today, involving indiscriminate searches and seizures and wholesale arrests and harassment of people for "quality of life" offenses, primarily in communities of color where people are often struggling to survive. Chris Fabricant of the Innocence Project argues that such practices constitute collective punishment because they maintain a punitive approach for an entire community when only a small number of persons may have committed violent crimes.[83] In linking this idea to the

Black Lives Matter movement and the challenge of environmental injustice, I would take Fabricant's argument further to extend the concept of collective punishment. First, I contend that it is largely immaterial whether crimes have occurred in these communities because the presence of police in communities of color has little to do with crime. Crime rates in the US have been dropping steadily for years and yet there has been a boom in prison construction and an attendant rise in mass incarceration.[84] In other words, the police presence in communities of color reflects the (racial) state's interests in controlling these communities rather than controlling crime.[85] Thus, contrary to the generally accepted legal definition of collective punishment, I maintain that it need not be viewed as a practice that emerges in response to any legal offense per se, other than the "offense" of being black in a white-dominated society. That is, I contest the assumption by legal scholars that collective punishment is always a response to crime. That assumption is problematic because it provides states practicing collective punishment the advantage of being seen as merely overzealous in otherwise justified and legitimate criminal apprehension and crime-reduction efforts. The assumption that a crime has occurred and the state's collective punishment is a response to that crime misses the crucial fact that *criminalization* of communities of color is ongoing and foundational to the racial state, and therefore no crime need be committed for collective punishment to take place.[86] Second, building on that first point, the evidence suggests quite strongly that multiple forms of racist state-sanctioned violence directed at African-Americans can be defined as a form of collective punishment (for the "offense" of being black – a condition of being interpreted as threatening to the state and its interests). If we accept that claim, then environmental racism, as a form of state-sanctioned racist violence involving the infliction of pain and suffering through the poisoning of air, land, water, food, and bodies, could also be defined as *collective punishment*. If we view environmental racism as collective punishment, then that facilitates the possibilities for broader conversations and actions around the problem of state-sanctioned violence for the Black Lives Matter movement, the Environmental Justice Movement, and Critical Environmental Justice Studies. To take this line of reasoning even further: my view is that collective punishment is a form of routine state violence that occurs even in the absence of legal infractions, and we should understand collective punishment itself as an offense or a harm inflicted on a population that must be addressed from within a broader social and political framework that exists outside of state-sanctioned legal discourse. In other words, while collective punishment is a term used primarily in the international law and human rights communities that seek legal, state-based remedies for these problems, a Critical EJ Studies perspective sees value in defining this problem and its solutions outside of that framework because states are the primary source of the harm and logically will be unlikely sites of justice for said harm.

A Critical Environmental Justice perspective on the phenomenon of the Black Lives Matter movement demonstrates how attention to multiple categories of difference and inequality (including more-than-human species and the built environment), consciousness of scale, and a focus on linking the entrenched character of social inequalities with transformative, anti-authoritarian and anarchist perspectives can produce an enriched, lively, and robust account of that movement's core concerns, its limitations, and its possibilities. In this perspective racial indispensability becomes evident. Black Lives Matter challenges the scourge of state-sanctioned violence against diversely constituted communities of African descent, with a primary emphasis on police brutality and mass incarceration. If we think of environmental racism as an extension of those state-sanctioned practices – in other words a form of violent and exclusionary control over bodies, space, and knowledge systems – then we can reframe it as a form of state violence. This would open up our capacity to pursue future visions and practices for EJ that foment change that limits, or goes beyond, the boundaries of state power.

3

Prisons and the Fight for Environmental Justice

The United States of America has the largest prison system of any nation on earth, the largest number of prisoners of any country, and one of the highest percentages of imprisoned persons of any nation.[1] Since 1970, the US has seen a 700 percent increase in people imprisoned,[2] a result of the growth in city police departments, a "get tough on crime" and "war on drugs" punitive approach to criminal justice, and a concerted effort to control and minimize the power of social movements and other forms of resistance from within communities of color.[3] The United States holds fully 25 percent of the world's prison population but has only 5 percent of the world's people. As of this writing there are more than 2.3 million people incarcerated in prisons, jails, immigration detention centers and other correctional facilities in the United States; if all of those prisoners were housed in one location, it would constitute the fourth largest city in the nation.[4]

What does all of this have to do with environmental justice? Until fairly recently, few scholars, activists, or government officials have linked prisons to environmental issues and environmental justice concerns, but this is changing. In January 2015, the Prison Ecology Project formed to investigate the links between the US prison system and environmental threats, uncovering and highlighting scores of cases across the nation where ecosystems, nearby communities, and prisoners themselves were placed at risk due to prison proposals, construction, and routine operations.[5] Panagioti Tsolkas is co-founder of the

Prison Ecology Project and a coordinator of the Campaign to Fight Toxic Prisons. He is a veteran activist with many years of direct action and community organizing experience. Tsolkas worked as an editor of the radical environmental movement's *Earth First! Journal*, as a trainer with the Ruckus Society, and as a chairperson of both the Palm Beach County Environmental Coalition and the Lake Worth Community Relations Board (a municipal board responsible for police oversight). I first met Panagioti Tsolkas in 2009 at the Walker Community Church at Minneapolis, when he and two other activists were producing the Earth First! Roadshow – a multimedia, action-packed, humorous, information-rich and inspiring presentation, and a series of grassroots workshops that motivated people around the country to join the Earth First! movement and to build on existing movements in our own communities. I spoke with Panagioti about EF!'s involvement in solidarity work and intersectional movement organizing that went beyond the traditional boundaries of environmentalism, and he educated me about this radical environmental movement's work with No More Deaths and other immigrant rights groups working on the US–Mexico border; he spoke about EF!ers' direct involvement in supporting the Umoja Village actions in Liberty City, Miami, where black residents were protesting housing evictions during yet another economic crisis and financial downturn – which always seem to hit working people and people of color the hardest. These were the stories of solidarity and coalition-building that we don't hear enough of from the environmental movement. Through the Prison Ecology Project, Panagioti has worked to bring together concerns over mass incarceration and environmental sustainability and justice, thus linking issues and movements that are not commonly thought of as connected. But well before the PEP was founded, there were important examples of activists, scholars, and policy-makers making these connections, which will be covered in the next sections. This chapter explores the relationship between the US prison and jail system and myriad environmental justice concerns, through an application of the four pillars of the Critical EJ Studies framework.

Early Linkages between Prisons and Environmental Justice: Mothers of East Los Angeles (MELA), Critical Resistance, and The Fight Over E-Waste Recycling

Juana Gutiérrez is the daughter of a Mexican farmer; she immigrated to the US at age fifteen. She remembers being instructed by her parents to stay out of trouble, but like many young persons she rebelled, and soon became a community organizer. In 1985, when California Governor George Deukmejian proposed to construct yet another prison in the predominantly Latino community of East LA, Gutiérrez, Aurora Castillo, and other Mexicana/Chicana grassroots activists started a social and environmental justice group called Mothers of East Los Angeles / Madres del Este de Los Angeles (MELA) with help from Monsignor John Moretta, a local Catholic parish priest with Resurrection Church. MELA activists were outraged at the Governor's plan and they built support for their efforts to oppose the prison through enlisting church members and anyone else who would listen. They leafleted and marched for months, protesting the decision to invest public funds to incarcerate people of color instead of using this funding for job creation, health care, and education. Eventually they won, and the proposal was stopped. Emboldened by this important victory, MELA took on additional threats to the community, including an above-ground oil pipeline that would have passed through areas with public schools, a hazardous waste storage facility, and a $20 million toxic waste incinerator that would have burned 125,000 pounds of hazardous substances each day (after six years of protests and lawsuits, MELA stopped the incinerator).[6] MELA went on to launch water conservation programs and a lead poisoning education campaign, building on earlier successes and linking multiple public health, environmental, and social issues and defining them as EJ concerns.[7] And it all started with a prison.

Critical Resistance is a social movement whose goal is to abolish the prison industrial complex (PIC) and support grassroots efforts to promote food, shelter, and freedom as more appropriate pathways to community safety and health. Founded in 1997, CR has worked to oppose the construction of numerous prisons around the US. In June 2000, CR filed an environmental lawsuit (*Critical Resistance et al. v. the California Department of Corrections*) to challenge the state's proposal to build a prison in Delano, California (in Kern County). That facility was called Delano II because it would be located in a town where a prison had already been built (North Kern State Prison, a medium-security facility, built in 1993). The lawsuit was part of a campaign that fused anti-prison and environmental justice organizing and aims, taking the novel approach of highlighting the combined environmental and social impacts of the proposed prison. The litigation challenged the state of California's environmental impact statement (EIS), claiming that it was defective in that it failed to pay sufficient attention to the effects of the prison on farmland (with a particular focus on the anticipated stress that a prison could place on the region's aquifer and water system, which the state's agricultural sector relied upon), traffic patterns and anticipated increased congestion and air pollution, school overcrowding, and threats to critical habitat for endangered species like the Tipton kangaroo rat and the San Joaquin Valley kit fox. Moreover, the plaintiffs argued that the California Department of Corrections should translate the EIS and hold public meetings in Spanish, given the fact that the population residing in the Delano area was overwhelmingly Chicano/Mexicano.[8] What was perhaps most fascinating and revealing about this campaign was the diversity and range of participants in the coalition, which included Critical Resistance, the California Prison Moratorium Project, the NAACP, the Rainforest Action Network, the National Lawyers Guild, and a group called Friends of the Kangaroo Rat.

A key moment during the campaign against Delano II was when two anti-prison groups – Critical Resistance and the California Prison Moratorium Project – collaborated with leading environmental justice groups (including MELA) to organize a conference: "Joining Forces: Environmental Justice and the Fight against Prison Expansion." In June 2001, a Bakersfield, California,

Superior Court agreed with the activists and ruled in their favor that the EIS was inadequate. Unfortunately, this victory was followed by a loss on appeal, two years later, and the prison project proceeded. The prison cost more than $700 million to build and was completed in 2004.[9] While that particular battle was lost, activists learned valuable lessons, such as maintaining a broad tactical and strategic approach that does not rely entirely on a legal or state-based effort, so that movement-building was just as important – if not more so – as demanding justice from the courts.[10] And, as Panagioti Tsolkas told me, activists won the war in the sense that "Delano II was the last state prison built in California – this was an important victory."[11]

Prison Labor and Electronic Waste Recycling

E-waste is the most rapidly growing waste stream in the world, and experts project continued growth into the foreseeable future.[12] The United States is one of the chief sources of e-waste, since US consumers purchase more computers than the citizenry of any other nation. Electronics industries in the US have been shipping these hazardous materials to nations of the global south for years. Responding to this problem, in the 1990s and 2000s activist groups like the Silicon Valley Toxics Coalition, the GrassRoots Recycling Network, and others came together under the Computer TakeBack Campaign banner and ran several initiatives aimed at putting a stop to the export of electronic waste to the global south. They also campaigned to ensure that it was recycled by governments and companies safely and responsibly. Dell Computer Corporation was a target of this effort and responded by recycling e-waste using prison labor.

Dell made the decision to work with UNICOR – a publicly subsidized prison industrial operator that runs a chain of plants in the federal penitentiary system – as its primary recycling partner. Activists countered by linking two issues – workplace/ prison toxics and the global/international environmental racism of e-waste exports. Grassroots leaders visited a prison in California where Dell contracted for this kind of work. Sheila Davis, then

Director of SVTC's Clean Computer Campaign in San Jose, California, stated, "We were appalled to witness the working conditions inside the federal prison at Atwater, California, where inmates were using hammers to smash computer monitors."[13]

One inmate/e-waste worker at the prison in Atwater reported,

> Even when I wear the paper mask, I blow out black mucus from my nose everyday. The black particles in my nose and throat look as if I am a heavy smoker. Cuts and abrasions happen all the time. Of these the open wounds are exposed to the dirt and dust and many do not heal as quickly as normal wounds.[14]

Prison inmates reported that those who sought to improve conditions in the e-waste recycling facility faced discipline and the threat of job loss. Inmates worked for $.20–$1.26 per hour at the Atwater prison,[15] toiling outside the protection of state and local environmental and labor regulations that private sector employers must obey. The laborers are not classified as employees and are not protected against retaliatory acts by their employer (UNICOR) under the Fair Labor Standards Act. Inmates are not allowed to unionize or serve on the prison health and safety committees. And UNICOR acknowledged that e-waste processed in its facilities is likely exported overseas to other nations.

In June 2003, the CTBC released "A Tale of Two Systems" – a report that contrasted Dell's prison-based recycling operations with Hewlett-Packard's free-market partnership with the firm MicroMetallics. Barely a week after the CTBC released this report announcing its concerns about the use of prison labor, the Dell Corporation announced that it would no longer rely on prisons to supply recycling workers for its program.[16] In 2004, the CTBC achieved a key victory by persuading Dell to join H-P in endorsing a Statement of Principles in support of Extended Producer Responsibility.

In less time than it takes to introduce a bill to a City Council, the CTBC forced what was at the time the largest computer company in the world to cease the use of prison labor; forced the company to choose another contractor altogether; persuaded that contractor to adopt the CTBC's pledge of stewardship and principles of environmental justice; and persuaded Dell to endorse a pledge of producer responsibility. This was remarkable. Dell was just one particularly high-value target. Ultimately, this movement succeeded in passing legislation and securing agreements with many US states, the University of California system, the European Union, and other companies who pledged to reject prison recycling and prohibit e-waste exports.

The work of activists at MELA, Critical Resistance, and the Computer TakeBack Campaign highlighted key intersections between prisons and environmental justice concerns. Many activists did not know that the United States Environmental Protection Agency (USEPA) was doing this as well at the same time.

The USEPA: One Step Forward, Two Steps Back

In 1999, in response to public complaints about the safety of prisons, the USEPA's Region III office (based in Philadelphia, its priorities are the Mid-Atlantic states) did a series of inspections across several prisons. The branch of Region III that conducted these inspections was the Office of Enforcement, Compliance, and Environmental Justice (OECEJ) and the effort was titled the Prison Initiative. Complaints they received that prompted these inspections included concerns about "noxious odors from overloaded sewage treatment plants to improper storage and disposal of hazardous waste."[17] It might surprise readers to know that OECEJ was particularly interested in investigating prisons with "a variety of manufacturing areas (industrial shops) that generated hazardous waste in some quantity."[18] That's right: prisons frequently produce hazardous waste from industrial activity occurring within their walls. That activity often involves the labor of inmates who are not afforded the same health and safety protections as nonprisoners in other industry sectors.

The EPA issued a report based on its Prison Initiative that read, in part,

Correctional institutions have many environmental matters to consider in order to protect the health of the inmates, employees and the community where the prison is located. Some prisons resemble small towns or cities with their attendant industries, population and infrastructure. Supporting these populations, including their buildings and grounds, requires heating and cooling, wastewater treatment, hazardous waste and trash disposal, asbestos management, drinking water supply, pesticide use, vehicle maintenance and power production, to name a few potential environmental hazards. And the inmate training programs offered at most institutions also have their own unique environmental challenges . . . the US Environmental Protection Agency has been inspecting correctional facilities to see how they are faring. From the inspections, it is clear many prisons have room for improvement.[19]

Garth Connor, the lead inspector for the Prison Initiative, later wrote in an article that USEPA staff completed six multimedia inspections at different kinds of prisons and found

egregious non-compliance with applicable environmental regulations. One inspected prison had been generating hazardous waste for over twenty years, but had never applied for or received an ID number to allow for proper disposal. Another prison had been a chronic violator of the effluent limits in its wastewater permit and its staff did not understand how to properly conduct the sampling and analysis portion of its permit. All six of the inspected prisons were in non-compliance with both the hazardous waste regulations of the Resource Conservation and Recovery Act (RCRA) and the oil-spill prevention requirements contained in the Spill Prevention Control and Countermeasure (SPCC) regulations.[20]

Connor concluded that one of the basic problems was that prison staff simply had little to no training in applicable environmental regulations. Connor notes that most prisons have industrial shops and are subject (in theory) to RCRA regulations. But some of the prisons were listed as "small quantity generators" of hazardous waste while the inspection revealed that in fact they were large quantity generators. A number of older and larger prisons in the US operate wastewater treatment plants onsite since prisons produce industrial and biological waste (sewage) that must be treated. These facilities are required to have National Pollution Discharge Elimination System permits. Wastewater treatment has been a major challenge in many prisons due to overcrowding (as a result of the rise of mass incarceration), with thousands of inmates producing biological waste that simply overwhelms the system. Prisons are also supposed to have SPCC plans in place to address accidents that might occur when there is a spill or rupture of a gasoline or diesel tank (used for powering prison vehicles) or of a heating oil tank (used for heating buildings). None of the inspected prisons had an SPCC plan. There were also a number of Clean Air Act violations stemming primarily from improper maintenance and operation of air conditioning units that were emitting CFCs into the atmosphere. The USEPA initiated enforcement actions against all of the facilities, fining them and taking steps to ensure compliance with regulatory requirements.

In fact, USEPA's Region III office continued to take numerous enforcement actions and other initiatives against prisons in the region between 1999–2011.[21] Moreover the EPA's OECEJ website repeatedly stressed the importance of its focus on *environmental justice*, which it defined as "the fair treatment and meaningful involvement of all people regardless of race, color, national origin, or income with respect to the development, implementation, and enforcement of environmental laws, regulations, and policies."[22] So one can imagine the surprise when activists working with the Prison Ecology Project were repeatedly told that the USEPA does not include prisoner populations in its environmental justice mandate.

The Prison Ecology Project vs. the USEPA

In July of 2015 and 2016, Paul Wright, Executive Director of the Human Rights Defense Center (of which the Political Ecology Project is a part) wrote a letter to the USEPA in order to request that the agency include prisoners in its EJ 2020 Action Agenda Framework to ensure that these populations "receive the protections that are intended under Executive Order 12898 and Title VI of the Civil Rights Act."[23] In those letters (signed by more than 130 other civil society groups and leaders), Wright laid out clear and detailed reasoning as to why prisoners should be deemed worthy of inclusion as a population facing environmental injustices and why the USEPA should be the agency to take the lead on addressing this gap. Moreover, Wright made the important argument that the families of prisoners should also be taken into account in the USEPA's decision on this matter, since the children and loved ones of prisoners bear particularly unique and troubling social, psychological, and financial burdens from having a family member incarcerated.

The Prison Ecology Project interviewed EPA Region III representative Donna Heron in February of 2015, and she explained that EJ guidelines were not being applied to prisoners because the agency uses census data, which excludes that population.[24] USEPA press officers Roy Seneca and Julia Valentine offered equally vague reasons for this oversight.[25] In June of 2016, Prison Ecology Project staff and supporters from several other organizations met with USEPA representatives in Washington, DC, to seek further guidance and progress on this question, with no luck.

Wright and the Prison Ecology Project find the USEPA's reasoning flawed and unacceptable. Wright asked, "If we can recognize the problem with forcing people to live in close proximity to toxic and hazardous environmental conditions, then why are we ignoring prisoners who are forced to live in detention facilities impacted by such conditions?" As Panagioti Tsolkas writes, "In fact, these risks may actually be in violation of environmental protections intended under Executive Order 12898. The Order, which passed under President Clinton in 1994 and became known as the Environmental Justice Act, was really just a clarification of an older and hard-won law: the Civil Rights Act of 1964. Title VI of that Act prohibits discrimination in the permitting of any activity that the federal government has a hand in."[26] The HRDC and the PEP believe that documenting environmental health impacts on prisoners could become critical to the social movement effort to block the construction of prisons and to shut others down. Furthermore, they believe that ongoing prisoner activities to support such documentation and to resist environmental hazards inside correctional facilities points to the centrality of prisoners as key participants in the movements to end mass incarceration and promote environmental justice.

The vast majority of prisoners in the US are low-income persons, people of color, and immigrants. They are clearly facing exposure to a range of environmental and public health hazards, as the USEPA itself has found. So why not include these populations under the banner of "environmental justice communities"? The USEPA's reasoning appears to be that prisons should be regulated as sources of environmental pollution *only* insofar as that pollution might harm surrounding ecosystems and public health and *not* the health of prisoners who are in greater proximity to those hazards. In January 2011, the USEPA and the US Department of Justice announced a settlement with Pennsylvania's Department of Corrections and the Department of General Services for alleged violations of the federal Clean Air Act at boiler plants that produce power, heat, and hot water at four correctional facilities (Muncy, Bellefonte, Huntingdon, and Somerset, PA). As a result of the settlement, each of the four prisons had to make changes at their boiler plants to reduce emissions of nitrous oxides, sulfur dioxide, and particulate matter because these pollutants can produce haze, respiratory problems, and contribute to asthma. The Pennsylvania Department of Corrections also paid a civil penalty of $300,000 under the agreement. Tellingly, Shawn M. Garvin, EPA Mid-Atlantic Regional Administrator, stated, "Today's settlement will improve the air quality in four Pennsylvania communities. It's important that all sources of air emissions, including prisons, comply with environmental regulations to ensure that the standards are met in nearby communities."[27] By "nearby communities" Garvin meant the surrounding residential communities, *not* the communities of prisoners *within* the prisons. This is clear evidence that, as Panagioti Tsolkas put it, "prisoners are viewed as less than human."[28] Prisoners are *not* afforded human rights or basic civil rights (they are arguably enslaved, after all). And if imprisonment of so-called "criminals" is a solution to the social problem of crime – and particularly given that the overwhelming number of prisoners are poor and people of color – then prisons become a form of waste management, a technology of containment and control of social contamination and social pollution. In other words, there is a double contamination threat being managed here by the USEPA, the Department of Justice, and Bureau of Prisons: 1) the environmental hazards associated with air, land, and water pollution that emanate from prisons that threaten surrounding communities (i.e., the USEPA jurisdiction) and 2) the social contamination and social pollution embodied in the prisoners themselves, who tend to be from populations that are criminalized (i.e., the DOJ and BOP jurisdiction).[29] So the EPA seeks to regulate prison pollution threats only insofar as they may affect nearby residential areas, while they ignore the plight of prisoners facing myriad toxic exposures, and the DOJ and BOP manage the social pollution problem via the construction of prisons and the incarceration of human "waste" in those facilities.

In January of 2015 when the Prison Ecology Project was launched, Panagioti Tsolkas likely had no idea that they would uncover so many cases of prison-related environmental injustices. A few examples: in the state of California, at least eight of the state prisons have documented major water pollution problems, including the facilities in Chino, Folsom, Norco, and San Luis Opisbo;[30] there are confirmed reports of water contaminated with arsenic, lead, and other pollutants at prisons in nearly twenty other states, including the now infamous case of Flint, Michigan, where the Genesee County jail's inmates were forced to drink toxic water while prison guards drank filtered water out of bottles;[31] in May 2014 the Escambia County, Florida jail was the site of severe flooding that contributed to a gas leak and explosion that killed two prisoners and injured others;[32] the Sing Sing Correctional Facility is close enough to the Indian Point nuclear plant in New York that the prison should have an evacuation plan in case of an accident – in 2012 that plan was exposed as woefully inadequate;[33] the Rikers Island jail in New York City was built atop a landfill that for years has produced methane gas explosions and is plagued with health complaints from cancer-stricken corrections officers;[34] the Victorville Federal Correctional Complex in

California was built on a former Weapons Storage Area (WSA) and is now a military superfund site;[35] the Northwest Detention Center is a privately operated facility designed to house more than 1,500 immigrant detainees and is built adjacent to a Superfund site known as Project Area #3 of the Tacoma Tar Pits.[36]

A traditional environmental justice studies approach to these cases might generally involve an analysis of the proximity between humans and hazards, a consideration of historical and social forces that led to this unfortunate intersection, and perhaps a proposal for tougher legislation or actual enforcement of existing legislation to remedy the problem. That is, an earlier-generation EJ Studies approach would place a primary emphasis on the degree to which there may be geographic concentration of prisons and environmental hazards (defined as Locally Unwanted Land Uses) in communities of color and low-income neighborhoods and what remedies might be sought through state-based policy mechanisms. In the next sections, I present a Critical Environmental Justice Studies approach to the prisons-environment problem and demonstrate how and why it offers a more comprehensive, rigorous, and transformative path to address this dilemma.

First Pillar: Categories of Difference

The first pillar of Critical Environmental Justice Studies opens up our scope of analysis to consider how multiple social categories of difference are intertwined in the making of (and in resistance to) environmental injustice. Among the numerous categories of difference I consider in this section are race, gender, sexuality, social class, age, citizenship, and more-than-human-spaces and species, because they are all operating in the context of the prison industrial complex. Furthermore, in extending beyond the category of the human to include the more-than-human world, the CEJ framework includes nonhuman animals, ecosystems, and – perhaps most important here – the *built environment* as subjects and instruments of oppression, and as agents of social change. In other words, prisons are an environmental justice issue because they are part of the built environment, a space where marginalized bodies are made even more vulnerable; prisons are also spaces where we live, work, learn, play, and pray. And they are spaces where we "do time." And unlike nonprisoners, prisoners do not have the freedom to leave this built environment and come and go as they please, so exposure to chemical toxins and pollutants, extreme weather events, social violence, and control are that much more pervasive.

Race, class, gender, sexuality, citizenship, species, and imprisonment
The US prison system is overwhelmingly made up of people who are poor and nonwhite.[37] One in three African-American men is at risk of being sentenced to at least one year in prison during his lifetime,[38] and the rate of incarceration for African-Americans is five times that of white Americans. The rate for Latinos is nearly twice that of whites. Another way of putting this is that white Americans are highly *under*represented in every one of the fifty US states' prison populations while black and brown people are *over*-represented.[39] The single greatest contributing factor to the rise of mass incarceration has been the racially discriminatory "war on drugs," which began in the late 1970s and early 1980s and led to intensified racially unequal arrests, convictions, and sentencing for alleged drug use, possession, and sale.[40] For example, while marijuana is currently being legalized and decriminalized in many states in the US where white Americans are freely purchasing, growing, smoking, and selling it, the reality for African-Americans is that they are nearly four times as likely as whites to be arrested on charges of marijuana possession, despite the fact that the two groups use the drug at similar rates.[41] In the early 1970s, New York State passed a series of draconian anti-narcotics statutes called the Rockefeller Drug Laws. While the majority of drug users in that state are white, 90 percent of the people incarcerated under those laws are African-American and Latina/o. Nationally, the same trends prevail. The political consequences of this unequal policing are profound and dire: in many states, one in four black men cannot vote because they have a past or present felony conviction that disqualifies them from participation in that most basic act of citizenship.[42] The US prison system has been castigated by

international human rights organizations and the United Nations as a site of routine human rights abuses associated with these vast racial disparities.[43]

And while these statistics and trends are concerning, they do not include the thousands of young persons who are locked up in juvenile detention facilities or the many thousands of people caged in immigrant detention centers. Also not included in these statistics are the more than five million people who are under formal surveillance through parole and mass probation.[44] While much of the anti-prison movement and criminal legal reform efforts have been focused on the racial disparities affecting African-American citizens, we must pay increased attention to the fact that the "browning of America" is also reflected in the browning of American prisons. Because of harsher immigration and crime legislation passed in the 1980s and 1990s, Latinas/os are now the largest ethnic/racial population in the federal prison system.[45]

Scholars and activists have pointed out that there has long been inattention to the presence of women in prisons, since this was generally a smaller inmate population when compared to male prisoners. Today, however, women constitute the single fastest growing group of prisoners in the US, largely as a result of massive job losses associated with deindustrialization and economic globalization and the gutting of key social service programs such as Aid to Families with Dependent Children – which have had deeply gendered effects on the demography of prisons.[46]

Ethnic studies scholar Martha Escobar presents a compelling argument that links the criminalization of African-Americans and Latina/os through racialized and gendered discourses that have sanctioned the condemnation of black and brown motherhood and the locking up of people of color to control, contain, and manage them. She writes, "The re-mapping of dependency and criminality onto (im)migrant women's reproductive bodies rationalized punitive policies and practices against Latina (im)migrants and their communities. Racialized and gendered (im)migration enforcement serves to contain and, in the case of incarceration and deportation, dispose of the 'threat.' *This directs our attention to the significance of incarceration as a mechanism for (im)migration control.*"[47]

As for research on women and gender-nonconforming prisoners, study after study finds that women and LGBTQ folk face extraordinarily high threats of sexual abuse and violence in the prison system. The first national survey of violence in the penal system, conducted in 2003, by the Bureau of Justice Statistics, concluded that sexual orientation was the single greatest determinant of sexual abuse in prisons, with 18.5 percent of LGBTQ inmates reporting they were sexually assaulted, compared to 2.7 percent of heterosexual prisoners.[48] Moreover, this violence is generally encouraged and often perpetrated by prison policies and staff members (I will discuss sexual violence in greater depth in the next section, on the Second Pillar).

The field of critical prison studies and the prison abolition movement are helpful for offering an innovative understanding of these trends, their historical roots, and their implications. Many of these scholars and advocates have also pushed to center the experiences of women, LGBTQ folk, and gender-nonconforming bodies and identities in the prison industrial complex (PIC), arguing that criminalizing and controlling these persons and their politics are central features of the PIC.[49] This framework departs conspicuously from a traditional or mainstream criminal justice and criminology perspective that often focuses on the social construction of individual crime and argues for reforming the PIC, sentencing guidelines, and other aspects of the PIC, to embrace civil rights and anti-discrimination values, but accepts the legitimacy and continued existence of the PIC. Critical prison studies and prison abolition activists go beyond this point and call for the dismantling of the PIC altogether.

Humans and more-than-humans linked

The effects of prisons on ecosystems include the ways in which sewage and other water discharges, chemical toxins, fossil fuels, air pollution, and hazardous waste affect nonhuman species and communities in waterways, ambient air, and nearby land bases. For example, the Delano II prison was anticipated to have negative impacts on the Tipton kangaroo rat and the San Joaquin Valley kit fox. Sewage overflows and water system spills and discharges have occurred at prisons across the country, which have placed aquatic and plant life at risk.[50] For example, the Monroe correctional complex, north of Seattle, has had numerous sewage spills into the Skykomish river since at least 2006. Amazingly, that same facility is believed to be the first prison in the United States to receive a Leadership in Energy and Environmental Design (LEED) Gold rating, which some observers have called a ridiculous case of greenwashing. As one journalist writes,

> The cache of state records obtained by . . . the Human Rights Defense Center (HRDC), reveals that roughly half-a-million gallons of sewage water and other contaminates have been negligently dumped or accidentally spilled from the Monroe prison's wastewater system over the last eight years, polluting rivers and wetlands. . . . The systemic breakdowns and human negligence include a nearly 400,000–gallon spill in 2012. Caused by an effluent pump failure, the spill went undiscovered for almost four days while nobody was minding the wastewater helm.[51]

The Skykomish River is well known for its healthy populations of steelhead trout and other wildlife. It is a popular destination for fishing, rafting, kayaking, and swimming, so when hundreds of thousands of gallons of sewage are dumped into this waterway, both human and nonhuman populations are placed at great risk.

Letcher County, Kentucky, is the site of a proposed federal prison project that will be placed on land where mountain top removal (MTR) coal mining has occurred, which is a destructive practice of blowing up mountains to extract coal, reducing ecosystems to poisonous rubble and dust.[52] The proposed 1,200–prisoner facility is also to be placed near an area that is largely low income – with a poverty rate that is higher than Kentucky's average – raising clear environmental justice concerns about multiple and layered uses over time that produce harm to local ecosystems and human health.[53] Eastern Kentucky is a region where the coal industry has dominated for decades but is now in decline, so state and corporate leaders are promising that this prison will bring sorely needed jobs and economic development.[54]

Activist Sara Estep, of the Letcher Governance Project, stated "Letcher County's economy used to be based on coal. Now we are fighting prisons in the area. This new prison would be the 4th in our area."[55] In fact, this would be only the latest in a series of prisons that are increasingly dotting the Appalachian landscape as part of a new revenue-generation strategy adopted by public officials in the region. The Prison Ecology Project has publicly opposed the project, joining with groups like Kentuckians for the Commonwealth and the Letcher Governance Project.

The Letcher County site is also home to second-growth forests that serve as habitat for the Indiana bat and grey bats, both of which are endangered species whose fate is further placed in jeopardy as a result of the spread of the deadly new bat disease, white nose syndrome.[56] The proposed prison therefore "would destroy habitat at a time that the bats are under substantial threat from WNS."[57] In total, this prison potentially threatens seventy-one different species.[58]

The fact that these nonhuman species and ecosystems are more vulnerable as a result of the prison industrial complex speaks to the ways in which human and nonhuman communities are linked through what David Nibert calls "entanglements of oppression."[59] I might expand Nibert's term, and say that what we see in these cases are "entanglements of oppression and privilege," since the incarceration of human beings and oppression of nonhuman natures also benefits (at least in the short term) other groups who designed those systems of domination as a solution to the problem of social control.[60] Communities are entangled within and across species in ways that reveal how the scholarship on environmental inequality and intersectionality can benefit from extending beyond the unnecessarily restrictive boundaries of the human.

Agency and resistance

An important part of the first pillar of CEJ studies is how people and nonhumans respond to and/or participate in this oppression. Prisoners have not accepted these conditions without a struggle. In 2005, eighteen prisoners at the St. Louis and Mid-Michigan Correctional Facility sued the prison system over what they claimed were unconstitutional conditions, including the fact that the city's drinking water was contaminated with p-CBSA, a byproduct of the banned insecticide DDT, and that was the same water prisoners were forced to drink. St. Louis schools switched to bottled water but the area prison officials did not, so the prisoners brought a lawsuit in US District Court.[61] In 2003, the women's correctional facility known as the William Hobby Unit experienced a water contamination crisis, since it received its water from the nearby town of Marlin, Texas, which was also contaminated. Prisoners brought a lawsuit against officials claiming that the water contamination caused serious injuries. One plaintiff, Helen Caples, stated that the prisoners were restricted to three six-ounce cups of water per day for all purposes and they were not allowed to flush toilets, which soon became backed up. Plaintiffs stated that maggots were in the showers, that rats ran rampant around the facility, and that birds flew through the mess hall, depositing droppings on the meal tables. Another prisoner, Jessica Garza, reported that she experienced stomach sickness, headaches, and dizziness when drinking the tap water. Moreover, during the heat waves of the summer of 2004, when temperatures reached 106 degrees Fahrenheit, there were four heat-related deaths and six suicides.[62] Federal authorities rejected the prisoners' lawsuit, but in 2014 there was a sewage backup, creating further problems.

These cases of water contamination reveal important observations. First, prisoners are not helpless victims and are often the most outspoken and active advocates working to challenge their conditions of confinement. Second, these troubling cases of environmental injustice in prison also reveal the ways in which nonhuman natures have agency – they also act and shape human lives and futures. Unfortunately, nonhuman nature's agency isn't always a welcome development. When sewage, toxic chemicals, contaminated water, and extreme weather conditions are at work, they can have major deleterious impacts on the health and well-being of prisoners, ecosystems, and surrounding communities. And finally, prisons and nearby towns often use the same water supply, so when policymakers and prison officials behave as if they are separate and distinct problems, harm for one or both populations is often the result.

From a Critical EJ Studies perspective, in order to include a discussion of the role of nonhuman natures and species in this analysis, one need not actually look beyond human beings because people of color, immigrants, women and LGBTQ folks are often viewed and treated as if they were not fully human.[63] This reflects not only a racial discourse of animality (see chapter 2) but sexualized and gendered discourses of animality as well. And since prisoners are treated as subhumans, when a person is an inmate and inhabits another one of these marginalized categories, that is a toxic combination for one's health and life chances. Consider the case of Duana Johnson, a working-class African-American transgender woman who was arrested for sex work in Memphis, Tennessee in 2008, and was physically and verbally abused in the Shelby County Criminal Justice Center by police officers who called her a "faggot" and a "he-she." Johnson later stated, "I couldn't breathe. . . . Nobody checked to see if I was OK. . . . *I didn't feel like I was a human being there.*"[64] Johnson was targeted for being a gender-nonconforming person and the violence she experienced was rooted in what legal advocates Joey Mogul, Andrea Ritchie, and Kay Whitlock call "queer criminal archetypes" – culturally ingrained images and representations that resonate widely and often produce strong emotional responses and associations with respect to LGBTQ folk. They write:

> Queer criminal archetypes promulgated through the media spread quickly through channels of pop culture, community gossip, and schoolyard banter. Their presence is often revealed by the use of particular words and phrases that promote paranoia-inducing images: *web, ring, network, recruitment, infiltration, takeover, underworld, nest, infestation, contagion, gang, and wolf pack.* They do not describe human beings; rather, they promote cold, terrifying abstractions that are the stuff of cultural nightmare: *perverts, predators, deviates, psychopaths, child molesters, bull daggers and bull dykes, pansies, girlie-men, monsters, he-shes, and freak shows.* The archetypes and their accompanying scripts are remarkably powerful in directing not only the initial gaze, but also subsequent interpretations

and actions, of police, prosecutors, judges, juries, and prison authorities. It is almost impossible to overestimate the societal clout of these symbolic representations.[65]

In other words, as Duana Johnson stated, LGBTQ folk are often treated as if they are not human, as if they are subhuman, or worse – monsters.

Second Pillar: Scales of History, Futures, Geography, and Bodies

The second pillar of Critical EJ Studies advances multiscalar analyses for generating a deeper grasp of the driving forces underlying environmental inequalities. This enables us to produce more radical and productive responses to them. Scale in this framework means an emphasis on temporal and spatial/geographic dimensions of environmental justice struggles, from historical perspectives on the PIC to micro- and macroscalar dynamics of the relationship between the PIC and environmental justice politics.

Histories

The Thirteenth Amendment to the Constitution of the United States of America is a key site for discussion of the relationship between imprisonment and oppression. The official interpretation is that this Amendment put an end to enslavement. The Amendment was passed and ratified by Congress in 1865, a major legal action signaling the end of the Civil War, and the end of the formal institution of chattel slavery. But the first section of the Amendment declares "Neither slavery nor involuntary servitude, *except as a punishment for crime whereof the party shall have been duly convicted,* shall exist within the United States, or any place subject to their jurisdiction."[66] The italicized portions reveal an inherent contradiction between the claim that slavery was truly abolished and the fact that the same Amendment clearly allows for the enslavement of human beings as long as they are being punished for a crime. Therefore prisons are legally sanctioned sites of enslavement through the incapacitation of human beings and through widespread forced labor. As neo-Abolitionist scholar

Joy James explains, "The Thirteenth Amendment ensnares as it emancipates. In fact, it functions as an enslaving antienslavement narrative."[67]

Soon after the Thirteenth Amendment was passed, the acceptance of the black vote and the resultant election of black politicians under what was called Reconstruction gave many people hope. The forces of white supremacy were upset with these developments and the process was soon reversed, as Southern states passed the Black Codes, which allowed governments to arrest newly freed African-Americans for all manner of petty crimes and alleged offenses, such as "vagrancy." Many of those arrested could not afford the fines levied against them so they were subjected to a convict leasing system, which saw prisons loaning out inmates to private businesses to do all manner of labor. Many historians have argued that the convict leasing system was actually worse than slavery, because private companies simply did not have the same investment in convicts as plantation owners did in enslaved human beings. Consequently, convicts could be worked much harder, abused, and even killed without raising the kind of concern that a plantation owner would have about their "investment" in human chattel. Many convicts were leased out to coal mining companies, doing dangerous, even life-threatening work to extract fossil fuels from the earth, thus undercutting free white labor's wages and political power while contributing to what we would later recognize as climate change. Journalist Douglas Blackmon called the convict leasing system "slavery by another name." He told the story of how John T. Milner, a Southern elite entrepreneur, took advantage of that system and used black labor in his coalmines and farms in Southern Alabama. Records of mistreatment at Milner's properties reveal that black men and women were frequently subjected to beatings, whippings, starvation, were often forced to strip naked, and at other times were barely clothed and suffered from lice infestations.[68] The exploitation involved in Milner's operation was mirrored in the broader convict leasing system, much of which was focused on the extraction of ecological wealth from ecosystems in the US South. Historian Mary Ellen Curtin observes,

Alabama used prison labor extensively in its coal mines. By 1888 all of Alabama's able male prisoners were leased to two major mining companies: the Tennessee Coal and Iron Company (TCI) and Sloss Iron and Steel Company. For a charge of up to $18.50 per month per man, these corporations "leased," or rented prison laborers and worked them in coalmines.[69]

Years later, scholar, activist, former political prisoner, and prison abolitionist Angela Davis made some powerful personal connections between her own biography and this brutal history. She writes,

> I grew up in the city of Birmingham, Alabama. Because of its mines – coal and iron ore – and its steel mills that remained active until the deindustrialization process of the 1980s, it was widely known as "the Pittsburgh of the South." The fathers of many of my friends worked in these mines and mills. It is only recently that I have learned that the black miners and steelworkers I knew during my childhood inherited their place in Birmingham's industrial development from black convicts forced to do this work under the lease system.[70]

And while many scholars and activists rightly point to the Thirteenth Amendment as an indisputable site where the enslavement of other human beings is legally enshrined, others go back even further and argue that the issue is broader and deeper than that, contending that the logic of centuries of colonial practices – from the founding of the US through the current era – reveal that "violent captivity has always been central to the making of the United States."[71] The intersections between unfreedom and environmental justice struggles have long roots, reflecting the importance of attention to the scales of time. And as many scholars argue, confronting and abolishing the prison industrial complex today is an important effort to complete the work of slavery abolition begun centuries ago, in order to create a future where freedom is enjoyed by all.[72]

Geography and Bodies

A San Francisco-based artist recently told me that she met an African-American man at a workshop on environmental issues who stated that while he is concerned about climate change, his first battle is to stay alive and keep his body from being assaulted by police and other forms of racist violence. This story reflects the importance of thinking about environmental justice conflicts at the microscale, at the bodily level. An emphasis on the body reflects a core focus in feminist scholarship in general and on feminist environmental justice in particular. Rachel Stein argues that when we redefine our bodies as "lands" and "homes" and "environments," we can then more effectively personalize and politicize environmental justice for people whose personal well-being is often at risk from a range of threats.[73] Chicana feminist lesbian scholar Cherríe Moraga writes, "Land remains the common ground for all radical action. But land is more than rocks and trees. . . . For immigrants and natives alike, land is also the factories where we work, the water our children drink, and the housing project where we live. For women, lesbians, and gay men, land is that physical mass called our bodies."[74]

Critical EJ studies draws from this scholarship and views human bodies – particularly people of color, indigenous peoples, LGBTQ folk, women, immigrants, and working-class people – and bodies of land, water, and other animals as sites of environmental justice struggles. In this section, these ideas come together in two ways. First, let us consider the ways in which toxic chemicals contaminate the bodies of prisoners and ecosystems simultaneously. Second, we must focus on sexual abuse in prisons. Scale and the body come together powerfully and violently on the subject of prisoners and environmental injustice at the microscale, which is linked to policies, discourses, and practices operating at the macroscale.

Geography: Environmental contamination of bodies and landscapes
Paul Wright is Human Rights Defense Center Director and editor of *Prison Legal News* (PLN). He states,

Criminologist Jonathan Simon refers to prisons as human toxic waste dumps where the ruling class dumps its human waste: out of sight and out of mind. Sadly, toxic waste is not just a literary analogy when discussing American prisons and jails. As PLN has reported for several decades . . . many prisons and jails are built on toxic waste dumps, landfills and former mining sites, which negatively impact the health of prisoners and staff alike.[75]

Prisons produce and intersect with environmental impacts in myriad ways. One of these connections is through external *geography*: the bodies of land and landscapes where a prison is located, and how that produces threats to various communities both inside and outside the prison. With respect to risks outside of prisons, consider the facility that MELA opposed in Los Angeles in the 1980s. This was a locally unwanted land use because area residents concluded that it was a nuisance and an offense. They felt the state should be investing these taxpayer funds in more socially useful projects. Similarly, one of the many reasons activists opposed the Delano II prison in the San Joaquin Valley was its anticipated impacts on human communities (increased traffic congestion, school overcrowding, burdening families of prisoners), on ecosystems (threatening vulnerable species like the Tipton kangaroo rat and the San Joaquin Valley kit fox), and on both (placing stress on water systems, aquifers, and on agriculture and farmland).

Geography works the other way around as well – that is, the location of a prison and the spatial organization of a prison can produce internal threats to the bodies of prisoners and corrections officers who work and live on site. Texas prisoners face some of the worst heat and humidity of any inmates in the nation, because of extreme weather combined with a lack of air conditioning and deficient medical care at facilities throughout the state. In one investigation it was discovered that fourteen prisoners died between 2007 and 2014 due to extreme heat, and the Texas Department of Criminal Justice has done little to address the matter.[76] In another example, at the State Correctional Institution Fayette in Labelle, Pennsylvania, prisoners are forced to endure life next to a coal ash dump containing an estimated 40 million tons of waste and two coal slurry ponds. The Abolitionist Law Center and the Human Rights Coalition undertook a year-long investigation of the health consequences of this exposure and revealed that an unusually high percentage of prisoners report declining health and symptoms and illness consistent with exposure to toxic coal waste.[77] These symptoms include cancer; respiratory, throat and sinus conditions; thyroid disorders; blurred vision, fatigue, hair loss, dizziness, and headaches; gastrointestinal problems; and much more. Moreover, residents of the town of LaBelle suffer from the same health conditions. One inmate, Nicholas Morrissey, told investigators, "I can't even control my body anymore. . . . My life has been completely changed in the last year . . . I went from an athletic and healthy person to a frail sickly man who can barely walk." Another SCI Fayette prisoner stated, "I have four years left on my sentence and that could be a death sentence with the contamination here." A particularly noteworthy aspect of this study is that most prisoners' symptoms and illnesses did not emerge until after they arrived at SCI Fayette, and in numerous instances prisoners who left the facility experienced dramatic improvements in health. Finally, the report noted that prison staff routinely delay or even withhold medical care from prisoners with illnesses, exacerbating already serious conditions and constituting a possible violation of the Eighth Amendment prohibition against cruel and unusual punishment. In fact the report's authors argue that the scourge of environmental injustice in prisons more broadly may violate this basic right granted to all citizens under the US Constitution. The concept of scale is powerfully represented in this case, as the bodies of prisoners have been placed at considerable risk by exposure to coal ash, which is a byproduct of the fossil fuel industry, which has been blamed for contributing massively to the scourge of global climate change.

Furthermore, prisons generate hazards within their walls that pose substantial threats to ecosystems and human communities both inside and outside of prisons. Again, harms facing prisoners' bodies are linked with bodies of land and more-than-human communities beyond the prison gates. Many prisons are sites of water contamination stemming from overflowing sewage systems, or from importation of contaminated water that also often affects residents of those areas. Another set of internal hazards produced by prisons originates from e-waste recycling (mentioned earlier in this chapter), which exposes prisoners to a range of extremely dangerous chemicals and toxins (such as arsenic, barium, beryllium, cadmium, chromium VI, lead, mercury, nickel, and toner dust) that are also linked to the pollution of waterways and vulnerable ecosystems globally.[78]

The connections between prisons and environmental injustice are even more disturbing and direct when we consider the deliberate use of toxins on prisoners' bodies. A 2015 Human Rights Watch Report found that, in many US jails and prisons, inmates with mental disabilities are frequently and repeatedly subjected to punishment and pain compliance techniques that include the use of chemical sprays.[79] Pepper spray (or Oleoresin capsicum, OC) is the most common chemical agent in use in the prison system, one of at least three types. Effects of these sprays can include intense burning sensations, temporary blindness, second- and third-degree burns, positional asphyxia, and death. Moreover, experts conclude that the use of chemical sprays on mentally ill persons can produce additional and severe complications, including escalated anxieties and fears and psychotic episodes.[80] Jeremiah Thomas was an inmate in the Florida State prison system who suffered from mental illness and was subjected to repeated chemical spraying by correctional officers on several occasions, ultimately suffering third-degree burns. He recalled that the chemicals would "eat me up on the inside . . . it burn me real bad and it harmed me."[81]

Perhaps the question of scale with respect to prisons and EJ concerns is best captured by the fact that some prisons are located on or near former military waste dumps. For example, the Victorville Federal Correctional Complex in California was built on a former Weapons Storage Area (WSA) and is now a military superfund site, which means it is recognized by the federal government as contaminated land that poses a threat to human and/or environmental health.[82] The prison complex is built on the site where the George Air Force Base once was located and is on land where the US Department of Defense once buried and stored radioactive nuclear waste, creosote, tetraethyl lead, and munitions.[83] Numerous former employees of the base are now registering their public concerns about the fact that they were never made aware that nuclear weapons testing and decontamination practices were ongoing at the site and that people were unknowingly exposed to these hazards. Numerous officials have, in the past, denied this fact, but since recently declassified documents have exposed this history, the protests have become more intense.[84] Former environmental activist and political prisoner Eric McDavid stated, "I served time at FCI Victorville, which is on a Superfund site. The water is contaminated. It's what you shower in and you eat with it and you drink it. Two other prisons I served in also had contaminated water. I did a blood analysis after I got out and my copper levels were off the charts. I had to do a detox program for many months after that."[85]

This is a story of how scale functions to reveal the ways in which a prison in operation today is affected by a previous land use on the same property that involved some of the most dangerous and toxic substances known to humankind, that were developed with the express purpose of killing massive numbers of human beings through warfare. The Victorville site where prisoners are exposed to nuclear hazards against their will today speaks to the importance of paying closer attention to history, in particular the role of the US military and US empire as global forces supported by ecologically and socially destructive policies, practices, and aims. The production of the Cold War–era nuclear arsenal resulted in extraordinary destruction and contamination of lands, rivers, and peoples, particularly in Native American communities, where radiation has caused an epidemic of cancer among Navajo/Dine populations in the Southwest.[86] The at-risk bodies of prisoners at Victorville are linked to the exposed bodies of George Air Force Base employees and the devastated bodies of indigenous and nonindigenous humans and nonhumans sacrificed in the global nuclear arms race and the Cold War.[87] The significance of scale comes into sharp relief as we consider how US scientists split the atom to create a nuclear program with far-reaching global effects, from creating the cancer cells in human and nonhuman bodies to producing radiation that circulates through our global ecosystems.

A Critical EJ Studies framework seeks to link the macroscale to the microscale – but also does so through an expansion of the concept of environmental justice itself to include a focus on the body.[88] As we consider, in this next section, how sexual abuse in prisons constitutes a form of environmental injustice the need for this focus becomes even clearer.

Sexual violence: From the microscale of the body to the macroscale of population

Activist scholar and INCITE! Women of Color Against Violence leader Andrea Smith urges us to think more broadly about how we define sexual violence. Interpersonal violence and rape are of course sexual violence, but its basis and extension can be seen more broadly. Smith writes, "If sexual violence is not simply a tool of patriarchy but also a tool of colonialism and racism, then entire communities of color are the victims of sexual violence."[89] Smith argues that we can think of colonialism, racism, environmental injustice, and the destruction of people's ways of life and identities as forms of sexual violence. These processes involve the imposition of punishment on a population – the taking of something vitally important to that population – without consent. The core of sexual violence is the imposition of one's power and will over another's body without permission. What drives that violence? In many case, Smith contends, it is the culturally ingrained view that some bodies – particular those of indigenous peoples, but also those of other peoples of color and LGBTQ persons – "are 'dirty,' they are considered sexually violable and 'rapable,' and the rape of bodies that are considered inherently impure or dirty simply does not count."[90] Consistent with this view, Linda McFarlane, deputy director of Just Detention International (a group working to end sexual abuse in prisons) stated, "We've heard multiple times about officers openly expressing a belief that gay and transgender inmates cannot be raped, that they deserve to be raped due to their mere presence in the environment, or that if they are raped it's simply not a concern."[91] Amnesty International found that "lesbians and other women who are seen to transgress gender boundaries are often at heightened risk of torture and ill treatment," making them a target for sexual abuse.[92] The United Nations Special Rapporteur for Violence Against Women, Radhika Coomaraswamy, visited numerous immigrant detention centers and state and federal prisons in the US and concluded that "sexual misconduct by prison staff is widespread in American women's prisons."[93]

Angela Davis contends that the sexual violence in prison is not exceptional; rather it reflects the realities of the society more broadly. She writes, "prison is a space in which the threat of sexualized violence that looms in the larger society is effectively sanctioned as a routine aspect of the landscape of punishment behind prison walls."[94]

Another form of sexual violence in prisons is directed at population control. Martha Escobar argues that by locking up women of color in general and immigrant women in particular, the state and the PIC function to place limits and constraints on these groups' reproduction. This outcome is in some ways consistent with decades-old environmentalist and nativist logic that laid the blame for environmental crises at the feet of immigrant women and women of color: their reproductive practices were seen as harmful to ecosystems because they were believed to be contributing to "overpopulation." These movements sought to "fix" the problem through eugenics and population control.[95] The state of California has a history of coercive sterilizations of women in prison, of which the public was reminded in the fall of 2014, when Governor Jerry Brown signed S.B. 1135, which sought to end most forms of prisoner sterilization. A Center for Investigative Reporting study found that nearly 150 female prisoners in California were sterilized without proper approval.[96] The history of sterilizations in California goes further back than that. Between 1909 and 1964, 20,000 men and women in the state were sterilized because they were viewed as unfit to reproduce: they were people of color, poor, mentally ill, or "criminals." California was the state with the most sterilization cases, impressing Nazi Germany's leaders so much that they sought advice from the state with respect to the

Third Reich's own eugenics system.[97] This is yet another example of how ideologies of difference and exclusion reveal how unstable the category "human" is; so many people are treated as if they are not fully human. The CIR report quoted Crystal Nguyen, a former Valley State Prison inmate who worked at the prison's infirmary in 2007. She told investigators that she frequently heard medical staff asking prisoners who had served more than one term to undertake a sterilization procedure. Nguyen recalled thinking, "Oh my God, that's not right. . . . Do they think they're animals, and they don't want them to breed anymore?" Women of color constitute the majority of women in the state of California's prison system, so they have been disproportionately targeted by these practices.[98]

For observers who believe that prison reform can address the problem of sexual violence, Mogul, Ritchie, and Whitlock write,

> The grim reality is that even though prison policies prohibit all sexual activity and violence, in practice prison officials not only allow and count on forcible sex, but use it to reinforce their own authority. Not only is forcible sex currency in prisons, but *the prison system itself is predicated upon it. As a result, sexual violence is an entrenched and intractable feature of prison life.*[99]

If we take seriously the idea that the body is a site of EJ struggle, then all forms of captivity are environmental injustices, since they harm the body. That is a productive way of thinking about the link between prisons and EJ because it refuses reform and points to the necessity of abolition. Sexual violence directed at individual bodies of prisoners reveals the ways that such microscale environmental injustices are inescapably linked to and supportive of macroscale environmental injustices focused on entire populations of people. The effects of such violence targeting one person or one body ripples across populations and communities, through an ecology of repression and brutality that requires a transformative response.

Scales of human extractivism: Impacts on children and families as environmental injustice

Years ago a student who took a class on Environmental Racism that I taught asked me a simple yet profound question: since one of the things EJ scholars and activists are so concerned about is the disproportionate impacts of pollution from extractive industries around the globe, why not consider the effects of imprisonment as an *extractive* activity that could be reframed as an environmental injustice? After all, family members, friends, neighbors, co-workers, and colleagues are literally siphoned off from their homes and social networks every day; they are critical "resources" for maintaining the functioning of our communities. Why not think of that as a form of environmental injustice? I was stunned and I made a promise to consider that question seriously and to return to it someday.

Best-selling author, journalist, and activist Naomi Klein describes the dominant capitalist model of development as "extractivism," which I believe speaks to this idea quite effectively. She writes:

> Extractivism is a nonreciprocal, dominance-based relationship with the earth, one purely of taking. . . . It is also the reduction of human beings either into labor to be brutally extracted, pushed beyond limits, or, alternatively, into social burden, problems to be locked out at borders and locked away in prisons or reservations. In an extractivist economy, the interconnections among these various objectified components of life are ignored; the consequences of severing them are of no concern. Extractivism is also directly connected to the notion of sacrifice zones – places that, to their extractors, somehow don't count and therefore can be poisoned, drained, or otherwise destroyed.[100]

A number of scholars and activists studying and confronting the PIC have noted that imprisonment – whether in a county jail, a state or federal prison, or juvenile or immigrant detention centers – involves the extraction or siphoning of human beings from their families and communities. They contend that we need to take those impacts into account when discussing the consequences of incarceration. Generally speaking, women tend to be left responsible for caring for extended family members when relatives and community members are imprisoned.[101] Martha Escobar contends that the rise in the imprisonment of immigrant women serves to achieve the goal of population or reproductive control by restraining their ability to have children, but it also serves to separate these mothers from any children they already have.[102] In many cases where the prisoner is undocumented, the violence of that separation is intensified when those mothers are deported to another nation.[103]

In its letter to the USEPA requesting that imprisoned populations be considered for inclusion into the category of "environmental justice communities," the Human Rights Defense Center wrote,

> Statistics show that one in 28 children have a parent in prison – 2.7 million children are growing up in households in which one or more parents are incarcerated. One in nine black children has an incarcerated parent, compared to one in 28 Hispanic/Latino children and one in 57 white children. The absence of a parent due to incarceration has a significant impact on the communities where these children live. This factor should be considered among a review of the cumulative impacts that affect environmental justice communities.[104]

In another letter from the HRDC to the Bureau of Prisons (BOP) regarding the Environmental Impact Statement (EIS) for the proposed prison in Letcher County, Kentucky, Paul Wright argues that, rather than seeing this facility as a new economic opportunity for the region, it actually represents an unbroken chain of continuity with the history of extractivism in the Appalachian coal fields. He writes, "The EIS announces BOP's plans to continue with a new type of extractive activity. BOP's proposed project would take 1,200 prisoners, extracted from their homes and neighborhoods, and import them into Letcher County."[105]

The prison industrial complex is *mining* our homes and neighborhoods for human resources that fuel the carceral system, and prisoners, their friends, families, and our communities are paying the price. In that regard, through the lens of *scale*, we see that the prison is everywhere since its tentacles affect people and ecosystems globally.

With respect to scale as time, geography, bodies, and space, the logic of the prison or carceral form is increasingly linked to and influences a range of other institutions: schools, workplaces, and neighborhoods across this nation. What this suggests is that, in some respects, it is a mistake to think of prisons as a separate institutional form. The lines are increasingly blurred between prisons and other spaces across society in terms of the logic of domination, surveillance, punishment, security, repression, and control that permeates social reality. To fail to recognize this dynamic reflects a kind of dualism or separation between prisons and an allegedly "free" society – when in fact the borders between these sites are fluid and interlinked, just as pollution crosses boundaries of the human, nonhuman, and international borders and just as prisons are sites where products are manufactured for consumption and use throughout society (like furniture in universities and e-waste) and just as universities are sites where scholars develop ideas for the more effective functioning and strengthening of the criminal legal system.[106]

Third Pillar: Entrenched Inequalities and Politics of the State

The third pillar of Critical Environmental Justice Studies constitutes a call for a greater emphasis on the deeply entrenched character of social inequality – in this case, state power – and therefore signals an opportunity to think and act in ways that question our reliance on these social relations to imagine and achieve environmental justice. This section addresses how the intersections between prisons and environmental politics speak to these themes through the lens of state repression.

A particularly pronounced and chilling way in which prisons and environmental justice come together is through the methods the state deploys to criminalize, control, and often incarcerate people who, as lone activists or as part of a larger social movement, take measures to defend and "save" the environment and nonhuman animals.[107] In recent years, this state repression has been called the Green Scare, which includes surveillance, infiltration, intimidation, and imprisonment of activists in the radical earth and animal liberation movements. In 2005, a prominent federal government official named radical earth and animal liberation movements the number one domestic "terrorist" threat in the United States.[108] While these movements have not, to my knowledge, killed a single person in the US, they have produced significant economic losses through property damage directed at industries such as forestry, genetic engineering, and animal research. Through these actions and the discourse that supports them, these radical movements question what they view as the violence of capitalism, state power, multiple forms of oppression within human communities, speciesism, and ecological destruction.

Legislation such as the Animal Enterprise Terrorism Act (AETA) of 2006 declared it a crime of "terrorism" to harm the profits of an industry whose products are primarily based on the use of animals. This can include boycotting, picketing, and other forms of protest that lead to a decline in revenue for industries like furriers, circuses, animal research testing laboratories, and farms. Civil liberties advocates cried foul at this law as a breach of constitutional rights, but several activists have already been indicted, charged, or imprisoned under the AETA. They join the many other earth and animal liberation activists who have served time in federal penitentiaries, and who are commonly viewed as political prisoners by movement participants, attorneys, and scholars. One activist described the AETA as "basically hate crimes legislation for people who are compassionate toward animals. . . . What this literally means is if you're standing on KFC's property with a sign, and in an act of time-honored tradition of civil disobedience, you refuse to leave when told to leave . . . you can be charged with terrorism. A federal felony for standing with a sign."[109]

Political prisoners

Dozens of earth and animal liberation activists have been subpoenaed, indicted, charged, convicted, or imprisoned for their role in illegal activities aimed at defending or protecting nonhuman natures. Movement participants, attorneys, and scholars view many of the earth and animal liberation activists who have spent time in federal penitentiaries as political prisoners. Here I consider the cases of a few of these persons to illustrate the power of the state to repress social movements.

Marius Mason is a transgender environmental and social justice activist who has worked as an Earth First! organizer; a musician and writer; a volunteer for a free herbal health care collective;

and the parent of two children. Building on Judi Bari's legacy, Mason worked to engender solidarity between environmentalists and workers as an active member of the Industrial Workers of the World (IWW) and editor of the *Industrial Worker*, the IWW's newspaper. He was sentenced to 21 years and 10 months in prison for Earth Liberation Front (ELF) arson actions that targeted research on genetically modified agriculture and commercial logging. Of Mason's sentence, Heidi Boghosian, Director of the National Lawyers Guild, has said, "We are definitely seeing more severe sentences post-9/11, no doubt about it. . . . We have seen a trend of using the terrorist label and federalizing a lot of criminal activities that would have gotten a far less stringent sentence before."[110] Mason's support committee wrote:

> The judge has shown that if activists attempt to impede . . . the progress of the marketplace in altering the genetic code of all beings . . . [its] desire to turn all aspects of the natural world into commodities . . . [or its] extraction of natural resources from the land – then they will be treated exactly the same as murderers. Nothing can be more clear about our legal system's priorities.[111]

Mason continues to write poetry, paint, and offer words of inspiration in letters to supporters and activists worldwide.

Daniel McGowan has been active in numerous social movement causes. Originally from New York, he has worked for the Rainforest Action Network, trained with the Ruckus Society, and volunteered for an anti–domestic violence advocacy group. He is also an earth liberation activist, volunteered for the EF! Journal's political prisoner support page, and worked to support other political prisoners. In June 2007, McGowan was sentenced to seven years (with a terrorism enhancement) in prison for arson and property destruction actions claimed by ELF in 2001 in the name of protecting forests from timber companies in the Pacific Northwest.

McGowan spent time in one of the infamous CMUs – a federal Communication Management Unit – in Marion, Illinois. CMUs are secretive, "self-contained" housing units inside prisons, designed to hold prisoners who "require increased monitoring of communication" in order to "protect the public." Lauren Regan was Gowan's attorney; she stated that her client was "the only white guy there. Everybody else is Muslim and Middle Eastern."[112] The co-location of ELF and "jihadist" prisoners in the same unit speaks volumes about the racialized nature of the "war on terror" and the Green Scare.[113]

Rod Coronado is a Pascua Yaqui Indian activist who spent several years in federal prison for his activism and public statements associated with his participation in radical ecological politics. In March 1995, Coronado pled guilty to aiding and abetting an Animal Liberation Front (ALF) arson that caused over $100,000 in damage at Michigan State University.[114] The action targeted and destroyed thirty-two years of research documents that, in Coronado's words, were "intended to benefit the fur farm industry."[115] The ALF claimed responsibility for the raid, the seventh in a series of direct actions targeting fur farms and universities engaged in taxpayer-supported research jointly funded by the fur trade. It was known as "Operation Bite Back." Along with liberating animals, the actions deliberately targeted the fur industry's research and knowledge base. According to Coronado, the research the arson at Michigan State University halted involved "experiments where mink and otters are force-fed toxins and other contaminants until they convulse and bleed to death."[116] Drawing on a radical anti-statist perspective, Coronado stated,

We have no obligation to any government. We have every obligation to protect the earth that gives us life and our future generations. Adherence to laws that sanction the destruction of our one home planet are crimes unprecedented in human history and demand active refusal and resistance.[117]

Activists in both earth and animal liberation movements consciously draw inspiration from environmental and social justice movements around the world, both past and present. One early influence on these activists was MOVE – a black revolutionary group founded in Philadelphia in 1972 by John Africa. MOVE was organized around a commitment to improve public health;

challenge the state and capitalism; and fight the racism, home-lessness, police brutality, and industrial pollution they produce. Clearly an example of an early EJ organization, MOVE's mission statement reads:

> MOVE's work is revolution ... a revolution to stop man's system from imposing on life, to stop industry from poisoning the air, water, and soil and to put an end to the enslavement of all life. Our work is to show people how rotten and enslaving this system is and that the system is the cause of homelessness, unemployment, drug addiction, alcoholism, racism, domestic abuse, AIDS, crime, war, all the prob-lems of the world. We are working to demonstrate that people not only can fight this system, they must fight the system if they ever want to free themselves from endless suffering and oppression.[118]

Many MOVE members were vegetarians and staunch animal rights activists[119] and MOVE founder John Africa once wrote, "All living beings, things that move, are equally important, whether they are human beings, dogs, birds, fish, trees, ants, weeds, rivers, wind or rain. To stay healthy and strong, life must have clean air, clear water and pure food."[120] MOVE became the target of an infamous police repression campaign, including the bombing of their homes and the imprisonment of several members on questionable charges. Many of these activists are still behind bars as of this writing and are widely considered political prisoners today, including by the earth and animal liberation communities.

What unites these groups is the experience of state repression. Repression is not something that states practice on an occasional basis. For many scholars repression is at the core of what states do: modern nation states claim a "monopoly on the legitimate use of physical force."[121] The prison is a particularly vicious and tangible site and form of state repression; the fact that activists working to protect and defend vulnerable ecosystems and nonhuman animals have been targeted by the state and imprisoned suggests quite clearly to radical movements that embracing and reinforc-ing state power may be counterproductive for efforts to produce environmental justice. And prisoners – be they known as political prisoners or social prisoners – are subjected to treatment that suggests they are not viewed as fully human. Radical activists in the earth, animal, and other revolutionary movements know this quite well. As Black Liberation Army activist and political prisoner Jalil Muntaqim stated at his sentencing hearing, "the only thing we are guilty of is being human in an inhumane society."[122]

Fourth Pillar: Racial and Socioecological Indispensability

The fourth pillar of the Critical EJ Studies framework centers on the concepts of *racial* and *socioecological indispensability*. In other words, CEJ counters the discourses and practices that cast people of color and other marginalized communities – both human and more-than-human – as expendable and necessarily separate from the rest of us, with a view that all beings and things are indispensible for building a sustainable and socially justice future. Journalist, author, and activist Naomi Klein is often quoted declaring, "To change everything we need everyone" – which is a way of arguing for indispensability as a method, a metaphor for environmental and climate justice.

It is hard to imagine a more appropriate site for such a discussion than the prison industrial complex – that web of institutions within the criminal legal system and beyond that sustains the physical and ideological frameworks that support the incapacitation, incarceration, monitoring, surveillance, and control of massive populations of "criminals" and criminalized beings. The PIC is premised on the assumption that people who are labeled "prisoners," "inmates," and "detainees" are expendable, surplus, and detrimental to the functioning of a "free" society. A CEJ perspective challenges that assumption and argues that in order to successfully imagine and treat all people as indispensable members of our communities, the abolition of prisons and the prison industrial complex is in our best interests.

Angela Y. Davis refers to Norwegian criminologist Nils Christie, who argues that "in the criminal justice field, the raw material is prisoners"[123] – in the sense that they are needed to fuel the industry. It follows that the prison industry will do whatever is necessary to ensure the flow of that raw material – including lobbying for prison construction. Davis's response to that view is, "Whether this human raw material is used for purposes of labor or for the consumption of commodities provided by a rising number of corporations directly implicated in the prison industrial complex, it is clear that black bodies are considered dispensable within the 'free world' but are a major source of profit in the prison world."[124]

EJ studies scholar Sacoby Wilson often uses the term "environmental slavery" instead of "environmental racism" because he says the latter term "is too nice." He employs the term "environmental slavery" to capture the full impacts and realities of oppression as it concerns the intersections of environmental harms in communities of color.[125] If we were to take Wilson's idea and invitation seriously, we would have to go further than (re)labeling environmental racism as environmental slavery. We would have to ask what environmental justice could look like if we thought of environmental racism as a form of enslavement. We would, therefore, in my view, have to *think of environmental justice in the context of abolition.*

Numerous scholars and activists in the anti-prison movement have thought deeply about the idea of abolition in the context of prisons. Leading anti-prison scholar-activist Ruth Wilson Gilmore writes,

> The purpose of abolition is to expose and defeat all the relationships and policies that make the United States the world's top cop, warmonger, and jailer . . . abolition is a movement to end systemic violence, including the interpersonal vulnerabilities and displacements that keep the system going. In other words, the goal is to change how we interact with each other and the planet by putting people before profits, welfare before warfare, and life over death.[126]

Angela Davis concurs with Gilmore and contends that prison abolition is not a vision focused on simply removing prisons from society. It is predicated instead on undertaking the more difficult work of making prisons irrelevant and obsolete by transforming the social relationships outside of prisons, throughout society, which feed and fuel the prison system. As she writes, "rather than try to imagine one single alternative to the existing system of incarceration, we might envision an array of alternatives that will require radical transformations of many aspects of our society."[127] As one activist states, "if prison abolition requires creating a world where prisons are no longer needed, then the real work of abolition must be done away from prisons – in shelters, health clinics, schools, and in battles over government budget allocations."[128] Davis grounds her vision and analysis partly in the work of the pioneering scholar-activist W. E. B. DuBois, who coined the term "abolition democracy" to describe the kind of society that would be needed to truly embrace the freedom of newly emancipated African-Americans, since Reconstruction and the subsequent historical periods failed to do so. Thus abolition democracy in Davis's framework would be immensely beneficial to the abolition of the PIC because it would involve "the creation of an array of social institutions that would begin to solve the social problems that set people on the track to prison, thereby helping to render the prison obsolete."[129] Recall that the existence of prisons full of people of color today in full accordance with the Thirteenth Amendment to the US Constitution reveals that slavery itself has not yet been abolished.

Martha Escobar takes a "feminist abolitionist" approach to prisons by centering her analysis and advocacy around prison abolition on women and gender-nonconforming populations, which offers the opportunity to see how the PIC is a deeply gendered and sexualized phenomenon. She writes, "the prison abolition movement's resolve to organize around *all or none* – its refusal to leave anyone behind – provides direction for the (im)migrant rights movement and presents possibilities for collaborative work across movements."[130] The idea of "all of us or none" is a powerful declaration of solidarity and of indispensability. In fact, All of Us or None is the name of a grassroots civil and human rights organization that advocates for the rights of people who are either formerly or currently incarcerated, as well as for their families. In particular, they organize to confront and prevent discrimination against these populations, who are routinely denied access to housing, employment, public benefits, and the right to vote.[131] Confirming the logic of abolition, All of Us or None understands that it is not enough to get out of prison: formerly incarcerated peoples are not "free" while they have a mark on their record that facilitates their exclusion from myriad human and civil rights that many of the rest of us enjoy. In fact, because of the persistence of homophobia, transphobia, racism, patriarchy, and class bias, too many of us are denied those rights and access to basic liberties even when we do *not* have a prison record. Neoabolitionist scholar Joy James writes that African-Americans in particular face continued threats associated with the blurred lines between the supposedly "free" world and the PIC because "the black body shares a proximity of positionality with the felon/prisoner – that of the suspect or noncitizen. Consequently, contemporary radical penal narratives as (neo)slave narratives denounce the State for manufacturing slavery on both sides of prison walls."[132]

I want to return to the foundational problem of dehumanization because it gets at the root of how prisoners are perceived and treated, and it allows us to make the necessary linkages between and among race, class, gender, sexuality, citizenship, and species that are key to the Critical EJ studies framework. In chapter 2, I discussed what I term the "social discourse of animality" to describe the ways in which language reflects our understandings of social difference, which produces and reveals entanglements between humans and nonhumans that support violent hierarchies. For incarcerated peoples, this discourse takes on a particular flavor, since they are literally confined to cages. This can produce deep resentments and rebellion from time to time. Consider the prison uprising at Attica in 1971. This was an historic event during which several thousand Attica inmates took control of the prison in protest against brutality by the prison staff, racism, overcrowding, and the murder of prisoner, author, and theorist George Jackson at San Quentin prison earlier that year. During the rebellion, a committee of inmates drafted a list of demands that read, in part:

We, the inmates of Attica Prison, have grown to recognize beyond the shadow of a doubt, that because of our posture as prisoners and branded character as alleged criminals, the administration and prison employees no longer consider or respect us as human beings, but rather as domesticated animals selected to do their bidding in slave labor and furnished as a personal whipping dog for their sadistic, psychopathic hate.[133]

These rebels at Attica powerfully articulated the discourse of animality that reflects the connections among different forms of domination operating within and beyond the species boundary of the human form. While many readers would sympathize with incarcerated persons who rebel against horrific conditions such as those faced by the Attica inmates, a CEJ perspective would also not shy away from problematizing the way in which these oppressed persons also employ speciesist language that accepts some forms of domination (speciesism and dominionism) but rejects other forms (racism and prisoner abuses). What is always fascinating about the discourse of animality is that it demonstrates that those who are speaking are actually drawing intersections between different forms of power and hierarchy, but they tend to embrace one while confronting the other. A CEJ perspective seeks to both examine *and challenge* all forms of hierarchy.

Finally, connecting the idea of prison abolition to Critical EJ to create a path toward the abolition of environmental injustices, one could argue that instead of focusing on a specific set of institutions such as the prison system or the state agencies and corporations responsible for regulating and creating environmental injustices, any movement toward abolition of the PIC and environmental injustices would likely need to focus on the broader set of social relationships within the human community and across the species spectrum that give rise to relations of ruling and domination among both human and more-than-human populations. Critical Environmental Justice as abolition must analyze and confront all relations of dominance and support relationships, knowledge, and practices that are sustainable and just in order to render the PIC and environmental injustice both illogical and irrelevant.

4

The Israel/Palestine Conflict as an Environmental Justice Struggle

One of the most intractable cases of religious, geopolitical, social, and environmental conflict in the world is the Israel/Palestine struggle. Perhaps the single most important thing to keep in mind when considering this conflict is that *it is infinitely complex* with respect to the historical forces shaping it, its contemporary character, and its future implications. In other words, there are no simple answers to the questions "Why is this happening?" and "What is the solution?" While this conflict is often described in ethnic and religious terms, its *environmental* dimensions are far less well known but central to the disputes between these populations. The role of land in particular has always been at the center of the conflict between the State of Israel and the Palestinian Arab communities both inside and outside of Israel. In this chapter, I explore some of the key historical roots of this conflict and offer a Critical EJ Studies approach to understanding its causes, consequences, and possible futures.

Anti-Jewish State Violence and the Roots of Zionism

Anti-Jewish hatred (anti-Semitism),[1] exclusions, discrimination, violence, massacres, pogroms, and genocidal policies and practices have been hallmarks of world history for literally thousands of years. Jews have frequently served as a convenient outlet for nativist, racist, or nationalist hatred stemming from those who sought scapegoats for challenges facing their societies rather than addressing those problems head on. After enduring centuries of discrimination and racist state-violence, a number of Jewish leaders in Europe and Russia began to organize a movement to found a safe space for Jews – a nation state. Zionism was and is a political movement that seeks the creation of and support for a Jewish state. In the late nineteenth century, Zionist leaders debated options for a future Jewish state, considering locations in various parts of the world (including South America and East Africa), and eventually chose Palestine – part of the historic land of Israel (*Eretz Yisrael*). Viennese journalist Theodor Herzl was one of those leaders; he penned a pamphlet titled *The Jewish State: An Attempt at a Modern Solution to the Jewish Question*, in which he argued that, given widespread anti-Jewish hatred in Europe and Russia, Jewish assimilation in those regions was unrealistic and that, with international support, Zionists could establish a homeland for the world's Jewish population. He and other early Zionist leaders believed that the "present possessors" (Arabs in Palestine) of that land would benefit from the modernizing European influence Zionists would bring. That attitude – some might call it paternalist, others might call it racist – permeated Zionism and reflected the view that indigenous Arab populations were in need of development and advancement in education, government, law, and ethics, which European Jews could presumably offer.[2] Zionist leaders also felt that since the Jewish presence in the area preceded the Arab conquest by several centuries, their claims to the land were much stronger.

The first groups of Jews leaving Europe and Russia began migrating to Palestine in the 1880s (these migrant waves were called *aliyah*). There were small numbers of indigenous Jews in Palestine who were the descendants of people living in the ancient Jewish kingdom there. That kingdom was conquered by Rome in 70 CE, resulting in the expulsion of most of its inhabitants. By the nineteenth century, however, the vast majority of persons living in Palestine were Arabs and Christians. There were also a number of Bedouin and Druze communities. Palestinian Arabs are the descendants of the indigenous population of Palestine living under the Arab/Islamic Empire, which had ruled the area since the seventh century. This was for centuries a site of rich scientific and artistic activity and economic exchange, often associated with what is called the Golden Age of Islam (which ended in the thirteenth century).

The Zionist plans for Palestine were premised on the idea that this was a "land without a people for a people without a land"[3] so the non-Jews in the area were generally viewed either with indifference or as an obstacle to the eventual colonization of the land. Thus the stage was set for a prolonged conflict. As historian Alan Dowty describes it, "The core of the Israeli-Palestinian conflict is the claim of two peoples to the same piece of land. Stripped of other layers and dimensions added over the years, it was and is a clash between a Jewish national movement (Zionism) seeking to establish a Jewish state in *Eretz Yisrael* – the historic Land of Israel – and an Arab/Palestinian national movement defining the same territory as *Filastin* (Palestine) and regarding it as an integral part of the Arab world."[4] The Zionist movement won support from Britain when that country took control of Palestine after the defeat of the Ottoman Empire. In 1917, the British Balfour Declaration gave license to the Zionist movement for "the establishment in Palestine of a national home for the Jewish people ... it being clearly understood that nothing shall be done which may prejudice the civil and religious rights of existing non-Jewish communities in Palestine."[5] Unfortunately, the preservation of civil rights for non-Jewish communities would become a controversial issue that would come to haunt the State of Israel.

Over the course of four centuries of Ottoman Turkish rule, Palestine was "a distinct and identifiable region within the larger empire."[6] After the fall of the Ottomans during World War I, the British Mandate authorized London's control of the area until 1947 when the United Nations took over. The United Nations Partition Agreement that year divided Palestine into two sectors: one Jewish (55 percent of the land) and one Arab (45 percent of the land), with Jerusalem to be left under international management. A war among the parties broke out soon after and, in

1948, the State of Israel came into existence, taking 78 percent of the land that had been under the League of Nations-authorized British Mandate Palestine. The remaining 22 percent of land was made up of the West Bank and Arab East Jerusalem (governed by Jordan) and the Gaza Strip (a small area along the Mediterranean coast on the Egyptian border and controlled by Egypt). At the end of the June War of 1967 between Israel and its neighboring Arab nations, Israel took control of those remaining areas – the West Bank, Gaza, and East Jerusalem. The international community defines these areas as *occupied territories*. Despite claims to the contrary from the Israeli state and its close ally the United States, the vast majority of the international community as well as international courts have been clear that "Israel does not have the right, under international law or United Nations resolutions, to continue its occupation, let alone to use violent methods to enforce it."[7] Thus the relevance of the Israel/Palestine conflict to Environmental Justice Studies is the fact that this struggle involves power imbalances between different religious and ethnic communities over history, memory, land, water, agriculture, and the very right to exist. An earlier-generation EJ studies approach to this conflict would likely center on the spatial relationship between environmental threats and ethnicity, and how those dynamics were produced by policymaking over time. I do that as well, but a Critical EJ analysis incorporates a wider range of social categories of difference, the use of multiscalar methods, an anarchist orientation to the state, and an unwavering commitment to the indispensability of all sides of this conflict to ensuring just and sustainable futures.

First Pillar: Multiple Categories of Difference

The first pillar of Critical Environmental Justice Studies expands our lens of analysis to include a focus on the ways in which multiple social categories of difference are entangled in the production of and resistance to environmental injustice. Among the numerous categories of difference I consider in this chapter are religion, race/ethnicity, gender, and more-than-human species and ecosystems, because they are all centrally at stake in the Israel/Palestine conflict.

Religion, ethnicity, and race: Anti-Jewish hatred, exclusion, and violence

No discussion of the Israel/Palestine conflict can be taken seriously without a focused consideration of the long history and ongoing realities of anti-Jewish hatred and violence. This is, in fact, the reason why so many Jews migrated from Europe and Russia to Palestine in the first place. As one historian puts it, "the central thread of Jewish history, as seen by most Jews, is the omnipresent threat of persecution. Persecution lies behind Jewish population movements, demography, and geography."[8] While I would like to assume that most readers are familiar with the Nazi-led Holocaust (Shoah), wherein millions of Jews, and also Roma, Afro-Germans, and LGBTQ persons were slaughtered to make way for an ethnically "pure," heteropatriarchal Aryan nation state, the scale and expanse of Holocaust denialism and the denial of Jewish suffering more generally render any such assumption no longer valid, if it ever was. In addition to the horrific series of events known as the Holocaust/Shoah – the effects of which are still deeply present in the early twenty-first century – the longer history of anti-Jewish violence is extraordinary in its scope and impacts, and must be considered here as well. During the First Crusade, which began in 1096 – a Christian-led effort to retake the Holy Land from Muslims and other non-Christians – an estimated one-quarter to one-third of Jews in France and Germany were killed.[9] Between the thirteenth and sixteenth centuries, Jews were expelled from England, France, most of Germany, Saxony, Sicily, Provence, Tuscany, Sardinia, Milan, and Spain, among other places. There were multiple massacres of Jews in Poland throughout the seventeenth and eighteenth centuries as well. The reign of Tsar Alexander III in Russia during the late nineteenth century saw literally hundreds of pogroms committed against that nation's Jewish population.[10] As a wave of anti-Jewish hatred spread across Russia, it also took hold in Romania, Austria-Hungary, Germany, and France at that time. This was an era of the rise of the modern European nation state, and nationalism was a social force inspiring and mobilizing populations across the continent. Unfortunately, while nation states then and now function to variously assimilate groups on the margins into the dominant cultural framework (or exclude them if they are deemed a threat), in many places Jews were not considered assimilable. The drive to migrate to Palestine was an intense response.

The State of Israel as haven, site of violent exclusion, and nonhuman agency

After the Holocaust/Shoah the push to establish a safe haven for Jewish peoples was strong and understandable. Unfortunately, this effort was accompanied by a great deal of tension and violence. During the 1947–48 War, Zionist militias that would soon become part of the Israeli army participated in the expulsion of Arab communities from Palestine. All told, some 700,000–750,000 Arab Palestinians left their homes and neighborhoods, as a result of direct violence and threats or from fear of such violence at the hands of Zionist militias.[11] The Arabs who stayed behind constitute 20 percent of Israel's population and are the descendants of those who fled during what many of them call the *Nakba* or "Catastrophe." Those living in exile have not been allowed to return, despite protestations in international legal venues and United Nations resolutions. Moreover, Israel's admission to the United Nations in 1948 was made possible by its promise to honor UN General Assembly Resolution 194, which calls for the right of return and compensation for those exiled Arab communities. Israeli Arabs are citizens of that nation, who enjoy the right to vote and run for elected office. In fact, numerous Palestinians have been elected to the Israeli Knesset or parliament. However, there are many rights that Israeli Arabs do not enjoy, since the legal system frequently favors Jews over non-Jews (a direct violation of the understanding put forth under the Balfour Declaration) through what are called "nationality rights," which discriminate against non-Jews with respect to access to *the right to own land, access to water*, access to bank loans and education, military service, social services, and more.[12] What is called "Class A" citizenship is for Jews (full citizenship based on one's religious affiliation as Jewish) while "Class B" citizenship (partial citizenship) is for everyone else, the vast majority of whom are Arabs.[13] Under the Absentees' Property Law of 1950, there are two additional terms of relevance here. One is the category of "present absentee" – those Arab citizens of Israel who live within Israel and are disallowed full access to their properties, and the other category is "absentee" – those Arabs who are not Israeli citizens but are among the refugees who fled or were expelled from Palestine and who also have no access to those properties.

The idea that a nation should exist exclusively or primarily for one religious or ethnic/racial group seems deplorable to many of us, but that is the premise upon which the State of Israel was founded and continues to function. Israel defines itself as a "Jewish state" and encourages Jewish migration from anywhere in the world under what is known as the Law of Return (passed in 1950).[14] Regardless of whether one has familial or ancestral ties to Israel or not, Jews from anywhere on Earth can claim Israeli citizenship upon arrival and can claim the right to "all of the privileges of being Jewish in a Jewish state, including state-financed language classes, housing, job placement, medical and welfare benefits, etc."[15] The Law of Return is premised on the claim that since Jews were expelled from Eretz Ysrael during the Roman conquest, people in the Jewish Diaspora should have the right to return to their symbolic homeland. The Law of Return does not, then, apply to indigenous Palestinians who were expelled or fled from their homes in Palestine during the 1947–48 and 1967 wars, despite specific guarantees of that right as embodied in United Nations Resolution 194 and, more generally, in the Universal Declaration of Human Rights.[16]

No less troubling and perhaps more revealing of the uneasy foundation the Jewish state rests upon under the Law of Return (which has been amended over the years), Palestinian non-Jews and specifically Arab "absentees" are excluded from full citizenship. Major groups of Jews are also excluded from full citizenship, including Jews born "out of wedlock," persons who are Jewish but whose mothers are not, Jews whose mothers have converted to another faith tradition, and Jewish converts who did so under the guidance of conservative or reform Rabbis since only the Jewish orthodox conversion procedure is recognized by the State of Israel. Thus, the question of who is a Jew reveals the entanglements of race, ethnicity, religion, gender, sexuality, and heteropatriarchy and has troubled the State of Israel since at least 1950.[17] Finally, age, ethnicity, and geography intersect in unpleasant ways under Israeli law, as Palestinian children from the West Bank are systematically treated more harshly under the Israeli military justice system than Palestinian children from Jerusalem and Jewish Israeli children more generally. This fact came to light during 2015–16, when a wave of violence that resulted in the deaths of around thirty Israelis was linked to stabbings, shootings, and vehicular attacks from Palestinian youths in response to continued tensions over the Occupation and the growth in Jewish settlements. Speaking about the case of a twelve-year-old Palestinian girl who was jailed after a failed attempt at stabbing an Israeli guard at the Karmi Tzur settlement, Sarit Michaeli of the Israeli human rights group B'tselem said, "Nobody doubts what she did . . . but if she was an Israeli child, it would be impossible under Israeli law to sentence a child this young for an actual jail term. They don't see a small girl. . . . They think of them as terrorists."[18]

Given this complex history, one can see that invoking calls for "peace" and "an end to the violence" between Israel and Palestine is, to say the least, limited and ill-informed. That approach overlooks long histories of (and ongoing) anti-Jewish hatred and the problems of military occupation and institutional racism that prevent Palestinians from enjoying full access to legal rights in Israel and independence in the Palestinian Occupied Territories.

While scholars disagree over whether the Zionist control over Palestine should be described as a form of European colonization – since no single European state was involved in the process – in many ways Zionism mirrored some of the key drivers and practical outcomes of settler colonialism elsewhere in the world. As historian Nur Masahla writes,

European settler colonies uprooted and almost completely destroyed indigenous peoples in North America and Australia. Land-grab was

117

the driving force behind these European settler-colonial societies. In Palestine *land, demography and water* were (and still are) at the heart of the struggle between the European Zionist settlers and the indigenous Palestinians. For the European Zionist colonizer, who is "returning" after 2,000 years to redeem the "land of the Bible," the indigenous inhabitants of Palestine earmarked for dispossession were usually invisible. They are simultaneously divested of their human reality and national existence and classed as a non-people. ... In a sense, Zionism's long-lasting battle against the native Palestinians was a battle for "more land and fewer Arabs."[19]

Thus the quest and struggle for land to found a Jewish state was inextricably linked to the struggle for control over water sources (primarily the Jordan River). Both of these struggles were necessarily competitions over who would occupy that land. Regardless of one's views on this struggle, these three forces and actors – land, people, and water – reflect the relevance of an environmental justice analysis for the Israeli-Palestinian conflict. Furthermore, the US, Britain, and other Western nations serve as allies to the State of Israel to, at least in part, ensure access to oil supplies and a solid military and economic foothold in the Middle East among many Arab and Muslim-majority nations whose support may wax and wane with each election. Franklin Delano Roosevelt's administration is said to have once referred to Middle Eastern oil as "the greatest prize in human history."[20] With OPEC being dominated by nation states that are sometimes hostile to Western capitalist state interests, the alliance with Israel serves to maintain the power and presence of the West in the region and a mode of access to a critical ecological resource that literally fuels the global economy and shapes global geopolitics. Thus, land, water, and oil should not just be viewed as prizes to be won in a battle among rival human communities; they are also *agents* or *actors* themselves, literally shaping our imagination, policymaking, and the material contours of nation states.[21]

Again, we must keep in mind the *complexity* of this story and place at the front and center the harsh realities of virulent and widespread anti-Jewish hatred and violence that drove people to leave Europe and Russia for a safe place. Without consistent attention to this fact, there can be little understanding of the Israeli-Palestinian conflict. Israel may be a nation state, but its majority comes from a population that has faced extraordinary oppression around the globe for many centuries. The concept of *intersectionality* from Women of Color Feminism is also useful here because it reminds us that privilege and oppression are always multifaceted phenomena that can often result in the important concept of "the oppressed as oppressor." For example, while Native American, African-American, Asian American and Latino men have historically been targeted by the US state for violence, exclusion, and marginalization, some of those oppressed men can and often have participated in the oppression of women, children, and LGBTQ members of their communities. Similarly, Jews fleeing racist violence and genocide in Russia and Europe experienced unspeakable horrors at the hands of mobs and state agents, but many of them also eventually participated in and benefited from the oppression of Palestinian Arab communities through the founding of the State of Israel. It is important to note that, from the beginning of the nineteenth-century Zionist movement to this day, many Jews opposed Zionism and even the founding of the State of Israel. Many Orthodox Jews, for example, believe that only God can intervene on behalf of their people and that Jews taking steps to found a state is a therefore a grave mistake. Other Jews – some of them a part of the International Jewish Anti-Zionist Network (IJAN) and others from the Reform tradition – have openly stated their opposition to the oppression of any human beings, including and especially Arabs, and therefore embrace human rights and the movement to end the Israeli Occupation. The key points here then, are that 1) oppression and privilege are complex experiences such that the same individual or population can simultaneously experience both phenomena, and 2) principled criticism of the State of Israel and of the political movement known as Zionism should not be mistaken for criticism of Jews or Judaism (i.e., anti-Jewish hatred, or anti-Semitism) since millions of Jews are also critical of Israel and opposed to the Occupation (although to be sure, some criticism of the State of Israel is definitely driven by anti-Jewish hatred). Thus, in the Israeli-Palestinian conflict the social categories of race, gender, religion, ethnicity, and nationality are entangled with land, water, oil, and history through conflict, inequality, privilege, oppression, resistance, and solidarity. Zionism can be thought of as a form of environmental injustice wherein different racial/ethnic and religious populations are afforded uneven access to land and other ecological wealth.

Zionism as environmental injustice

Since the first European Jewish settlers arrived in historic Palestine in the 1880s, the discourse of Zionism has often contained strong rhetoric about the necessity of displacing the indigenous Arab populations of the region in order to allow for the large-scale settlement of Jewish immigrants to live in peace. This displacement (some scholars have called it ethnic cleansing) was realized during the 1947–48 war that preceded the founding of the State of Israel, when 750,000 Palestinian Arabs were evacuated, became refugees, and have never been allowed the right of return.[22]

But long before the struggle over land between the State of Israel and the Palestinian Occupied Territories of the late twentieth and early twenty-first centuries, the foundation was laid by an organization that remains at the center of the crisis today. In 1901, the Keren Kayemeth LeIsrael Jewish National Fund (KKL-JNF) was founded to promote land acquisition and property rights exclusively for Jewish settlements. It later evolved to embrace the practices of afforestation (converting land into forest), agricultural development, sustainable development, education, and tourism.[23] KKL-JNF describes itself as an environmental organization and enjoys tax-exempt status as such in more than fifty nations, but has always seen its work in the European green colonial tradition of transforming an otherwise "desolate and neglected Asiatic desert of Palestine into a blooming green European terrain of forest."[24] Unfortunately, this transformation has resulted in the planting of forests directly on sites where Palestinian Arab villages *and mosques* once stood, thus erasing the evidence of the Arab and Muslim presence in the name of environmental sustainability and Israeli Jewish sovereignty.[25] In a fascinating twist on the politics of indigeneity within and across species, the KKL-JNF planted non-indigenous conifers, pine trees (which are native to the northern hemisphere), and cypress trees on land where Arabs and indigenous trees were uprooted via the reported destruction of more than 500 Arab villages in areas that are now "forested."[26] It would seem that the KKL-JNF is fixated on producing landscapes generally found in Europe or European-dominated spaces in the heart of desert terrain in the Middle East.

The Palestinian Arab village of Lubya, located in the Lower Galilee, inside pre-1967 Israel, was depopulated and destroyed during the 1947–48 War. Lubya's residents who escaped to locations outside of Israel then became refugees or "absentees" and those who remain living within Israel became internally displaced and were defined as "present absentees" under Israel's Absentees' Property Law of 1950. At that site, where Lubya once stood, is the South African Forest. This forest was planted by the JNF, various agencies of the Israeli government,[27] and the Women's Zionist Organization of South Africa to honor the special relationship between the settler colonies of Israel and South Africa.[28] The forest's recreational area and children's playground are built directly on the ruins of Lubya.[29] A section of the South African Forest is fenced off and reserved as a grazing ground for cattle owned by nearby Zionist settlements Kibbutz Lavi and Moshav Sedeh Ilan. More than 9,000 acres of land from what was the village of Lubya have been distributed among the nearby Israeli settlements, including Giv'at Avni. For many scholars and activists, the South African Forest is a monument to the twin projects of state-sponsored racist violence and ecological management.

The Palestinian village of Tantura was also razed during the 1947–48 War and, according to Israeli historian Theodor Katz and other scholars, this was a site of a mass atrocity by Zionist militias.[30] Reportedly, more than two hundred bodies of Palestinian villagers were found buried in mass graves. Today that same spot is where the parking lot for Israel's Dor Beach is located.[31] On the igoogledIsrael.com travel website, there is an article about Dor Beach titled "One of Israel's Best Beaches." The article opens with the following paragraph: "If you're looking for a truly great beach in Israel and even have a couple of days spare for a romp up north,

— Befor the 30 year old war in Europe (west phalica)

may of public property in 1800's?

What is Critical Environmental Justice?

you should consider checking out Dor Beach (*Hof Dor,* often known as *Hof Dor Tantura*). Located between the Mediterranean and Mount Carmel, Dor Beach is surely a contender for one of Israel's best beaches."[32] This site of recreation and pleasure today is also a site of the erasure of Palestinian life and death.

*Reminds me of the
Hedges that blocked may of*

Since 1948 the JNF has planted hundreds of thousands of trees, many of them not only concealing destroyed Palestinian villages such as al-Tira in the Haifa region (which has been transformed into Carmel National Park) and six villages where the Birya Forest now stands,[33] but in many cases, tree planting is linked symbolically to the Holocaust/Shoah, as many trees are planted in memory of lost communities and individual victims who died at the hands of the Nazis.[34]

Thus the JNF has, since its inception, been at the core of the colonization of Palestinian land. Moreover, at the center of Israeli-Zionist collective memory is the narrative that views the State of Israel as undertaking the important work of transforming the desolate desert of Palestine into a blooming terrain of European-inspired forests, which the previous Palestinian owners of the land are said to have neglected to do.[35]

The forcible conversion of depopulated and razed villages to green space and recreational lands is nothing new. Environmental justice studies scholar Dorceta Taylor writes that the creation of New York's Central Park was made possible by the expulsion of African-American and other marginalized communities and the destruction of their neighborhoods.[36] The creation of the National Park systems in the United States and South Africa went hand in hand with the eviction of indigenous peoples from those lands, or with severe reductions in their territories. Environmental groups such as the World Wildlife Federation and Conservation International continue to advocate such ecological conservation "solutions" in countries around the world today.[37] This is an example of what Betsy Hartman has called "coercive conservation"[38] and what Lisa Sun-Hee Park and I call "environmental privilege"—practices that exclude undesirable people from accessing green space and other coveted environmental amenities that are reserved for a chosen elite.[39] For scholars and others commit-

122

ted to social and environmental justice, this pattern is disturbing. It appears to reflect a mindset that casts indigenous peoples as threats to ecological sustainability, and as lacking the capacity to sustain and protect such lands. Thus they are often summarily evicted in "green/conservation" plans.

This framework shapes the social and ecological geography of Israel's urban Arab and Jewish communities today. The predominantly Arab city of Nazareth has a population that is double the size of its majority Jewish neighboring community of Upper Nazareth, but only 5 percent of the land, while Upper Nazareth's residents enjoy many more public parks and public services.[40] According to B'Tselem, an Israeli human rights organization, "Jerusalem's Jewish population, who make up about 70 percent of the city's 700,000 residents, are served by 1,000 public parks, 36 public swimming pools and 26 libraries. The estimated 260,000 Arabs living in the east of the city have 45 parks, no public swimming pools and two libraries."[41]

More traditional examples of environmental inequality abound as well in the region. For example, as a result of Israeli government practices, there is highly uneven and insufficient access to water for farming and a lack of sewage treatment among many Israeli Arab communities.[42] There are also instances where chemical factories and heavily polluting industries that have been outlawed inside Israel later relocate to the West Bank and other Palestinian communities.[43] And that age-old environmental justice issue of human waste and garbage rears itself in other, disturbing ways that intersect with the violence of Palestinian displacement and dispossession. Havah Ha-Levi was a Jewish Israeli woman who wrote a memoir about her experiences living in a kibbutz near an old Palestinian Arab village, Sarkas, which was evacuated and bulldozed by Zionist forces during the 1947–48 War. Ha-Levi recalled that the site of the ruins of Sarkas was soon used for another purpose. She writes,

The destroyed village was made into the kibbutz garbage dump. . . . Never, not once, while standing there among the ruins and the dust under the scathing sun did we talk or think of the inhabitants of the

123

Sarkas who lived here: where are they? Where did they go? Why? . . . Today I remember these Arab women and I ask myself: where did they come from? Who were they? Were they exiled inhabitants of the village? . . . The Arabs were something whose temporary provisional existence was eternal. . . . The entire area was leveled down, and around the huge factory orange groves were planted, and there is not one single cut stone left as testimony. Yet, I remember. I testify.[44]

Human and more-than-human exploitation, resistance, and agency

A core part of the first pillar of Critical EJ studies is the role of multi-species agency. People have resisted the occupation of Palestinian lands since the very beginning. As noted earlier, many Jews around the world oppose Zionism and the Occupation, and the majority of Jewish Israeli citizens favor returning the Occupied Territories to the Palestinian people.[45] Even before the rise of Zionism in the nineteenth and twentieth centuries and the successful formation of the Jewish state, a movement some called *Palestinism* was emergent. Palestinism is described as a discourse and belief that Arab Palestinians are a group of people, distinct from other Arab populations, who have a right to their own nation state.[46] A part of the broader pan-Islamic and pan-Arab movements that took hold during the twentieth century, Palestinism was reinforced by Zionism and in some ways is a parallel movement, focused on claiming the same land that Zionist Jews desire to hold onto. Better-known organizations focused on resisting the Occupation are the Palestine Liberation Organization (PLO), Hamas, and the Palestinian Authority (PA). Hamas is a nationalist Palestinian Islamist organization rooted in the idea that religion should be the basis for social and political change. Founded in 1987 in Gaza during the popular Palestinian uprising known as the first intifada (1987–93), Hamas outplayed the older PLO and became the popularly elected governing body in Gaza, providing many basic services and public needs that the occupying power, Israel, refused to make available to the people there, including social welfare agencies, schools, clinics, hospitals, and mosques. The Palestinian Authority is the governing body in the West Bank and was created out of the 1993 Oslo Peace Accords.

Rooted in the pan-Islamic Muslim Brotherhood (an Egypt-based group founded in the mid-twentieth century), Hamas is openly hostile to Zionism and is viewed as a "terrorist" organization by the US and Israel, which therefore officially only engage in government-to-government interactions with the PA.

Other forms of resistance to the Israeli occupation come in the form of groups like the International Jewish Anti-Zionist Network (IJAN) and the Boycott, Divestment, and Sanctions (BDS) movement. IJAN is an international network of Jews who "are committed to the dismantling of Israeli apartheid, the return of Palestinian refugees, and to ending the Israeli colonization of historic Palestine. We coordinate and support Jewish participation in local and international efforts to challenge Zionism, Islamophobia and other racism, separatism and militarism, and work towards a society premised on the economic, political, social, cultural and environmental rights of all people."[47] IJAN has affiliates and chapters in the US, Latin America, India, Europe, and New Zealand, among other places. They have produced reports that purport to document Israel's involvement in the violations of human rights, international law, and the repression of social change movements in Israel, Palestine, and many other nations around the globe.[48]

In 2004, the International Court of Justice ruled that Israel's separation wall violates international law.[49] A year later, in July of 2005, Palestinian civil society groups followed up on that decision with a call for Boycott, Divestment, and Sanctions (BDS) against Israel, until both equal rights and an end to the occupation are realized.[50] The movement quickly gained steam, with supporters from around the globe joining in. For example, in 2012, an international Quaker organization divested from Veolia Corporation and Hewlett-Packard, protesting those companies' involvement in the occupation. Veolia is a French corporation that does business in Israel providing water management, waste management, and energy services, and Hewlett-Packard supplied Israel with checkpoint systems technology, which is used to restrict Palestinian freedom of movement in the name of Israeli security. In 2013, TIAA (a large financial services company and retirement fund) dropped Veolia from its Social Choice Fund. Veolia also operates buses in Israel that are segregated by ethnicity, allowing only Jews on the buses servicing the settlements of Giv'at Ze'ev and Mevo Horon via what are called "settlers only" bus routes. Veolia is also being targeted for allegations of environmental racism in Palestinian communities. As one report stated, "Veolia owns and operates the Tovlan landfill in the Jordan Valley of the occupied Palestinian territory. The Tovlan landfill is used to dump Israeli waste from both within Israel and Israeli settlements."[51] The landfill has been said to produce negative health impacts among Palestinian workers at the site, Palestinian villagers who live near the site, and among their nonhuman animals. As another report stated,

> Rather than benefiting the Palestinians living next to the landfill, its existence in the area is deeply problematic for them. The two families who live nearest to Tovlan are forced to move elsewhere in the summer when the smell from the waste becomes too bad, only to move back during the winter season when it is bearable. Mohammed also testifies to the harmful health impact of the site. "Before I was dismissed from my job," he says, "I could only work for four minutes at a time without taking a small break as the smells were so bad. My health has improved a lot since I left." In Abu Ajaj, the closest village to Tovlan, the negative impact has also been noted. Since the landfill was established, its people have begun suffering from persistent coughs and breathing difficulties. The worst thing, however . . . is the impact it has on their animals: the animals now live for a shorter time than before and an increase in stillborn babies has been recorded, a very serious development for a small community relying on animal breeding. A heavy increase in flies and mosquitoes attracted by the landfill has further complicated their existence there.[52]

In the wake of the founding of the State of Israel, much of the land that Palestinians owned included olive and fruit orchards that were taken over by the Israel Custodian of Absentee Property agency. The harvest and sale of these goods is said to have contributed significantly to amassing wealth that secured the economic stability of the State of Israel. For example, in 1949 the olive produce from "absentee" Arab-owned groves was Israel's third-largest export, just after citrus fruit and diamonds. And fruit from "absentee" Arab land exported abroad produced nearly 10 percent of Israel's foreign currency earnings from exports in 1951.[53] Palestinian scholar Edward Said reflected on this externally imposed control over the Palestinian people and the fruits of their labor:

> when in London and Paris I see the same Jaffa oranges or Gaza vegetables grown in the *bayarat* (orchards) and fields of my youth, but now marketed by Israeli export companies. . . . The land and the peasants are bound together through work whose products seem always to have meant something to other people, to have been destined for consumption elsewhere . . . the carefully wrapped eggplants are emblems of the power that rules the sprawling fertility and enduring human labor of Palestine.[54]

Said continued with his thoughts on an article written by Israeli human rights attorney Avigdor Feldman about Israeli Laws 1015 and 1039, which "stipulate that any Arab on the West Bank and Gaza who owns land must get written permission from the military governor before planting either a new vegetable – for example, an eggplant – or fruit tree. Failure to get permission risks one the destruction of the tree or vegetable plus one year's imprisonment."[55] Drawing on the field of Political Ecology, one could say that the formerly Palestinian and now Israeli agricultural sector produced – through the combined efforts and labor of humans, plants, soil, water, fertilizers, and other beings and things – significant financial and state-supporting benefits that enabled one group to exercise dominance over the other, resulting in furthering the Zionist project of displacing Palestinians and controlling their land. In other words, human beings – particularly Israeli Jews – and more-than-humans both exercise agency in this scenario marked by conflicts and deep inequalities among multiple species.

In another example of more-than-human agency, one author describes how, despite the JNF's efforts, some flora resist eradication and expulsion with great tenacity:

It is possible to bulldoze a Palestinian village to the ground and cover the ruins with a JNF forest. It is not possible to eradicate the native Palestinian village cactus, the *sabr*, which has traditionally served also as a hedge to demarcate the boundaries of family compounds and agricultural plots. Tear the *sabr* down, and it will always re-emerge. And indeed, as one wanders through the South African Forest, as through many other JNF forests, one repeatedly comes across hedgerows of *sabr*, growing vigorously under the shadow of the pine forests planted by the JNF.[56]

Unfortunately, not all stories of human / more-than-human agency end well. Michael Mountain is the editor of the website EarthinTransition and works for the Nonhuman Rights Project, a group dedicated to advocating for the legal rights of more-than-human animals. He recently recounted the following events that occurred in the Palestine/Israel conflict:

A donkey suicide bomb and a farmyard massacre – two examples of how nonhuman animals have become targets in the current war between Israelis and Palestinians . . . a reporter for *The Daily Telegraph* came across a devastated farmyard where dozens of cows had died of their wounds after Israelis had bombed the Sha'af region of Gaza. . . . The farmer said: "My brothers and I have lost 100 dairy cows and 70 oxen for meat, as well as several camels. . . . This is a family business that we have inherited from our father, who built it up from money he earned working in Saudi Arabia. It's all we know." Another report was of a donkey, fitted with a suicide bomb, who'd been sent on her way toward a group of Israeli soldiers. The soldiers blew her up. . . . All across Gaza, the dead bodies of donkeys, horses and other animals litter the streets. No one knows how many dogs and cats lie buried under rubble or how many farm animals have been blown up or abandoned to die.[57]

If Israel's Separation Wall is a violation of international law, according to the International Court of Justice (ICJ), it is also a violation of the "laws" of ecology, separating people and more-than-humans from communities and spaces they are inescapably linked to. One could say the same for the entire occupation of Palestinian lands as well. And since this struggle is so multi-faceted, it requires a multiscalar analysis.

Second Pillar: Multiscalar Analyses of Temporal and Spatial Environmental Inequalities

The second pillar of Critical EJ Studies embraces multiscalar analyses for producing more robust understandings of the drivers of environmental inequalities and for developing more effective responses to them. The concept of scale here includes both spatial/geographic dimensions and temporal understandings of this phenomenon. This section of the chapter explores micro and macro spatial and historical-temporal scales of the Palestine/Israel conflict through a CEJ lens.

Microscale of the occupation

Under the Israeli Occupation, the lives of Palestinians are controlled even at the microscale through the use of checkpoints, the presence of a police and military force, and control over ports, trade, and flows of people, goods, and services. As Phyllis Bennis puts it, "Military occupation means complete Israeli control over every facet of Palestinian civil and economic life."[58]

During and after the Six Day War of June 1967, Israel occupied the West Bank, Gaza, and East Jerusalem through military control of these areas. Between 1967 and 1993 Israel issued roughly fifteen hundred military orders that regulated myriad aspects of political, economic, and civilian life among the Palestinian population, including the power to exercise full control over the allocation and use of water and land, control of the banking system, control over the export and import of goods, administration of local and municipal councils, the banning of political activity, and the issuing of identity cards and permits for work, travel, and professional activities.[59] Supporters of Israeli state policy have argued that the occupation no longer is in effect since, in the summer of 2005, Israel unilaterally withdrew its soldiers and settlers from the Gaza Strip. Observers and interested parties continue to debate whether, according to international law, Palestinian lands are still under occupation since, according to Article 42 of the 1907 Hague Regulations, a "territory is considered occupied when it is actually placed under the authority of the hostile army. The occupation extends only to the territory where such authority has been established and can be exercised."[60] Many supporters of the Israeli state argue that Israel exercises no formal authority over Palestinian life, while others point to the fact that Israel continues to exert enormous power over the Palestinian economy in the form of border controls, closures of entire towns and roads, Gaza's airspace and airport, the sea waters off the coast of Gaza and the seaport, and through an economic embargo in place since 2006. The United Nations, the International Court of Justice, and the International Committee of the Red Cross refer to the West Bank and Gaza as "occupied territories" and as "Israeli-controlled territories," articulating the view that the Palestinian people are not in control of their collective fates.[61] Moreover, Israel imposes restrictions on access to water for Palestinian farmers; restrictions on water, electricity, food, trade, and medical needs for the broader Palestinian population; and demolishes the homes of suspected "terrorists."[62]

In June 2016, media reports indicated that

Tens of thousands of Palestinians living in the Israeli-occupied West Bank are without access to safe drinking water during the Holy Month of Ramadan, after Israel's national water company began siphoning off water supplies to multiple West Bank cities and villages. Meanwhile, European Union officials are warning that 95 percent of the water in the Israeli-occupied Gaza Strip is currently not fit for human use. This comes as US officials announce breakthroughs in talks over increased US military funding to Israel.[63]

The Palestinian people's claims that the Israeli occupation violates their rights and is contrary to international law have been validated on a number of occasions. In one of many documents that speak to the *microscale* of the occupation, in 2004 the International Court of Justice (ICJ) issued an Advisory Opinion that concluded that Israel's separation wall violates international law, as well as Palestinians' rights to free movement, adequate standards of living, property, and self-determination. The summary document of that Advisory Opinion states, in part,

That construction, the establishment of a closed area between the Green Line and the wall itself, and the creation of enclaves, have moreover imposed substantial restrictions *on the freedom of movement* of the inhabitants of the Occupied Palestinian Territory (with the exception of Israeli citizens and those assimilated thereto). . . . In the view of the Court, the construction of the wall would also deprive a significant number of Palestinians of the *"freedom to choose [their] residence."* . . . There have also been serious repercussions for agricultural production, and increasing difficulties for the population concerned regarding access to *health services, educational establishments and primary sources of water.*[64]

Solid waste management reflects another example of how the State of Israel shapes the *microscale* of Palestinian life. The sewage problems in Gaza are now legendary. A combination of factors such as a fast-growing population, chronic shortages of electricity and fuel, halted development projects, and Israeli restrictions on critical imports of necessary equipment (via its blockade of the Gaza Strip) have resulted in the Gaza Strip's sewage system being incapable of managing and treating the area's waste. As a consequence, large volumes (90,000 cubic meters) of untreated and partially treated sewage spew forth into the Mediterranean Sea every day, threatening sea life and human health. Leaking pipes in the sewage treatment infrastructure also result in groundwater contamination of the coastal aquifer – the sole source of fresh drinking water for the population, placing agricultural crops and human health at significant risk. A severe lack of potable water, in combination with these other threats, has led the United Nations to warn that in a few years Gaza may no longer be livable.[65] The volume of sewage waste has also made it hazardous for residents who may want to swim or spend time on the beach. The Israeli blockade of Gaza has made life difficult for Palestinian fisherfolk like Foad al-Amodi, the president of the fishermen's syndicate in Khan Younis. He explained, "[The sewage] has a big effect. It annihilated the algae that feeds the small fish. The sewage kills the small fish, which is what the big fish feed on. With sea creatures such as shrimp and squid, the sewage wiped out their eggs." Amodi complains of skin rashes and infections that he and his fellow fisherman suffer from.[66] Moreover, the State of Israel has imposed a three-nautical-mile limit on how far out fisherfolk can travel to fish. Exacerbating the situation are the numerous wars that Gaza has endured in recent years. During the 2014 conflict with Israel alone, 26 municipal drinking wells and 183 agricultural wells were damaged or destroyed, while upwards of 30 percent of sanitation and water pipes were harmed as well. Three sewage treatment centers and 500 septic tanks were also destroyed during the conflict.[67] Guillaume Pierrehumbert, the International Committee of the Red Cross's water and habitat coordinator for the Gaza Strip, says, "The equation is simple. The shortage of electricity prevents water from being cleaned, evacuated, treated, desalinated and restored to homes, hospitals and businesses. There is an overall lack of water, and the water that is available is salty, dirty or dangerous to drink."[68]

If, following the wisdom of EJ scholars and activists, we define "the environment" as those spaces and places where we live, work, pray, learn, and play, then the Palestinian people in the Occupied Territories are living under environmental conditions that are largely outside of their control, having their access to the basic necessities of life – food, water, housing, shelter, land, recreation, and sites of spiritual, historical, and cultural significance – constrained by an occupying power. Perhaps the single most important aspect of the Palestinian situation is that much of the wastes and other environmental hazards this population is exposed to are generated from *within* the community – the problem is that the Israeli government's restrictive control over Palestinian environmental management systems reduces the Palestinian community's capacity to properly handle, treat, and dispose of these materials.[69] Thus, the Israeli military occupation is an environmental justice concern and one that has impacts for people and more-than-human natures at the microscale.

The occupation and Israeli state actions on a global scale

There are multiple ways in which the Israeli-Palestinian conflict is relevant for a global scalar analysis. For example, since 1976, Israel has been the top recipient of US foreign aid, now ranging from between $3 and $5 billion annually.[70] The US government has traditionally viewed Israel as an ally through which US state agencies, the military, corporations, and investors can maintain a geopolitical and financial foothold in the Middle East for the purpose of accessing global petroleum markets (along with the US ally Saudi Arabia and others). Aside from these political economic ties, the so-called "unbreakable relationship" between the US and Israel has long held deep cultural and religious significance through which Christians and Jews in the US can gain access to holy sites and visit family members. Thus, Israel's cooperation with the US has been critical for sustaining US influence if not hegemony over the region.

The US support of the State of Israel has been a flashpoint for domestic US criticism and activism for decades. During the 1960s the Student Nonviolent Coordinating Committee (SNCC), the Black Panther Party, and a number of other organizations focused on racial justice in the US openly criticized the US Congress and the White House for support of Israel on the grounds that Zionism was a form of racism, imperialism, and contrary to any semblance of an embrace of civil and human rights.[71] Activists pointed to the hypocrisy of the US Congress and President claiming support for civil rights at home while undermining Palestinian humanity in the Occupied Territories. In the 1980s, prominent feminist authors and scholars such as Carol Haddad, June Jordan, Alice Walker and others spoke out against Israel's occupation of Palestine and its brutal invasion of Lebanon at that time. This sparked a major debate within feminist circles and within the National Women's Studies Association that divided many participants over the now familiar tension between the perception that anti-Zionism was the equivalent of anti-Jewish hatred versus the insistence that support for Palestinian rights and criticism of Israeli policy were justified and principled.[72]

While the US's support of Israel has long been a sore spot for human rights and Palestinian rights advocates around the world, perhaps an even more troubling aspect of the Israeli state's approach to the question of human rights is how it manifests itself on a *global scale*. Israel has ranked as one of the world's top ten arms exporters,[73] which is surprising given that it is a small nation around the size of New Jersey. Many analysts argue that one reason for Israel's high profile in this regard is because it treats the Occupied Territories of the West Bank and Gaza as "laboratories" in which they test and refine weapons and methods of state repression that become "combat proven" and "battle-tested," making them that much more marketable to governments around the world in search of counterinsurgency techniques and resources. According to numerous sources, Israeli military manufacturers have sold arms to a number of nations led by repressive regimes, including apartheid–era South Africa, Rwanda, Serbia, and Equatorial Guinea – a country described as one of the most unequal, corrupt, and dictatorial in all the world.[74] No less controversial have been Israeli arms sales, military training, and other forms of support for pro-US repressive governments and guerrilla armies in Angola, Chile, El Salvador, Mozambique, and Nicaragua.[75]

Israel's arms exports to Africa doubled between 2012 and 2013, and have continued to rise since that time. Analysts fear that these arms shipments will fuel war, genocide, and mass atrocity, and that they will prop up undemocratic governments. Thus far the evidence seems to suggest they have good reason to be concerned.[76] A number of respected scholars and journalists claim that, during the early 1990s, Israeli leaders Shimon Peres (then foreign minister) and Yitzhak Rabin (then prime minister) approved the transfer of arms to Rwanda and Serbia while those genocides were in progress.[77] The ongoing conflict in South Sudan has involved numerous human rights abuses and mass atrocities, prompting the European Union to instate an arms embargo and issue sanctions against that nation's military officials. Despite those facts, according to the United Nations, automatic rifles produced in Israel have been documented in the possession of the Sudan People's Liberation Army, the National Police, and the National Security Service during the conflict.[78]

Israel's sometimes-close relationship with the apartheid government of South Africa is not well known but is well documented.[79] While numerous scholars have debated whether Israel's occu-

134

pation of Palestine and its treatment of Arab Israeli citizens constitutes a form of apartheid, I will not venture down that path here, except to say that 1) both the South African and Israeli systems of racial dominance were fundamentally centered on controlling and linking people and land[80] (which is as central an environmental justice concern as any) and 2) the alliances and cooperative agreements between those two governments speak for themselves and reflect state-based racially informed projects to support settler colonial societies. Israel was openly critical of the apartheid government of South Africa during the 1950s and 1960s as the Jewish state constructed partnerships with many newly post-colonial African governments. But most African states cut off ties with Israel after the 1973 Yom Kippur War and when it became clear that the government in Jerusalem "began to take a more benign view of the isolated regime in Pretoria."[81] In 1976, the Israeli government hosted John Vorster – a former Nazi sympathizer and former commander of the Ossewabrandwag (an Afrikaaner organization in South Africa that sided with Hitler during WWII) – during an official state visit. Israel's prime minister, Yitzhak Rabin, toasted Vorster at a state banquet, celebrating "the ideals shared by Israel and South Africa: the hopes for justice and peaceful coexistence."[82] Israel also provided critical technology and expertise to South Africa's apartheid regime in its development of nuclear bombs.[83] Nuclear weapons' threat to global ecological and public health is profound and troubling, to say the least.[84] Finally, the US-Israeli relationship goes both ways, as the US global "war on terror" at home and abroad – in terms of military operations and domestic surveillance of Muslim and Arab American communities – has drawn directly from technology and training provided by the Israeli Defense Forces and their practices in the West Bank. Most of the weapons Israel uses to maintain its occupation, such as F-16 fighter jets, Apache helicopter gunships, wire-guided missiles, and armored Caterpillar bulldozers for demolishing Palestinian homes are manufactured in the US and purchased with US aid funds.[85] Moreover, the US "contracted out the construction of major homeland security infrastructure like the border wall between the United States and Mexico to Israeli security corporations, transiting discourses of racial profiling in the process."[86]

The scales of time

In many ways, the Israel/Palestine conflict is not only a struggle over land, but also a conflict over interpretations and control of *history*, the *future*, and *time* itself. Both Arabs and Jews claim the same land as their birthright, based on historical and ethno-religious arguments. Jews were present in historic Palestine 3,500 years ago and were forced out by the Romans who conquered the area in 70 CE, while Arabs migrated to the area in the seventh century. Once the Zionist movement facilitated the "return" of Jews to the area, this was deemed justified by those who interpreted history in a way that sees Jews as the rightful and exclusive occupants of the land (regardless of whether one's ancestors actually once lived there). But since Arabs have lived in Palestine for well over a millennium, they see themselves as longtime and indigenous inhabitants of the land as well, thus creating a deeply and seemingly irresolvable tension over narratives of origin and belonging. Palestinian displacement (Nakba) and the ongoing Israeli occupation of the land have produced serious concerns that Palestinians be allowed their own "right of return." Thus both groups have claims to a "right of return" after expulsion. This disagreement also points to the socioecological character of time; in other words, our understandings of and engagements with time, history, and the future have highly consequential environmental justice implications. Specifically, from both the Zionist and pro-Palestinian perspectives, the relationship between time and environmental justice is one that sees exclusion and persecution as linked to dispossession from the land, and that the cause of environmental justice can only be supported and realized when these wrongs have been addressed and the rightful owners of the land are allowed to inhabit that territory without threats to their existence. The major difference with respect to time is that the Zionists see their current dominance and occupation of the land as just while the Palestinian community generally views that occupation as unjust. Thus the problem is that both groups have experienced persecution, making it difficult to frame one as the perpetrator and the other the victim, and there appears to be little room for a solution in which justice can be defined as a situation in which both populations share the same land.

The temporal scale is deeply linked to history but also to memory and the politics of remembering. For example, Israeli policy prohibits government funding for organizations that commemorate the Nakba.[87] Every spring, when Zionists celebrate Israeli Independence Day, Palestinians in the Occupied Territories and around the world commemorate Nakba Day. One event celebrates freedom and deliverance, the other calls attention to the "catastrophe" of Palestinian expulsion.

Scales of resistance and cultural politics

As discussed earlier, resistance to the occupation of Palestine has occurred from the beginning, dating back to the 1880s and continuing today. This has taken many forms, including the Palestine Liberation Organization (PLO), Hamas, and the Palestinian Authority (PA), but also the first and second Intifadas (or popular uprisings, from 1987–93 and 2000–05), and today the Boycott, Divestment, and Sanctions (BDS) movement. No less important than Palestinian resistance against the occupation is the *Jewish* resistance to that phenomenon, from the local scale within Israel via the Israeli Peace Movement and groups like B'Tselem, to the global scale via groups like IJAN, Jewish Voice for Peace, and many Orthodox Jews around the world. These multiple scales of resistance are important for understanding how far the occupation's impacts reach and how broad the refusal to accept it has become. John Collins uses the term "Global Palestine" to capture the ways in which Palestine has become both "a concrete 'local' place and . . . a thoroughly globalized space"[88] around which institutions, states, corporations, and activists mobilize throughout the world. As Phyllis Bennis writes,

Today Palestine stands at the symbolic center of much of Arab and Muslim consciousness, giving it a regional and indeed international significance far beyond its size. Palestine is also, since the independence

137

of East Timor in 1999, one of the last remnants of a once far more common phenomenon: what the UN used to call "non-self-governing territories." In other words, colonies occupied by another nation.[89]

Thus spatial and temporal scales offer a technique and lens through which to understand the Palestine/Israel conflict as an environmental justice concern as it reveals entanglements of race/ethnicity, religion, state and corporate violence, war, genocide, and ongoing tensions over efforts to secure the control and management of human and nonhuman bodies, land, water, waste, history, and memory.

Third Pillar: From Entrenched Inequality to Questioning the Social Order

The third pillar of Critical Environmental Justice Studies constitutes a call for a greater emphasis on the need think and act in ways that question the social order and the power of the state so as to imagine and achieve environmental justice. In this section, I consider how the Palestine/Israel conflict reflects these dynamics and opportunities for theory and action. Specifically, I examine the relationships among Jewish and Arab nationalism, state-building, European imperialism and colonization, anti-Jewish and anti-Arab racism, and ecological politics.

Race, gender, religion, nation, and land

Zionism began as a nationalist project, rooted in the idea that the Jewish people share a common history and should seek to form a state for their protection and defense. The irony of this project was that, while it evolved directly out of the need to ensure the survival of Jewish people and act against racist policies and practices by other states, Zionism itself was a form of racial nationalism. It therefore ran counter to the ideals of liberal nationalism in western Europe, in which full citizenship was to be enjoyed regardless of race, ethnicity, or religion, and therefore not based on "common descent." Zionism borrowed from German *volkisch* theory and from other forms of romantic nationalism in Central and Eastern

138

Europe that, like nationalism elsewhere, constructed a narrative that bound a people together based on a newly invented tradition and history.[90]

Racial nationalism also is a deeply gendered project, and Zionism has been no exception. Israeli feminist scholar Ronit Lentin describes the State of Israel's vision as an effort that embraced the view of the Jewish Diaspora as a "feminized" and weak Other in the face of European anti-Jewish hatred and the Holocaust, and sought to replace that Other with a "New Hebrew" symbolism exemplified by the Israeli masculine and militarized nation state.[91] In other words, Lentin contends that the Israeli nation-building project spurned the figure of the Diaspora Jew as a feminized gendered subject that was unable to successfully resist the assaults that led to the Shoah and therefore resurrected a new model of Jewry that explicitly saw its survival and existence as linked to state-based, masculinized violence, thus justifying the Occupation. Lentin argues that the "New Hebrew Man" was cast as a "man of iron" who was no longer meek and effeminate but now ready to defend *his* homeland by any means necessary. Russian Zionist leader and author Ze'eve Jabotinsky's 1923 essay "The Iron Wall" spoke to this newly emergent "muscular Zionism" and, as Israeli historian Avi Shlaim put it, "This, in a nutshell, was Jabotinsky's policy regarding the Arab question: to erect an iron wall of Jewish military force."[92]

The Zionist desire for a homeland and nation state was driven in large part by a sense that Jews, like any other population, would remain vulnerable as long as they were stateless. This view is of great importance for any scholar taking anarchist theory and politics seriously because it reflects a long-held view that states provide security, but ignores the view of many scholars that states have also perpetrated many of the greatest acts of social and ecological violence in history.[93] The claim that a state would provide the necessary protections to ensure the survival of the Jewish people took root in the late nineteenth century not only because this was a time of heightened Jewish persecution but also because it was an era when the idea of the nation state as a basic unit of world politics and national self-determination was being rediscovered and taken as common wisdom.[94] During that historical moment, that sentiment resulted in the unification of existing states like Italy and Germany. These strong nationalist movements left indelible imprints on Jews and Arabs at the time. Arab nationalism experienced an upsurge at this time as a number of nations – Greece, Serbia, Bulgaria, and Romania – successfully emerged out of secessionist movements seeking independence from a declining Ottoman Empire that ruled over most of the world's Arabs. Jewish and Arab nationalisms have strong parallels, including the way they reflected the views of many members of both groups who sought to recapture the status of a long-ago "golden age" when they enjoyed greater stature in the region. National determination seemed like the best way to achieve that goal. The point from a Critical Environmental Justice studies perspective is two-fold: 1) both Jewish/Israeli and Arab/Palestinian nationalism were tied to the quest for territory and therefore ethnicity/race and religion were inescapably linked to land – historic Palestine; and 2) while these nationalist movements grew strong in the late nineteenth century, their imaginaries are rooted in the respective histories of peoples who claim a presence and birthright to the land that extends back several centuries, even millennia. Thus the competing Arab/Palestinian and Jewish/Israeli nationalisms are deeply entrenched and based on longstanding struggles and long historical memories. In other words, the role of the state was firmly rooted in the desire for cultural integrity and sovereignty of a people. Not surprisingly, then, the Israeli nation state that emerged from this conflict was and remains intent on self-preservation and expansion. Those goals and the very form and functions of a state generally require authoritarianism, violence, and exclusion and erasure of populations unwilling to assimilate (or disallowed from doing so).

Racial/ethnic and religious politics in the Zionist context are complex indeed, but function to maintain Arab/Palestinian marginality and disempowerment, particularly with respect to land. Uri Davis writes about the category of "present absentees" – Palestinian Arabs who are classified as "absentees" under the Absentees' Property Law of 1950, their right to the title of their movable and immovable properties acquired until 1948 inside Israel have been nullified, their "presence" in Israel as citizens notwithstanding. . . . They are "present absentees," namely, internally displaced persons. . . . *It is important to note that the status of "absentee" is inherited. Children of "absentees," whether born inside or outside the State of Israel, are similarly classified as "absentees."*[95]

The irony of Israel's Absentees' Property Law of 1950 and the displacement of thousands of Palestinian refugees during the State of Israel's founding is that Israeli Jews shifted from a position of statelessness to one of statehood that was predicated on producing stateless Palestinians. And since the status of "absentee" is inherited, this raises troubling questions about the State of Israel's participation in a system of exclusion linked to reproduction that would ensure a caste-like element of permanent marginalization.

The question of reproduction is always linked to the racial/ethnic/religious demographic battles in Israel/Palestine. Itzhak Kanev was a scholar, activist, and architect of the early welfare state in Israel. Among other goals, he sought to use science and technology to increase the productivity of the land and increase Jewish Israeli women's reproduction. He aimed to improve land productivity through industrialized agriculture (including biological engineering, the use of chemical-intensive fertilizers, herbicides, and pesticides) and aimed to increase women's reproduction through pro-natal social policies, including "monthly child allowances, one-time birth grants, tax assistance for large families, rent subsidies, laws protecting pregnant women and new mothers in the workplace, paid maternity leaves, and subsidized daycare . . . [as well as] investment in fertility technologies and programs encouraging establishment of families and childbearing."[96] These programs and efforts reflected a "clear and consistent desire to increase Jewish fertility."[97] Israel is hardly the first nation state to employ the logic of eugenics by promoting the fertility of certain racial/ethnic groups while discouraging the same for less desirable populations.[98] The associations among demographics, gender, race/ethnicity, ecology, and the state come into equally sharp relief when one pays close attention to the Israeli military – the Israeli Defense Forces – and the role it has played in controlling and harming Palestinian people, local ecosystems, and the use of Jewish Israeli women's military service "not as an equalizing factor but rather as a mechanism for reproducing their subordination."[99]

Tensions and divisions within the Jewish State

Zionism is a political movement that seeks the creation and support of a Jewish state. In that regard, the movement has been successful since it ushered in the founding of the State of Israel in 1948. It has been less successful at defending the claim that a Jewish state can also be a *democratic* state, since it builds anti-Arab/Palestinian/Muslim discrimination into its structure. No less disturbing, though, is the question of whether Israel's government is democratic with respect to the wishes of its own Jewish citizens. According to various opinion polls, the majority of Jewish Israeli citizens are willing to end the occupation of the West Bank, Gaza, and East Jerusalem, but successive Israeli governments do not seem to be so inclined.[100] This is an exceedingly important observation since it would seem to indicate that it is the *state* – not the Jewish majority of Israel – that continues to advance the occupation. One must raise questions about how state interests conflict with the interests of the citizenry. One must also recognize that modern nation states are also racial states and this brings its own violence and exclusions that must be acknowledged. Recently, the Israeli Supreme Court rejected an appeal by twenty-one Israeli citizens who sought to be identified in the national registry as "Israeli" rather than by religion or ethnicity. The Court's rejection was based on its reasoning that delinking ethnicity and religion from citizenship "would have 'weighty implications' and could endanger the state's founding principles."[101]

Nationalism and nature

The Jewish National Fund (KKL-JNF), discussed earlier in this chapter, offers a case study in the deep links among nation, race/

142

ethnicity, and land. The Jewish National Fund (KKL-JNF) website states,

> A vital part of Zionist history, JNF achieved its goal of purchasing the land that would become the State of Israel, then helped to develop that land into a thriving nation – by planting over 240 million trees, building more than 200 dams and reservoirs, developing more than 250,000 acres of land, and creating over 1,000 parks. ... In 1960, Israel's Knesset adopted a Basic Land Law based on JNF-KKL's principle of national land, which stated that land owned by the Jewish People and maintained by JNF-KKL cannot be sold, but only leased for periods of 49 years at a time.[102]

The Jewish National Fund's work is part of a broader effort that reveals deep linkages between Zionism and the ideology of a superior European Jewish cultural force exerting positive and productive control over land and people of Palestine. David Ben-Gurion was one of the primary founders of the State of Israel and its first Prime Minister. He expresses this view in the following statement:

> No square inch of land shall we neglect; not one source of water shall we fail to tap; not a swamp that we shall not drain; not a sand dune that we shall not fructify; not a barren hill that we shall not cover with trees; nothing shall we leave untouched. An intensive agriculture, planned in accordance with a scientific and practical scheme worked out by the Government, operated by pioneering labour, and maintained by the full strength of the State ... will be the fundamental basis of a national economy created by the State ... under a Jewish Government.[103]

Elsewhere, Ben-Gurion further supported these sentiments by stating, "The demand of the Jewish people is based on the reality of unexploited economic potentials, and of unbuilt-up stretches of land that require the productive force of a progressive, cultured people."[104]

The inequalities of race, ethnicity, religion, gender, citizenship, and class in Israel are tightly linked to the development of the Israeli nation state and its expanding thirst for land and water. Nation states are, in the view of many scholars, inherently authoritarian, racially exclusionary (as much as they are inclusive of certain groups), and rooted in anti-ecological principles.[105] A Critical Environmental Justice perspective contends that closer attention to the ways that nation states are drivers of environmental injustice is necessary. CEJ also contends that analyses and politics that favor certain groups over others are unsustainable.

Fourth Pillar: Racial and Socioecological Indispensability

Critical Environmental Justice Studies advances the concepts of racial and socioecological indispensability as a commitment to an analysis and politics that views humans and more-than-human actors as *indispensable* to the present, and necessary to the building of sustainable, just, and resilient futures. Indispensability is a direct counter to the often prevailing views by dominant institutions and cultural frameworks that certain human populations (particularly people of color, indigenous peoples, migrants, refugees, women, and queer folk) and nonhuman species are of lesser value than others and that they are surplus, excess, or worse: threats to the stability and security of a given society or nation. CEJ Studies maintains that, even and especially during moments when seemingly irreparable conflicts and rifts emerge to divide various populations, it is imperative that we engage one another as indispensable members of a collective community whose futures are linked.

Throughout this chapter, I have reminded the reader that one cannot begin to grasp the roots of the Israel/Palestine conflict without careful attention to the long histories of anti-Jewish hatred around the globe that resulted in pogroms, massacres, exclusionary and discriminatory policies, expulsions, mass atrocities, and genocide directed at Jewish people. There can be no more blatant an indicator of rendering and defining a people as expendable than the Nazi's "Final Solution" to the Jewish Question – a policy of extermination. The seemingly unending power of anti-Jewish hatred has underscored the continuation of discourses and practices of expendability and therefore the need for a framework and embrace of *indispensability*. Unfortunately, the founding of the State of Israel was followed by the massive displacement of Palestinians and a government apparatus to control that population and limit their human rights. Yosef Weitz was director of the JNF's Land Settlement Department and the Afforestation Department. He later became head of Israel's "Transfer Committee" in 1948. On the Palestinian Question Weitz made it clear that ethnic cleansing was the only option for a secure Jewish homeland in Israel. His diary entry for December 20, 1940, states, in part:

> it must be clear that there is no room for both peoples in this country. . . . After the Arabs are transferred, the country will be wide open for us. . . . Not a single village or a single tribe must be left. . . . And only then will the country be able to absorb millions of Jews . . . there is no other solution.[106]

In describing Zionism's relationship to the Palestinian people, historian Nur-eldeen Masalha echoes the perspectives that many Ethnic Studies scholars present when focused on people of color in the US; they contend that the settler colonial state views the nondominant racial/ethnic and/or indigenous communities as subhuman and deserving of erasure. Masalha writes, "The immigrant-settler nation-state of Israel is a blatantly racist state, regarding its indigenous people – once by far the overwhelming majority population of historic Palestine – as less than human, as disposable, expendable and 'transferable.'"[107]

But as much as the two populations remain locked in conflict and tension, there are reasons for hope. Clearly the histories and memories of the Jewish Shoah and the Palestinian Nakba are distinct, but as John Docker argues, these histories illuminate one another because, in the first place, the Hebrew word for the Holocaust, *shoah*, translates to "catastrophe," which is identical to the Arab word, Nakba.[108]

One of the most dynamic and inspiring sites of discourse and action around the concept of indispensability comes from activists, scholars, and religious leaders on all sides of the Palestine/Israel conflict. For example, celebrated Palestinian scholar Edward Said once wrote about the bravery of Jews who reach across the divide to support their Palestinian relations despite the unpopularity of such a move:

> Most Palestinians have their own special instance of the Israeli who reached out across the barricade most humanly. For some it is the intrepid Israeli lawyer defending Palestinian political prisoners, or trying to prevent land expropriations and collective punishment; for others it is . . . an Israeli in a position of authority (prison guard or army officer) who prevented some atrocity or showed some clear sign of humanity and fellow feeling. For my part . . . I think of all the Israeli (or non-Israeli) Jews whose articulate witness to the injustice of their people against mine has marked out a communal territory. The result has usually been a friendship whose depth is directly proportional to the admiration I feel for their tenacity of conscience and belief in the face of the most slanderous attacks.[109]

The International Jewish Anti-Zionist Network (IJAN) is a global network of Jewish activists that describes itself as "uncompromisingly committed to struggles for human emancipation, *of which the liberation of the Palestinian people and land is an indispensable part.*" IJAN opposes the Israeli occupation of Palestinian lands but also works toward a future premised on respect for "the economic, political, social, cultural and environmental rights of all people, beginning with the most vulnerable communities." IJAN organizes using the principle of "joint struggle," a perspective that recognizes

> the particular stakes of different communities and sectors in the general struggle against Zionist repression, militarism, and imperialism. The stake of each movement is specific, but we share a commitment to principles of universal liberation, justice, equity, never sacrificing any aspect of one community or movement's struggle for freedom for the sake of advancing another's. We recognize that our struggles are bound together, and that we must find ways of organizing together that strengthen all of our movements.[110]

Michael Lerner is an American rabbi, author, and outspoken advocate of a just and sustainable peace in Israel/Palestine. He has criticized the Israeli occupation for years while also critiquing the US left for being driven, in part, by anti-Jewish hatred. He calls for all people to work together from various traditions – both religious and secular – to have open and honest conversations about the trauma that both Arab Palestinians and Jewish Israelis have experienced. His vision of the future of the region and its peoples is one of indispensability. He writes, "One reason that I've chosen to refer to the Holy Land as Israel/Palestine is that I insist on the ultimate oneness of both peoples and believe that their fate is intrinsically linked."[111] Lerner calls his approach the "Strategy of Generosity," which is "about empowering our most loving, kind, and generous instincts, honoring the spiritual wisdom of our traditions (both religious and secular) that teach us that every human being on the planet is equally precious and deserving of well-being and fulfillment."[112] He is clear that, in order to realize the promise of that strategy, we must build political and economic arrangements to facilitate social equality, justice, and ecological sustainability. Finally, Lerner declares, "We need this transformation not only in regard to our neighbor, but our dealings with all the people on the planet – because they are equally precious and equally created in the image of God and because our well-being depends on the well-being of everyone else on the planet."[113] Lerner demonstrates that indispensability is an ethical, spiritual, political, social, and ecological principle.

Concluding Thoughts

The Israel/Palestine conflict is a case where religion, race/ethnicity, and environmental justice concerns intersect because the State of Israel was established as a Jewish state and has created a system of laws, policies, and practices that exclude many non-Jews from access to critical social services, property, land, clean air, clean water, functioning utilities, and, in some cases, food and agricultural products. Moreover, the Jewish National Fund's raison d'être is explicitly focused on making land and nonhuman natures available to people of the Jewish faith. Thus religion is correlated with one's relationship to environmental threats versus environmental privileges. This case also underscores the difficulty, if not impossibility, of separating ethnicity from religion, thus complicating and deepening our understanding of the ways that environmental injustice conflicts play out in various contexts.

A Critical Environmental Justice Studies perspective on the Israel/Palestine conflict blends together the urgency of combating historical and contemporary oppressions facing Jews, Arabs, and the more-than-human-natures in that region with the hopefulness and possibilities of taking racial and socioecological indispensability seriously and making it a reality.

Conclusion

This book offers a new framework for the field of Environmental Justice Studies. It does so through the consideration of three case studies: 1) the challenge of racist state violence and the Black Lives Matter movement; 2) the prison system in the US; and 3) the Israel/Palestine conflict. What links these cases, aside from the fact that they reflect the intersections of social inequality and environmental politics?

Policing, Prisons, and Palestine

First, I wanted to explore sites and issues that are rarely connected to and theorized as examples of environmental justice struggles. After all, what scholarly and practical staying power does an academic field of study hold if we cannot extend its reach into spaces and topics well beyond what were previously believed to be its boundaries? Second, what is present across the issues of police brutality, incarceration, and the Israel/Palestine conflict is the power of the state to define reality for humans and more-than-just-humans, and to manage, manipulate, and control those beings, bodies, and the ecosystems that support them. This reflects my view that EJ studies must take more seriously the role of the state as a frequent impediment to environmental justice, and my view that the inseparability of humans from the more-than-human world must be at the center of our work. Third, across each of these three cases is the opportunity to push the boundaries of reformist thinking and action in the face of deeply entrenched, violent, and unsustainable policies and practices. In other words, timid half-steps will not move us very far intellectually or politically, so my goal is to present challenging subject matter here that requires a bold and transformative response.

Critical Environmental Justice, Critical Ecological Justice

Critical EJ Studies is a framework whose goal is to address important limitations and tensions within EJ studies. There are four key issues from earlier generations of EJ studies that Critical EJ Studies speaks to that I focus on in this book.

First is the tendency for EJ scholars to focus on only one or two social categories of difference (for example, race and/or class), when in fact, environmental injustices are driven by and affect actors across multiple forms of inequality (race, class, gender, sexuality, age, nationality, citizenship, ability, species, etc.). While a small but growing number of scholars are exploring the ways that, for example, gender and sexuality shape EJ struggles,[1] that work is still in its early stages. Further, the category of species remains almost entirely at the margins of the field despite the very clear ways that EJ conflicts reflect tensions and intersections between humans and the more-than-human world.[2] The evidence and perspectives from fields such as Ecofeminism, Political Ecology, Critical Race Theory, Ethnic Studies, Critical Race Feminism, the Environmental Humanities, and Critical Animal Studies suggest that multiple forms of inequality fuel environmental injustice and shape the experiences of the actors involved. EJ Studies would thus surely be strengthened with greater attention to these dynamics.

Second is the lack of consistent attention to multiscalar analyses in EJ studies. While there are numerous excellent local case studies, regional analyses, and national and even transnational studies of environmental inequality, the scholarly work that brings these multiple spatial scales together with attention to the body as a site of EJ struggle is impressive but rare.[3] Moreover, while there are outstanding historical studies of EJ conflicts and environmental inequalities in various communities, few scholars have linked historical work with multiscalar spatial approaches. Multiscalar methods and theoretical orientations to environmental injustice are critical because they facilitate our capacity to observe and engage the spatial and temporal ecology of EJ issues. That is, they point to the ways in which environmental injustices link people and the more-than-human world across geographic space and time. The evidence from fields such as Cultural and Critical Geography, Political Ecology, and the Environmental Humanities (particularly environmental history) suggests that a greater awareness of and engagement with scale is vital to the future of EJ studies.[4]

Third is the tendency within EJ Studies to name and critique the problems of social inequality and power imbalances as embodied in the state, paired with a hesitation to see those social relations as fundamental obstacles to achieving environmental justice. In other words, despite a strong condemnation of the scourges of racism, class domination, and the abuse of state and corporate power in the literature, EJ studies generally offers prescriptions for change that rely on dominant institutions and social systems serving as partners and collaborators in forging a just and sustainable future. The evidence and analysis from fields such as Anarchist Studies, Critical Race Theory, Critical Race Feminism, Ethnic Studies, and Critical Animal Studies suggests that these inequalities are foundational to the formation and maintenance of states and capital and that therefore it would likely be counterproductive for environmental justice scholars and advocates to seek solutions from dominant institutions. A Critical EJ Studies approach asks whether scholars and activists aiming for transformational analyses and social change should expect the very institutions that are largely driving socioecological inequalities to offer remedies for these harms (and what the implications of doing so might be). Social movements can strategically harness the power of states to produce positive outcomes, but should always be cautious about doing so and work to limit a reliance on the state.

Fourth, EJ studies suggests that certain human populations are devalued via environmental racism, yet stops short of theorizing this point beyond that claim and the problem of "sacrifice

zones" – highly contaminated communities that have been abandoned by society. A CEJ perspective takes this point further by
linking it to scholarship that concludes that these bodies and
entire *populations* are rendered expendable, not just particular,
localized communities and spaces. CEJ links that ideological and
institutional othering to the more-than-human world as well, and
confronts that hegemonic view with the perspective that these
bodies, populations, and spaces at risk are indispensable to our
collective futures.

Accordingly, Critical EJ Studies builds on and extends earlier-
generation EJ Studies via the above four pillars by 1) paying
greater attention to how multiple social categories of difference
are entangled in the production of, and in challenges to, environmental injustice, including race, gender, sexuality, ability, class,
and species; 2) embracing multiscalar methodological and theoretical approaches to studying EJ issues in order to build a more
substantive grasp of the complex spatial and temporal causes,
consequences, and possible resolutions of EJ struggles; 3) taking
the view that social inequalities and power relations that inhere
in the state, for example, are deeply embedded in the foundations
of society, suggesting that transformative analyses and visions
of environmental justice might seek to function (at least at some
level) beyond the state, capital, and the human through a broad
anti-authoritarian perspective; and 4) articulating a viewpoint that
all humans and more-than-human actors are *indispensable* to the
present and for building sustainable and just resilient futures.

Finally, Critical Environmental Justice Studies can aid scholars
and advocates in thinking through a *redefinition of the concept
of environmental justice itself* to reflect and encompass the above
four pillars. Following Rob White and Avi Brisman, perhaps any
discussion regarding the future of EJ Studies and the EJ movement might begin by connecting earlier-generation framings of
environmental justice – which center primarily around the intersection of human inequality and environmental harm – with the
concept of *ecological justice*, which engages more deeply with the
uneven relationships of human beings to the broader nonhuman
world and embraces a more respectful and egalitarian relationship

between the two.[5] These two concepts – environmental justice and ecological justice – are infinitely productive for each other. In my view, Critical EJ Studies would offer a redefinition or expansive view of environmental justice that reached out to and merged with ecological justice. This model of analysis and politics begins with humans taking responsibility for practicing transformative socioecological political work and extends to understanding inequalities within and across species and to making space to imagine and struggle for a more democratic multi-species world. Nonhuman species and ecosystems may not engage in politics the way humans tend to, but they can and do exert influence in many ways.[6] Consider, for example, the impacts of fossil fuels on the daily lives of human beings and on the political systems and economies of every nation on Earth. Ecological justice destabilizes the notion of the human as a biological category at the pinnacle of a human/nature hierarchy and, instead, embraces it as a political category that engages with the broader ecological community. This model of politics is also wary of the state as an arbiter of justice and inclusion. Generally speaking, states have managed, included, excluded, homogenized, and controlled humans and nonhuman natures for the benefit of a small elite. That should be reason enough to embrace an anti-statist, anarchist, or broadly anti-authoritarian approach to socioecological change. Curiously, this concept of ecological justice closely mirrors and parallels the Principles of Environmental Justice – a sort of founding document of the US EJ movement.[7] This suggests that, in many ways, the EJ movement and EJ Studies have yet to catch up to the vision of the EJ movement's founding principles, which are largely aligned with a Critical EJ perspective. My hope is that scholars and activists will pursue analyses and politics that produce relationships, practices, organizations, and institutions that are supportive of (and, when necessary, critical of) these ideas through conversation, discourse, and peaceful action that works to deepen multi-species democratic possibilities and futures.

Notes

1. Critical Environmental Justice Studies

1 Pellow and Brulle 2005.
2 Adamson 2011; Holifield, Porter, and Walker 2010.
3 See, for example, Brisman 2008; Bullard 2000; Gottlieb 1994; Shabecoff 2003.
4 Alkon and Agyeman 2011; Anguelovski 2014; Sze 2007.
5 Roberts and Parks 2007; Di Chiro 2016.
6 See The Principles of Environmental Justice 1991, http://www.ejnet.org/ej/principles.html.
7 Bullard 1996: 495.
8 Institute of Medicine 1999: 1.
9 Pellow 2000.
10 Holifield 2001.
11 Bullard 1996: 497.
12 Bullard 2000; Bullard and Wright 2012; Fothergill and Peek 2004; Fothergill et al. 1999; Harlan et al. 2006; Hunter 2000; Klinenberg 2002.
13 Bullard et al. 2007; Crowder and Downey 2010; Downey 2006; Mennis and Jordan 2005; Mohai and Saha 2007.
14 Bullard et al. 2007.
15 Adamson 2011; Bell 2013; Bell and Braun 2010; Brown and Ferguson 1995; Buckingham and Kulcur 2010; Gaard 2004; Holifield, Porter, and Walker 2010; Krakoff 2002; Krauss 1993; Park and Pellow 2011; Smith 2005; Stein 2004; Taylor 1997.
16 Pellow and Park 2002.
17 Buckingham and Kulcur 2010.
18 Bell and Braun 2010, Brown and Ferguson 1995.
19 Stein 2004, p. 2.
20 Smith 2005.

21 Gaard 1993 and 2017.
22 Adamson et al. 2004.
23 Bullard, Mohai, Saha, and Wright 2007; Figueroa 2001; Hunter 2000; Park and Pellow 2011; Pellow and Park 2002.
24 Alkon and Agyeman 2011.
25 DuBois 1977; LaDuke 1999; Pellow and Park 2002; Smith 2005.
26 Hurley 1995; Pellow 2002; Pellow and Park 2002; Taylor 2009; Washington 2003. The idea of a "long Environmental Justice movement" is inspired by the earlier concept of the "Long Civil Rights Movement," proposed by historian Jacquelyn Dowd Hall (2005).
27 Agyeman et al. 2010; Walker 2009.
28 See Buckingham and Kulcur 2010; Holifield, Porter, and Walker 2010; Walker 2010.
29 Brown and Ferguson 1995; Krauss 1993.
30 Cable and Cable 1995; Bullard 1990/2000; Pellow and Park 2000.
31 Gottlieb 1994; Hurley 1995; Park and Pellow 2002; Pellow 2000; Pulido 1996; Szasz 1994; Szasz and Meuser 1997.
32 Krakoff 2002; Pellow 2000; Schwab 1994.
33 Taylor 1997.
34 Chavez 1993; Fox 1991; Hossfeld 1990; Pellow 1998; Pellow and Park 2002; Robinson 1991; Wright and Bullard 1993.
35 Agyeman 2005; Agyeman et al. 2003; Schlosberg 2004.
36 Banerjee 2014; Harrison 2011; Schlosberg 2004, 2007; Walker 2010.
37 Čapek 1993.
38 Schlosberg 2007.
39 Schlosberg and Carruthers 2010.
40 Schlosberg 2004, 2007.
41 Schlosberg 2004: 529.
42 See Cole and Foster 2000; Lavelle and Coyle 1992; Lombardi, Buford, and Greene 2015.
43 Pellow 1999a and 1999b.
44 Young 2001: 683.
45 Scott 2009.
46 Cacho 2012, p. 8.
47 Espiritu 2005.
48 For a critique, see Mohai, Pellow, and Roberts 2009.
49 Best et al. 2007; Gaard 2004 and 2017.
50 See Angelo and Wachsmuth 2015.
51 Herod 2011; Sze 2016.
52 Sze 2006.
53 Beck 1996: 31; Beck 1995, pp. 23–23.
54 Dunlap and McCright 2010; Dunlap and McCright 2015; Levin, Cashore, Bernstein, and Auld 2012; Norgaard 2011; Oreskes and Conway 2010.

55 Newell 2005: 88.
56 Ciplet, Roberts, and Khan 2015; Pellow 2007; Roberts and Parks 2006.
57 Harrison 2008; Hooks and Smith 2004.
58 Caniglia et al. 2014.
59 Nibert and Fox 2002:13.
60 Heynen, Kaika, and Swyngedouw 2006.
61 Sze 2016, p. 178.
62 Sze 2016.
63 Kurtz 2003.
64 Sayre 2005.
65 Sze 2006: 792.
66 Yusoff 2013.
67 Imarisha 2015, p. 3.
68 While many EJ studies scholars have embraced anti-oppression principles – including an anti-capitalist framework – few have extended their support to anarchism.
69 Goldberg 2002; Smith 2011.
70 Amster et al. 2009; Goldberg 2002; Scott 1999 and 2010; Weber et al. 2004.
71 See Cole and Foster 2000; Lavelle and Coyle 1992; Lombardi, Buford, and Greene 2015.
72 Benford 2005.
73 Scott 2014, p. xiv.
74 Here I am influenced by David Graeber's (2002) writings in which he argues that anarchism is primarily focused on ". . . exposing, delegitimizing and dismantling mechanisms of rule while winning ever-larger spaces of autonomy from it" (p. 68). He continues, "this is a movement about reinventing democracy. . . . It is about creating and enacting horizontal networks instead of top-down structures like states, parties or corporations; networks based on principles of decentralized, non-hierarchical consensus democracy" (p. 70).
75 Author interview with scott crow, January 1, 2011.
76 Anguelovski 2015.
77 Márquez 2014.
78 See blacklivesmatter.com; Cacho 2012; Da Silva 2007; Mills 2001; Vargas 2010.
79 Mills 2001.
80 DuBois 1935.
81 Smith 2005.
82 Davis and Moore 1945; Parsons 1954.
83 King 1963.
84 My observations and claims here are also derived in large part from Ulrich Beck's Risk Society thesis (1995, 1996) and the concept of the "democra-

tization of risk," which contends that despite the reality of environmental injustices, there is no escaping at least some impacts of the hazards of contemporary industrialization.

85 Harlan, Pellow, and Roberts 2015.
86 Dunlap and McCright 2010; Dunlap and McCright 2015; Norgaard 2011; Oreskes and Conway 2010.
87 Principles of Working Together 2002.
88 The Flood Wall St. West Welcoming Committee 2015.
89 See Cacho 2012; Da Silva 2007; Márquez 2014; Mills 2001; Vargas 2010.
90 Pellow and Brulle 2005; Adamson 2011; Holifield 2010.
91 Bell 1993; Crenshaw 1991; Delgado and Stefancic 2012; Espiritu 2005; Goldberg 2002; Harris 1993; Lipsitz 2006; Márquez 2014; Mills 1999 and 2001; Omi and Winant 1994; Andrea Smith 2005; Williams 1992.
92 Anzaldua 2012; Collins 2008; Connell and Pearse 2014; Mohanty 2004; Wing 2003.
93 Amster et al. 2009; Scott 2010; Smith 2011; Torres 2007.
94 Adamson 2001 and 2011; Adamson, Evans, and Stein 2004; Nixon 2011.
95 Bennett 2009; Blaser and Escobar 2016; Heynen 2016; Heynen, Kaika, and Swygedouw 2006; Robbins 2007; Swyngedouw and Heynen 2003.
96 Gaard 1993, 2004; MacGregor 2006; Sandilands 2016; Sturgeon 1997.

2. Black Lives Matter as an Environmental Justice Challenge

1 See, for example, Hurwitz and Peffley 2005. An earlier version of this chapter was published in the DuBois Review (see Pellow 2016).
2 At a White House panel on criminal justice reform, President Barack Obama stated, "I think the reason that the organizers used the phrase 'black lives matter' was not because they were suggesting nobody else's life matters. Rather, what they were suggesting was there is a specific problem that is happening in the African-American community that's not happening in other communities. We as a society – particularly given our history – have to take this seriously . . . It's real, and there's a history behind it" (Superville 2015). In August 2015, the Democratic National Committee offered a formal endorsement of the Black Lives Matter movement, largely in response to numerous BLM activists interrupting public events featuring Democratic presidential candidates like Hillary Clinton and Bernie Sanders.
3 Garza 2014, blacklivesmatter.com
4 For an important exception see Dillon and Sze 2016.
5 Collins 2008; Crenshaw 1991.
6 Melamed 2011: 226; see also Hong 2006.
7 Garza 2014, blacklivesmatter.com.
8 Ferguson 2004: 22–23.
9 Ferguson 2004: 27.

10 Ferguson 2004: 37, 40–41.
11 www.blacklivesmatter.com.
12 New York City Police Department 2012. *Annual Firearms Discharge Report.*
13 Friedersdorf 2015, emphasis added. In 2016, the US Justice Department issued a report of the Baltimore Police Department that found systematic gender bias as well, in the form of woefully inadequate investigations of rape and sexual assault claims and persistent transphobia directed toward survivors of such violence (Stolberg and Bidgood 2016).
14 Smits 1994: 312; see also White 1993.
15 This is a point that Orrin Williams, a colleague of mine, explained to me during a personal communication in August 2015.
16 Adams 2010; Ascione 1997; Ascione and Arkow 1999; Lockwood and Ascione 1998.
17 Komorosky, Woods, and Empie 2015.
18 Upadhya 2014.
19 Currie 2012.
20 See Pellow 2016.
21 Fantz, Howell, and Shoichet 2014.
22 Change.org 2015.
23 Nichols 2015.
24 Williams 2015.
25 Fuller 2016.
26 Griswold 2015.
27 Griswold 2015, my emphasis.
28 Galarza 2015.
29 see Pellow 2014.
30 Craven and Bellware 2015.
31 McCarthy and Zald 1977; Morris 1984.
32 Swyngedouw and Heynen 2003.
33 Freudenburg, Frickel, and Gramling 1995.
34 Pellow and Park 2002; Smith, Sonnenfeld, and Pellow 2006.
35 Mock 2014.
36 Nixon 2011.
37 Ellison and Jones 2015, emphasis added. See also Dillon and Sze 2016.
38 Lombardi, Buford, and Greene 2015.
39 Harlan, Pellow, and Roberts 2015.
40 Schelling 1971; Massey and Denton 1998.
41 See Park and Pellow 2011.
42 Kang 2005.
43 Thomas and Thomas 1928: 571–2.
44 Lamothe 2014; Redden 2015.
45 Nazaryan 2014.

46 Childs 2015; Escobar 2016; Gilmore 2007; James 1996; Rodriguez 2006.
47 Williams 2015.
48 Brydum 2015.
49 Collins and Williams 1999; LaViest 1989; Williams and Collins 1995 and 2001.
50 Phelps 2013.
51 Garza, Alicia. 2015. Interview on Democracy Now! July 24.
52 Rios 2011.
53 Alexander 2012.
54 Moore and Cullors 2014.
55 After the November 2015 police killing of Jamar Clark, an African-American man in Minneapolis, BLM protesters built a people's occupation at the 4th precinct to demand justice. Soon after, a group of white vigilantes shot and wounded five protesters, sparking further outrage, but the police response included bulldozing the encampment and evicting the activists. In a Facebook posting calling for a protest of all of the above at the Mall of America (where, in 2014, hundreds of BLM activists staged a protest deemed illegal by the MOA officials and the city), the call reiterated several demands, including: "Prosecute the police involved without a grand jury by a special prosecutor. Federal domestic terrorism charges against white supremacists who shot 5 protestors" (#BlackXmas2: #Justice4Jamar, posted on December 17, 2015).
56 Moore and Cullors 2014.
57 Moore and Cullors 2014.
58 Black Lives Matter National Demands. N.D.
59 Black Lives Matter. 2015. "DOJ: Protect Black Activists . . ."
60 Cullors, Patrisse. 2015. Interview on Democracy Now! July 24.
61 Moore and Cullors 2014.
62 Lyiscott 2014.
63 Weber et al. 2004.
64 Mills 1997: 84–5.
65 By "police existence" I mean the existence of the police force as an institution.
66 Dahl 2005; Hunter and Dahl 1962.
67 For a critique, see Bachrach and Baratz 1962; Domhoff 2013.
68 Collins 2008; Goldberg 2002; Mills 1999 and 2001; Scott 1999 and 2010; Smith 2011.
69 Tometi 2015.
70 For exceptions, see Downey 2015 and Smith 2005.
71 Márquez 2014.
72 See blacklivesmatter.com; Cacho 2012; Da Silva 2007; Marquez 2014; Mills 2001; Vargas 2010
73 Gilmore 2007.

74 BLM 2015.
75 Mann, Weil, and Russell N.D.
76 Bailey 2004, p. 56.
77 Cooper 1893.
78 Garza 2014, December 6, emphasis added.
79 Klein 2004.
80 Cacho 2012; Marquez 2014; Vargas 2010.
81 Brydum 2015.
82 Geneva Convention 1949; The Hague 1907a.
83 Fabricant 2011.
84 Alexander 2012; Gilmore 2007.
85 Goldberg 2002.
86 Cacho 2012; Marquez 2014; Mucchetti 2005; Roberts 1999; Taslitz 2008.

3. Prisons and the Fight for Environmental Justice

1 Walmsley 2015. I follow the Human Rights Defense Center's definition of "prisoner," which refers to people held in jails, prisons, detention centers, civil commitment facilities, and other spaces where human beings are placed against their will as punishment or while awaiting court-related proceedings such as trials, sentencing, or deportation (see Wright 2015a).
2 Travis, Western, and Redburn 2014.
3 Alexander 2012.
4 "Top 100 Biggest Cities." http://www.city-data.com/top1.html, accessed June 25, 2016.
5 Tsolkas 2016.
6 Shrader-Frechette 2007.
7 Figueroa 2001; Gutierrez 1994.
8 This effort mirrors an argument that was pivotal in the environmental justice movement's victory in the earlier case of *El Pueblo Para el Aire y Agua Limpio v. County of Kings* (1991) in which the largely Latino and Spanish-speaking town of Kettleman City was the site of a proposed Waste Management Inc. incinerator and waste disposal facility and the project was halted when the court ruled under the California Environmental Quality Act (CEQA) that the defendants had not provided Spanish translations of public hearing documents thus making it impossible for the local community to have adequate knowledge of and inclusion and participation in the proceedings (Cole and Foster 2000).
9 Martin 2004.
10 Braz and Gilmore 2006; Cole and Foster 2000.
11 Comment by Panagioti Tsolkas as facilitator of "Prisons and the Environment" panel at the "Fight Toxic Prisons" convergence, June 11, 2016. Washington, D.C.

12 Baldé et al. 2015.
13 Computer TakeBack Campaign. 2003. "New Report Documents Dell's Use of High-tech Chain Gang." June. http://www.computertakeback.com/the_solutions/hp_and_dell.cfm). Sheila Davis was later appointed Executive Director of SVTC.
14 Computer TakeBack Campaign. 2003. "The Solutions." June. http://www.computertakeback.com/the_solutions/prison_sum.cfm.
15 Ibid.
16 *San Diego Union Tribune.* 2003. "Dell Cancels Contract for Inmate Labor." July 5.
17 Connor 2003, p. 3. Connor writes, "Several of the prisons were also targeted because they had a history of enforcement actions as a result of past noncompliance with environmental regulations" (ibid.). This is revealing because it indicates that government regulators had included prisons in their enforcement activities and data gathering on compliance prior to the OECEJ inspections.
18 Connor 2003, p. 3.
19 http://www.epa.gov/region3/compliance_assistance/prisons.htm. The USEPA removed this site shortly after the Prison Ecology Project publicized the fact that the agency has a history of regulating prisons because officials recently decided this is no longer within its purview.
20 Connor 2003, p. 4.
21 Some examples of USEPA actions include: the Region III office announced in October 2000 that it was citing the Pennsylvania Department of Corrections for Clean Water Act and RCRA violations at Graterford State Prison (USEPA Region III 2000); in June 2003 the USEPA announced that in a consent agreement, the Maryland Department of Public Safety agreed to pay a $34,125 fine and implement a $420,000 environmental management system at 34 prisons and other facilities under its jurisdiction that would ensure employee training in environmental compliance, annual audits, and the launch of a pollution prevention program. The EPA cited the Maryland Department of Public Safety for its failure in the case of the Maryland Correction Institute facility at Jessup, Maryland, to "properly close, inspect, label and date drums containing chromium and lead hazardous waste, stored near the prison's maintenance shop . . . [and] to provide required training to personnel on hazardous waste storage and disposal, [and] failed to submit necessary hazardous waste reports and failed to have a hazardous waste emergency plan" (USEPA Region III 2003). In that same press release, the EPA announced an issuance of citations against the West Virginia Division of Corrections (WVDC) for violations of hazardous waste storage regulations that were found during an inspection of the Mt. Olive Correctional Complex in Fayette County, West Virginia in September 2002 (ibid.); in July 2007 the USEPA announced an agreement with the US

Department of Justice and the Bureau of Prisons to undertake voluntary audits for environmental compliance (to avoid harsh enforcement actions) at 16 federal prisons across the states of Maryland, Pennsylvania, Virginia, and West Virginia (housing an estimated 20,000 prisoners). The agreement allows the prisons to disclose any violations of regulations and meet compliance requirements within 60 days. Unfortunately, this was part of a larger trend of "self compliance" and "voluntary agreements" that the USEPA was allowing a range of other industry sectors to pursue as a business-friendly approach to stronger government action. An EPA document announcing this agreement stated that "Potential environmental hazards at federal prisons are associated with various operations such as heating and cooling, wastewater treatment, hazardous waste and trash disposal, asbestos management, drinking water supply, pesticide use, and vehicle maintenance" (USEPA Region III 2007); finally, in January 2011 the USEPA announced a settlement with the Pennsylvania Department of Corrections concerning Clean Air Act violations at four correctional facilities (USEPA Region III 2011).

22 Source: http://www.epa.gov/Region3/compliance_assistance/prisons.htm. Again, note that this source is no longer active since the USEPA removed it from their website. The author can provide the document upon request.
23 Wright 2015b.
24 Wright 2015b.
25 Tsolkas 2016.
26 Tsolkas 2016.
27 USEPA Region III 2011.
28 Comment by Panagioti Tsolkas as facilitator of "Prisons and the Environment" panel at the "Fight Toxic Prisons" convergence, June 11, 2016. Washington, D.C.
29 See Higgins 1994 and Mills 2001 for a discussion of how some populations are viewed as contaminated and therefore their communities are logical destinations for the dumping of environmental health hazards.
30 Prison Ecology Project. 2016. "Examples of Prison Pollution and Environmental Justice Issues in US Prisons."
31 Democracy Now! 2016.
32 Pearson, Murgatroyd, and Lavandera 2014.
33 Edelstein 2011, 2012.
34 Deutsch 2011.
35 Wright 2015a; Homefacts.com N.D.
36 Henterly 2015; Kamb 2012.
37 Alexander 2012; Cole 1999; Gilmore 2007; Western 2007.
38 The Sentencing Project 2013.
39 Sakala 2014.
40 Mauer and King 2007.

41 Wegman 2014.
42 Manza and Uggen 2008.
43 Amnesty International 2016.
44 CR10 Publications Collective 2008, p. xii; Phelps 2013.
45 Escobar 2016, p. 10; Lopez and Light 2009; Light, Lopez, and Gonzalez-Barrera 2013.
46 Davis 2003, p. 65.
47 Escobar 2016, p. 11, emphasis added.
48 Mogul et al., p. 99; source: Myers 2008.
49 Silliman and Bhattacharjee 2002; Harris 2011; Richie 2012; and Sudbury 2005
50 Dannenberg 2007.
51 Anderson 2015.
52 Scott 2010.
53 Wright 2015a – in particular see the EIS Table 4–7 and Table 4–3.
54 Simmons 2016.
55 Estep 2016.
56 Conley 2011.
57 Wright 2015a, p. 15.
58 Tsolkas 2015.
59 Nibert 2011.
60 Escobar 2016; Gilmore 2007.
61 Dannenberg 2007.
62 Dannenberg 2007.
63 Gaard 2004.
64 Mogul, Ritchie, and Whitlock 2011, p.142, emphasis added.
65 Mogul, Ritchie, and Whitlock 2011, pp. 25–26, emphasis added.
66 Greene and McAward. N.D. "The Thirteenth Amendment." http://constitutioncenter.org/interactive-constitution/amendments/amendment-xiii, accessed July 2, 2016. Emphasis added.
67 James 2005, p. xxii.
68 Blackmon 2009, p. 52.
69 Curtin 2000, p. 1.
70 Davis 2003, p. 35.
71 Escobar 2016, pp. 31–32.
72 Davis 2005.
73 Stein 2004, p. 2.
74 Moraga 1993.
75 Wright 2016.
76 Human Rights Clinic 2015.
77 Abolitionist Law Center and Human Rights Coalition 2014.
78 Smith, Sonnenfeld, and Pellow 2006.
79 Human Rights Watch 2015.

80 Human Rights Watch 2015, p. 72.
81 Human Rights Watch 2015, p. 75.
82 Wright 2015.
83 http://www.georgeafb.info/victorville-federal-correctional-complex/, accessed July 6, 2016.
84 Vera III 2016.
85 McDavid 2016.
86 Eichstaedt 1994; LaDuke and Cruz 2013; Voyles 2015.
87 Welsome 2010. For information on indigenous peoples in Victorville, California see Blomberg 1987.
88 Sze 2006: 792.
89 Smith 2005, p. 8.
90 Smith 2005, p. 10.
91 Myers 2008.
92 Amnesty International 2001.
93 Coomaraswamy 1999.
94 Davis 2003, p. 78.
95 Park and Pellow 2011.
96 Johnson 2013.
97 Johnson 2013.
98 Escobar 2016, p. 35.
99 Mogul, Ritchie, and Whitlock 2011, p. 103, emphasis added.
100 Klein 2015, p. 169.
101 Incite! Women of Color against Violence and Critical Resistance 2008, p. 23; Richie 2002. "The Critical Resistance Incite! Statement on Gender Violence and the Prison Industrial Complex." Pp. 15–29 in CR10 Publications Collective 2008. *Abolition Now!*
102 Escobar 2016, p. 27.
103 Escobar 2016, p. 54.
104 Wright 2015b. Source for statistics on racial disparities: Pew Charitable Trusts 2010. A major public health study found that women with family members who were currently incarcerated reported a greater likelihood of diabetes, hypertension, heart attack or stroke, obesity, and fair or poor health (Lee et al. 2014).
105 Wright 2015a.
106 For example, the controversial "broken windows" theory of policing was developed by two scholars, James Q. Wilson and George Kelling (1982). In another example of a scholar participating in the strengthening of the PIC, Dr. Edward Schein is infamous in the anti-prison community for having developed theories of brainwashing and behavior modification that amount to deprivation and torture. His 1961 presentation at a meeting convened by the Bureau of Prisons led to the widespread adoption of his techniques in prisons throughout the U.S (James 2003, pp. 191–193). For an excellent

analysis of the many connections that exist between universities and the prison industrial complex, see Sudbury 2009.

107 Best 2004, p. 309.
108 Schuster 2005.
109 Author interview with Bruce Friedrich of PETA, June 9, 2009.
110 Ibid.
111 "Support Marie Mason" flyer. N.D.
112 Author interview, April 2, 2009. On March 30, 2010, on behalf of Daniel McGowan and several other plaintiffs, the Center for Constitutional Rights and the Civil Liberties Defense Center sued the Bureau of Prisons challenging the policies and conditions at two CMUs, as well as challenging the establishment of CMUs. A court dismissed the suit on July 15, 2013 (Philips, Tim. 2013. "Daniel McGowan's Claims against the Bureau of Prisons Dismissed." Activist Defense. July 15).
113 An article in the ELF journal *Resistance* puts it this way: "Think of what goes through your mind when you hear the term terrorist. Usually it relates somehow to racist beliefs and stereotypes about Arabs, about airline hijackings, violence, and about how terrorists need to be caught and/or killed to be kept away from society. So when the federal government and the mainstream press immediately label actions of the ELF as eco-terrorism all this can do is create a negative stereotype in the minds of the public." (N.A. *Resistance*. #5).
114 This figure comes from a government official's testimony (Jarboe 2002).
115 Coronado 1995. The professor whose research laboratory was targeted- -Dr. Richard Aulerich – at that time was the recipient of the second highest number of Mink Farmers Research Foundation grants and had ongoing government contracts to study the effects of PCBs and other toxins on mink, with his own published work revealing the details of violent deaths these animals suffered as a result of these experiments (Kuipers 2009, p. 189; N.A. 1992. "Michigan State: Animal Rights Raiders Destroy Years of Work." *New York Times*, March 8).
116 Coronado 1995.
117 Coronado 2000.
118 MOVE website, www.onamove.com, accessed August 2011.
119 Ibid.
120 From the MOVE organization's website, http://onamove.com/move-9/, accessed July 10, 2016.
121 Weber et al. 2004.
122 Muntaqim 2010, p. 218.
123 Davis 2003, p. 94.
124 Davis 2003, p. 95.
125 Wilson 2016.

126 Gilmore 2014, pp. vii and viii.
127 Davis 2003, p. 108.
128 Lee 2008, p. 111.
129 Davis 2005, p. 96.
130 Escobar 2016, p. 13.
131 http://www.prisonerswithchildren.org/our-projects/allofus-or-none/, accessed on July 15, 2016.
132 James 2005, p. xxxv.
133 Attica Liberation Faction 1971.

4. The Israel/Palestine Conflict as an Environmental Justice Struggle

1 Because the terms "Semite" and "Semitic peoples" actually apply to many different ethnic groups – including Jews *and* Arabs – I use the phrase "anti-Jewish hatred" to specify an ideology that is directed specifically at Jewish people.
2 Dowty 2012, p. 43.
3 Garfinkle 1991. Israel Zangwill was an early Zionist leader who is often quoted as having made the statement that historic Palestine was "a land without a people for a people without a land." He was the playwright and author of the celebrated play *The Melting Pot*, which sees Jewish assimilation in the US as the answer to their troubles. He was criticized for this by Jews who resisted assimilation, but as a Zionist, he supported the colonization of Arab land and their dispossession, while being celebrated in the US as the father of the Melting Pot concept, which was later taken up by sociologists, elected officials, policymakers, and others. According to historian Amos Elon, this slogan is said to have influenced early Zionists around the turn of the twentieth century, but receded in importance after that point (Elon 1983), although opponents of Zionism appear to have zeroed in on it in their criticisms of Israel (Muir 2008).
4 Dowty 2012, p. 4.
5 Bennis 2009, p. 175.
6 Bennis 2009, p. 14.
7 Bennis 2009, p. 8.
8 Dowty 2012, p. 28.
9 Riley-Smith 1991.
10 Ettinger 1976, pp. 881–8.
11 Khalidi 1992.
12 Bennis 2009, pp. 10–11.
13 Davis 2003, p. 89.
14 Sachar 2007.
15 Bennis 2009, pp. 17–18.

16 United Nations Resolution 194 states that "refugees wishing to return to their homes and live at peace with their neighbors should be permitted to do so at the earliest practicable date, and that compensation should be paid for the property of those choosing not to return."
17 Davis 2003, p. 71.
18 Hadid 2016.
19 Masalha 2012, pp. 61–62, my emphasis.
20 Haddad 2004.
21 Coronil 1997; Nixon 2011.
22 Pappé 2007.
23 jnf.org 2015, accessed November 2015.
24 Massad 2004, p. 61; see also Tal 2002.
25 Davis 2003.
26 Masalha 2012, p. 61.
27 These include the Israeli Ministry of Education, the Sports Authority, Regional Council of Lower Galilee, and Local Council of Kefar Tavor.
28 Davis 2003, p. 53.
29 Davis 2003, p. 53.
30 Pappé 2001.
31 Davis 2003, p. 24.
32 No author. "One of Israel's Best Beaches." http://igoogledisrael.com/2009/08/one-of-israels-best-beaches-hof-dor-tantura/, accessed on March 5, 2015.
33 Those Palestinian villages include Biriyya, 'Alma, Dishon, Qaddita, 'Amqa, and 'Ayn Zaytun.
34 Elon 1983, p. 200.
35 Massad 2004, p. 61. See also Cohen 1993; Lehn and Davis 1988; Pappé 2007.
36 Taylor 2009.
37 See Hari 2010 and Dowie 2011.
38 Hartmann 2003.
39 Park and Pellow 2011.
40 Rudoren 2014.
41 McGreal 2006a. "Worlds Apart."
42 Tal 2002, pp. 332–340.
43 Lorber 2013.
44 Ha-Levi 1981.
45 Bennis 2009, p. 22.
46 Kimmerling and Migdal 1993, p. xviii.
47 International Jewish Anti-Zionist Network (IJAN) 2012.
48 IJAN 2012.
49 International Court of Justice 2004.
50 Boycott Divestment Sactions 2014.
51 MacDonald 2012.
52 Corporate Watch 2010.

53 Davis 2003, p. 35.
54 Said 1999a, p. 28.
55 This quote comes from Said 1999a, p. 28, which was recounting what Avigdor Feldman wrote in his article (see Feldman 1983).
56 Davis 2003, p. 55.
57 Mountain 2014.
58 Bennis 2009, p. 14.
59 Jerusalem Media and Communications Center 1994; Rosenfeld 2004, p. 35.
60 The Hague 1907b.
61 International Committee of the Red Cross (ICRC) 2015.
62 ICRC 2015; Kershner 2015.
63 Democracy Now! June 16, 2016.
64 International Court of Justice 2004: 11, emphasis added.
65 United Nations 2012.
66 Marlowe 2015.
67 Marlowe 2015.
68 International Committee of the Red Cross (ICRC) 2014.
69 Tarabeih 2013; World Bank 1993.
70 Green 2016.
71 See Feldman 2015.
72 See Haddad 1983; Beck 1983; Jordan 1989; Smith 1983; and Women Against Imperialism 1982.
73 Opall 2009.
74 Auron 2015; McGreal 2006a and 2006b; Melman 2008; United Nations Security Council 2015.
75 Bennis 2009, pp. 86–87.
76 Khalek 2015.
77 Auron 2015.
78 United Nations Security Council 2015.
79 Davis 2003; Feldman 2015; McGreal 2006a and 2006b; Masalha 2012. This includes, for example, the collaborations among the Jewish National Fund and the Women's Zionist Organization of South Africa (Davis 2003) and the close relationship between the British Zionist leader Chaim Weizmann and General Jan Smuts, an advocate of racial segregation and prime minister of South Africa (Masalha 2012, p. 55)
80 Bennis 2009, p. 48.
81 McGreal 2006a.
82 McGreal 2006a.
83 McGreal 2006a.
84 Beck 1995; Perrow 1999.
85 Bennis 2009, p. 87.
86 Feldman 2015, p. 226. See Abunimah 2014; Apuzzo and Goldman 2013; and Fusté 2010.

87 Rudoren 2014.
88 Collins 2011, p. 14.
89 Bennis 2009, p. 80.
90 Said 1999b, pp. 6–7.
91 Lentin 2001.
92 Shlaim 1999.
93 Smith 2011.
94 Dowty 2012.
95 Davis 2003, p. 100. Emphasis added.
96 Orenstein 2013, pp. 94–95; see also Fargues 2000 and Portugese 1998. Ironically, the child allowances tended to benefit Arabs and Ultra Orthodox Jews, who have historically had higher birth rates and generally were excluded from the Zionist project (Orenstein 2013, p. 95).
97 Orenstein 2013, p. 95.
98 For a disturbing analysis of eugenics practices in the US directed at African Americans see Roberts 1998.
99 Gordon 2013, p. 247. See also Yuval-Davis 1985.
100 Bennis 2009, p. 22.
101 Rudoren 2014.
102 www.jnf.org, accessed November 8, 2015.
103 Ben-Gurion 1938, p. 63.
104 Ben-Gurion 1973, p. 7. Note: the original publication date was 1918 in *Der Yiddisher Kempfer*.
105 Goldberg 2002; Smith 2011.
106 Weitz 1940, pp. 1090–91.
107 Masalha 2012, p. 15.
108 Docker 2010.
109 Said 1999a, p. 43.
110 www.IJAN.org, accessed on March 15, 2016.
111 Lerner 2012, p. 1.
112 Lerner 2012, p. 3.
113 Lerner 2012, p. 307.

Conclusion

1 Adamson, Evans, and Stein 2004; Buckingham and Kulcur 2010; Stein 2004.
2 Best et al. 2007; Gaard 2004 and 2017.
3 Angelo and Wachsmuth 2015.
4 Barca 2016; Swyngedouw and Heynen 2003; Stein 2004.
5 White 2008 and Brisman 2008.
6 Bennett 2009; Braun and Whatmore 2010; Robbins 2007.
7 www.ejnet.org 1991.

Bibliography

Abolitionist Law Center and Human Rights Coalition. 2014. *No Escape: Exposure to Toxic Coal Waste at State Correctional Institution Fayette.* Pittsburgh, Pennsylvania.

Abunimah, Ali. 2014. *The Battle for Justice in Palestine.* Haymarket.

Adams, Carol. 2010. *The Sexual Politics of Meat: A Feminist-Vegetarian Critical Theory.* Bloomsbury Academic, 20th anniversary edition.

Adamson, Joni. 2001. *American Indian Literature, Environmental Justice, and Ecocriticism: The Middle Place.* University of Arizona Press.

Adamson, Joni. 2011. "Medicine Food: Critical Environmental Justice Studies, Native North American Literature, and the Movement for Food Sovereignty." *Environmental Justice* 4(4): 213–219.

Adamson, Joni and Kimberly N. Ruffin (eds.). 2013. *American Studies, Ecocriticism, and Citizenship: Thinking and Acting in the Local and Global Commons.* Routledge.

Adamson, Joni, Mei Mei Evans, and Rachel Stein (eds.). 2004. *The Environmental Justice Reader: Politics, Poetics, and Pedagogy.* University of Arizona Press.

Adeola, Francis. 2000. "Cross-National Environmental Justice and Human Rights Issues—A Review of Evidence in the Developing World." *American Behavioral Scientist* 43: 686–706.

Agyeman, Julian. 2005. *Sustainable Communities and the Challenge of Environmental Justice.* New York: New York University Press.

Agyeman, Julian, Robert Bullard, and Bob Evans (eds.). 2003. *Just Sustainabilities: Development in an Unequal World.* MIT Press.

Agyeman Julian, Peter Cole, Randy Haluza-DeLay, and Pat O'Riley (eds.). 2010. *Speaking for Ourselves: Environmental Justice in Canada.* University of Washington Press.

Ahmed, Sara. 2012. *On Being Included: Racism and Diversity in Institutional Life.* Duke University Press.

Bibliography

Air Force Real Property Agency. 2003. "Buried Radioactive Weapons Maintenance Waste." Fact Sheet. May 8.

Alexander, Michelle. 2012. *The New Jim Crow: Mass Incarceration in the Age of Colorblindness*. The New Press.

Alkon, Alison Hope and Julian Agyeman (eds.). 2011. *Cultivating Food Justice: Race, Class, and Sustainability*. MIT Press.

Amnesty International. 2001. *Crimes of Hate, Conspiracies of Silence: Torture and Ill-Treatment Based on Sexual Identity*. London.

Amnesty International. 2016. "Mass Incarceration in the USA." http://www.amnestyusa.org/our-work/issues/military-police-and-arms/police-and-human-rights/mass-incarceration-in-the-usa, accessed June 23, 2016.

Amster, Randall, Abraham DeLeon, Luis A. Fernandez, Anthony J. Nocella II, and Deric Shannon (eds.). 2009. *Contemporary Anarchist Studies*. Routledge.

Anderson, Rick. 2015. "Greenwashing Washington State's Prison System in a River of Sewage." *Prison Legal News*. August.

Angelo, Hillary and David Wachsmuth. 2015. "Urbanizing Urban Political Ecology." *International Journal of Urban and Regional Research* 39(1): 16–27.

Anguelovski, Isabelle. 2014. *Neighborhood as Refuge: Community Reconstruction, Place Remaking, and Environmental Justice in the City*. MIT Press.

Anguelovski, Isabelle. 2015. "Tactical developments for achieving just and sustainable neighborhoods: the role of community-based coalitions and bottom-to-bottom networks in street, technical, and funder activism." *Environment and Planning C* 33: 703–725.

Anzaldúa, Gloria. 2012. *Borderlands/La Frontera*. Aunt Lute Books, fourth edition.

Apuzzo, Matt and Adam Goldman. 2013. *Enemies Within: Inside NYPD's Secret Spying Unit and Bin Laden's Final Plot Against America*. Touchstone.

Ascione, Frank. 1997. Battered Women's Reports of Their Partners' and Their Children's Cruelty to Animals. *Journal of Emotional Abuse* (1)1: 119–133.

Ascione, Frank and Phil Arkow (eds.). 1999. *Child Abuse, Domestic Violence, and Animal Abuse: Linking the Circles of Compassion for Prevention and Intervention*. Purdue Research Foundation.

Attica Liberation Faction (Donald Noble, Peter Butler, Frank Lott, Carl Jones-El, and Herbert Blyden X). 1971. *The Attica Liberation Faction Manifesto of Demands and Anti-Depression Platform*. Appendix 1. Attica Prison, New York.

Auron, Yair. 2015. "Shimon Peres, Apologize for Israel's Enablement of the Rwandan and Serbian Genocides." *Haaretz*. January 26.

Bachrach, Peter, and Morton Baratz. 1962. "Two faces of Power." *American Political Science Review* 56(4): 947–952.

Bailey, Cathryn. 2004. "Anna Julia Cooper: 'Dedicated in the Name of My Slave Mother to the Education of Colored Working People.'" *Hypatia* 19(2): 56–73.

Baldé, C. P., F. Wang, R. Kuehr, and J. Huisman. 2015. *The global e-waste monitor – 2014*. United Nations University, IAS – SCYCLE, Bonn, Germany.

Bibliography

Banerjee, Damayanti. 2014. "Toward an Integrative Framework for Environmental Justice Research: A Synthesis and Extension of the Literature." *Society and Natural Resources* 27: 805–819.

Barca, Stefania. 2016. "History." Pp. 132–135 in Joni Adamson, William Gleason, and David N. Pellow (eds.). *Keywords for Environmental Studies*. New York University Press.

Beck, Evelyn Torton. 1983. "'No More Masks': Anti-Semitism as Jew-Hating." *Women's Studies Quarterly* 11(3): 11–14.

Beck, Ulrich. 1995. *Ecological Enlightenment: Essays on the Politics of the Risk Society*. Humanities Press.

Beck, Ulrich. 1996. "World Risk Society as Cosmopolitan Society? Ecological Questions in a Framework of Manufactured Uncertainties." *Theory, Culture, and Society* 13(4): 1–32.

Bell, Derrick. 1993. *Faces at the Bottom of the Well: The Permanence of Racism*. Basic Books.

Bell, Shannon Elizabeth. 2013. *Our Roots Run Deep as Ironweed: Appalachian Women and the Fight for Environmental Justice*. University of Illinois Press.

Bell, Shannon Elizabeth and Yvonne A. Braun. 2010. "Coal, Identity, and the Gendering of Environmental Justice Activism in Central Appalachia." *Gender & Society* 24(6): 794–813.

Ben-Gurion, David. 1938. *The Peel Report and the Jewish State*. Vol. 10. London: Palestine Labour Studies Group.

Ben-Gurion, David. 1973. *My Talks with Arab Leaders*. Third Press.

Benford, Robert. 2005. "The Half-Life of the Environmental Justice Frame: Innovation, Diffusion, and Stagnation." Pp. 37–53 in David N. Pellow and Robert J. Brulle (eds.), *Power, Justice, and the Environment: A Critical Appraisal of the Environmental Justice Movement*. MIT Press.

Bennett, Jane. 2009. *Vibrant Matter: A Political Ecology of Things*. Duke University Press.

Bennis, Phyllis. 2009. *Understanding the Palestinian-Israeli Conflict: A Primer*. Olive Branch Press.

Best, Steven. 2004. "It's War! The Escalating Battle Between Activists and the Corporate-State Complex." Pp. 300–339 in Steven Best and Anthony Nocella II (eds.), *Terrorists or Freedom Fighters? Reflections on the Liberation of Animals*. Lantern Books.

Best, Steven, Anthony Nocella, Richard Kahn, Carol Gigliotti, and Lisa Kemmerer. 2007. "Introducing Critical Animal Studies." *Journal for Critical Animal Studies*, 1.

BlackLivesMatter. 2015. "DOJ: Protect Black Activists from White Vigilante Violence." www.blm.com, accessed on December 16, 2015.

#BlackLivesMatter, 2015. "National Demands." blacklivesmatter.com/demands, accessed on August 25, 2015.

Bibliography

BlackLivesMatter. N.D. "All #BlackLivesMatter: This is Not a Moment, but a Movement." www.blacklivesmatter.com/about, accessed on July 24, 2015.

BlackLivesMatter. 2015. "State of the Black Union." January 22. http://black livesmatter.com/state-of-the-black-union/, accessed on August 12, 2015.

Blackmon, Douglas A. 2009. *Slavery by Another Name: The Re-enslavement of Black Americans from the Civil War to World War 2*. Anchor Books.

Blaser, Mario and Arturo Escobar. 2016. "Political Ecology." Pp. 164–167 in Joni Adamson, William Gleason, and David N. Pellow (eds.) *Keywords for Environmental Studies*. New York University Press.

Blomberg, Nancy. 1987. "A Historic Indian Community at Victorville, California." *Journal of California and Great Basin Anthropology* 9(1): 35–45.

Boycott Divestment Sanctions. 2014. "Tear Another Break From the Wall! Boycott and Divest for Palestinian Rights." www.bds.net. July. Flyer.

Boykoff, Jules. 2007. *Beyond Bullets: The Suppression of Dissent in the United States*. AK Press.

Braun, Bruce. 2002. *The Intemperate Rainforest: Nature, Culture, and Power on Canada's West Coast*. University of Minnesota Press.

Braun, Bruce, and Sarah J. Whatmore (eds.). 2010. *Political Matter: Technoscience, Democracy, and Public Life*. University of Minnesota Press.

Braz, Rose and Craig Gilmore. 2006. "Joining Forces: Prisons and Environmental Justice in Recent California Organizing." *Radical History Review* 96 (Fall): 95–111.

Brisman, Avi. 2008. "Crime-Environment Relationships and Environmental Justice." *Seattle Journal for Social Justice* 6(2): 727–817.

Brown, Phil and Faith Ferguson. 1995. "Making a Big Stink: Women's Work, Women's Relationships, and Toxic Waste Activism." *Gender & Society* 9: 145–172.

Brownstone, Sydney. 2015. "How Black Lives Matter is Changing Environmentalism." Thestranger.com. April 29.

Brune, Michael. 2014. "Why We Can't Be Silent." From the blog *Coming Clean*. December 6.

Bruyneel, Kevin. 2007. *The Third Space of Sovereignty: The Postcolonial Politics of U.S.-Indigenous Relations*. University of Minnesota Press.

Brydum, Sunnivie. 2015. "Alicia Garza Taking Black Lives Matter into Another Dimension." *The Advocate*. December 9.

Buckingham, Susan and Rakibe Kulcur. 2010. "Gendered Geographies of Environmental Justice." In Ryan Holifield, Michael Porter, and Gordon Walker (eds.), *Spaces of Environmental Justice*. Wiley-Blackwell.

Bullard, Robert D. 1996. "Symposium: The Legacy of American Apartheid and Environmental Racism." *St. John's Journal of Legal Commentary* 9: 445–474.

Bullard, Robert D. 1990/2000. *Dumping in Dixie: Race, Class, and Environmental Quality*. Westview Press, third edition.

Bibliography

Bullard, Robert D., Paul Mohai, Robin Saha, and Beverly Wright. 2007. *Toxic Wastes and Race at Twenty, 1987–2007*. New York: United Church of Christ.

Bullard, Robert D. and Beverly Wright. 2012. *The Wrong Complexion for Protection: How the Government Response to Disaster Endangers African American Communities*. New York University Press.

CR10 Publications Collective. 2008. *Abolition Now! Ten Years of Strategy and Struggle against the Prison Industrial Complex*. AK Press.

Cable, Sherry and Charles Cable. 1995. *Environmental Problems, Grassroots Solutions*. St. Martin's Press.

Cacho, Lisa. 2007. "'You just don't know how much he meant': Deviancy, Death, and Devaluation." *Latino Studies* 5: 182–208.

Cacho, Lisa. 2012. *Social Death: Racialized Rightlessness and the Criminalization of the Unprotected*. New York University Press.

Caniglia, B. S., Frank B. Delano, and B. Kerner. 2014. "Enhancing Environmental Justice Research and Praxis: The Inclusion of Human Security, Resilience and Vulnerabilities Literature." *International Journal of Innovation and Sustainable Development* 8: 409–426.

Čapek, Stella. 1993. The "Environmental Justice" Frame: A Conceptual Discussion and an Application." *Social Problems* 40(1): 5–24.

Change.org. (2015). "Terminate Officer Jennifer Lynne Silver." Online petition to Baltimore Mayor Stephanie Rawlings-Blake. April.

Chavez, Cesar. 1993. "Farmworkers at Risk." In Hofrichter, Richard (ed.), *Toxic Struggles: The Theory and Practice of Environmental Justice*. New Society Publishers.

Childs, Dennis. 2015. *Slaves of the State: Black Incarceration from the Chain Gang to the Penitentiary*. University of Minnesota Press.

Ciplet, David, J. Timmons Roberts, and Mizan R. Khan. 2015. *Power in a Warming World: The New Global Politics of Climate Change and the Remaking of Environmental Inequality*. MIT Press.

Cohen, Shaul Ephraim. 1993. *The Politics of Planting: Israeli-Palestinian Competition for Control of Land in the Jerusalem Periphery*. University of Chicago Press.

Cole, David. 1999. *No Equal Justice: Race and Class in the American Criminal Justice System*. New Press.

Cole, Luke and Sheila Foster. 2000. *From the Ground Up: Environmental Racism and the Rise of the Environmental Justice Movement*. New York University Press.

Collins, Chiquita, and David Williams. 1999. "Segregation and Mortality: The Deadly Effects of Racism?" *Sociological Forum* 14: 495–523.

Collins, John. 2011. *Global Palestine*. Columbia University Press.

Collins, Patricia Hill. 2008. *Black Feminist Thought: Knowledge, Consciousness, and the Politics of Empowerment*. Routledge.

Bibliography

Colwell, Kate. 2014. Friends of the Earth News Release. November 13. http://www.foe.org/news/news-releases/2014-11-friends-of-the-earth-international-expresses-solidarity-with-the-people-of-ferguson-missouri, accessed on July 31, 2015.

Conley, Lindsay R. 2011. "Bat Species Diversity in Old-Growth vs. Second Growth Forests in Lilley Cornett Woods, Letcher County, Kentucky." Online Theses and Dissertations. Paper 47. Eastern Kentucky University.

Connell, Raewyn and Rebecca Pearse. 2014. *Gender in World Perspective*. Polity Press, third edition.

Connor, Garth. 2003. "An Investigation and Analysis of the Environmental Problems at Prisons." *National Environmental Enforcement Journal* (May): 3–7.

Coomaraswamy, Radhika. 1999. *Report on the Mission to the United States of America on the Issue of Violence Against Women in State and Federal Prisons, in accordance with Commission Rights resolution 1997/44*. January 4.

Cooper, Ana Julia. 1893. *A Voice from the South*. The Aldine Printing House.

Coronado, Rod. 1995. "Spread Your Love Through Action." *The Militant Vegan* #8, March, pp. 10–11.

Coronil, Fernando. 1997. *The Magical State: Nature, Money, and Modernity in Venezuela*. University of Chicago Press.

Corporate Watch. 2010. "Veolia's Dirty Business: The Tovlan Landfill." January 28. https://corporatewatch.org/news/2010/jan/27/veolias-dirty-business-tovlan-landfill, accessed January 8, 2016.

Craven, Julia and Kim Bellware. 2015. "We Weep for African Lions, but What About Black Lives?" huffingtonpost.com, July 29.

Crenshaw, Kimberlé. 1991. "Mapping the Margins: Intersectionality, Identity Politics, and Violence Against Women of Color." *Stanford Law Review* 43(6): 1241–1299.

Crowder, K., and Liam Downey. 2010. "Inter-neighborhood Migration, Race, and Environmental Hazards: Modeling Micro-level Processes of Environmental Inequality." *American Journal of Sociology* 115(4): 1110–1149.

Cullors, Patrisse. 2015. Interview on Democracy Now! July 24.

Currie, Cheryl L. 2012. Corrigendum to "Animal Cruelty by Children Exposed to Domestic Violence." *Child Abuse & Neglect* 36(11–12): 800.

Curtin, Mary Ellen. 2000. *Black Prisoners and Their World, Alabama: 1865–1900*. University of Virginia Press.

Da Silva, Denise Ferreira. 2007. *The Global Idea of Race*. University of Minnesota Press.

Dahl, Robert. 2005. *Who Governs? Democracy and Power in an American City*. Yale University Press, second edition.

Dannenberg, John. 2007. "Prison Drinking Water and Wastewater Pollution Threaten Environmental Safety Nationwide." *Prison Legal News*. November.

Bibliography

Davis, Angela Y. 2003. *Are Prisons Obsolete?* Seven Stories Press.

Davis, Angela Y. 2005. *Abolition Democracy: Beyond Empire, Prisons, and Torture.* Seven Stories Press.

Davis, Kingsley and Wilbert E. Moore. 1945. "Some Principles of Stratification." *American Sociological Review* 10 (April): 242–249.

Davis, Uri. 2003. *Apartheid Israel: Possibilities for the Struggle Within.* Zed Books.

De Genova, Nicholas and Nathalie Peutz (eds.). 2010. *The Deportation Regime: Sovereignty, Space, and the Freedom of Movement.* Duke University Press.

Delgado, Richard and Jean Stefancic. 2012. *Critical Race Theory: An Introduction,* second edition. New York University Press.

Democracy Now! 2016. "Exclusive Report: How Long Did Flint's County Jail Inmates Drink Poisoned Water?" February 4. New York. http://www.democracynow.org/2016/2/4/exclusive_report_how_long_did_flints, accessed June 28, 2016.

Deutsch, Kevin. 2011. "Correction Officers' Suit says Rikers Island Prison Is Built on 'Toxic' Landfill, Causing Cancer." *New York Daily News.* January 10.

Di Chiro, Giovanna. 2016. "Environmental Justice." Pp. 100–105 in Joni Adamson, William A. Gleason, and David N. Pellow (eds.) *Keywords for Environmental Studies.* New York University Press.

Dillon, Lindsey and Julie Sze. 2016. "Police Power and Particulate Matters: Environmental Justice and the Spatialities of In/securities in U.S. Cities." *English Language Notes* 54(2), Fall/Winter.

Docker, John. 2010. "The Two State Solution and Partition: World History Perspectives on Palestine and India." *Holy Land Studies: A Multidisciplinary Journal* 9(2): 147–168.

Domhoff, G. William. 2013. *Who Rules America? The Triumph of the Corporate Rich.* McGraw-Hill Education, seventh edition.

Dowie, Mark. 2011. *Conservation Refugees: The Hundred Year Conflict between Global Conservation and Native Peoples.* MIT Press.

Downey, Liam. 2006. "Environmental Racial Inequality in Detroit." *Social Forces* 85(2): 771–796.

Downey, Liam. 2015. *Inequality, Democracy and the Environment.* New York University Press.

Dowty, Alan. 2012. *Israel/Palestine.* Polity Press, third edition.

DuBois, W.E.B. 1977 [1935]. *Black Reconstruction: An Essay Toward a History of the Part which Black Folk Played in the Attempt to Reconstruct Democracy in America, 1860–1880.* Atheneum.

Dunlap, Riley and Aaron McCright. 2010. "Climate Change Denial: Sources, Actors and Strategies." Pp. 240–259 in C. Lever-Tracy (ed.), *Routledge Handbook of Climate Change and Society.* Routledge.

Dunlap, Riley and Aaron McCright. 2015. "Challenging Climate Change: The Denial Countermovement." Pp. 300–332 in Riley Dunlap and Robert J.

Bibliography

Brulle (eds.), *Climate Change and Society: Sociological Perspectives*. Oxford University Press.

Edelstein, Michael. 2011. "Testimony of Dr. Michael Edelstein in Support of Hudson River Sloop Clearwater, Inc.'s Contention Regarding Environmental Justice." December 22. U.S. Nuclear Regulatory Commission's Atomic Safety and Licensing Board.

Edelstein, Michael. 2012. "Rebuttal to Respondents to Testimony on the Environmental Justice Contention Report." Atomic Safety and Licensing Board, Nuclear Regulatory Commission. June 28.

Eichstaedt, Peter H. 1994. *If You Poison Us: Uranium and Native Americans*. Red Crane Books.

Ejnet.org. 1991. http://www.ejnet.org/ej/principles.html. The Principles of Environmental Justice. Adopted October 24–27. Washington, D.C., accessed September 9, 2015.

Elijah, Jill Soffiyah. 1990. "Conditions of Confinement." Testimony at the Special International Tribunal on the Violation of Human Rights of Political Prisoners and Prisoners of War in United States Prisons and Jails. December 7–10. Hunter College, New York, NY.

Ellison, Keith and Van Jones. 2015. "Pollution Isn't Colorblind: Environmental Hazards Kill More Black Americans." *The Guardian*. July 24.

Elon, Amos. 1983. *The Israelis: Founders and Sons*. Penguin.

Escobar, Martha. 2016. *Captivity Beyond the State: Criminalization Experiences of Latina (Im)Migrants*. University of Texas Press.

Estep, Sara. 2016. Presentation at the Fight Toxic Prisons conference. June 11. Washington, D.C

Ettinger, Shmuel. 1976. "The Modern Period." In H. H. Ben-Sasson (ed.), *A History of the Jewish People*. Harvard University Press.

Evans, Mei Mei. 2002. "'Nature' and Environmental Justice." Pp. 181–193 in Joni Adamson, Mei Mei Evans, and Rachel Stein (eds.), *The Environmental Justice Reader: Politics, Poetics, and Pedagogy*. University of Arizona Press.

Evans, Monica J. 1995. "Stealing Away: Black Women, Outlaw Culture and the Rhetoric of Rights." In Richard Delgado (ed.), *Critical Race Theory: The Cutting Edge*. Temple University Press.

Faber, Daniel. 1998. *The Struggle for Ecological Democracy: Environmental Justice Movements in the United States*. The Guilford Press.

Fabricant, M. Chris. 2011. "War Crimes and Misdemeanors: Understanding 'Zero Tolerance' Policing as a Form of Collective Punishment and Human Rights Violation." *Drexel Law Review* 3: 373–414.

Fantz, Ashley, George Howell, and Catherine Shoichet. 2014. "Gunshots, Tear Gas in Missouri Town Where Police Shot Teen." CNN.com. August 12.

Fargues, P. 2000. "Protracted National Conflict and Fertility Change: Palestinians and Israelis in the Twentieth Century." *Population and Development Review* 26(3): 441–482.

Bibliography

Feldman, Avigdor. 1983. "The New Order of the Military Government: State of Israel against the Eggplant." *Koteret Rashit*. August 24.

Feldman, Keith P. 2015. *A Shadow Over Palestine: The Imperial Life of Race in America*. University of Minnesota Press.

Ferguson, Roderick. 2004. *Aberrations in Black: Toward a Queer of Color Critique*. University of Minnesota Press.

Ferguson, Roderick. 2012. *The Reorder of Things: The University and its Pedagogies of Minority Difference*. University of Minnesota Press.

Fields, Liz. 2014. "Half of Sexual Abuse Claims in American Prisons Involve Guards, Study Says." ABC News. January 26. http://abcnews.go.com/US/half-sexual-abuse-claims-american-prisons-involve-guards/story?id=21892170, accessed July 5, 2016.

Figueroa, Robert Melchior. 2001. "Other Faces: Latinos and Environmental Justice." Pp. 167–183 in Laura Westra and Bill E. Lawson (eds.), *Faces of Environmental Racism: Confronting Issues of Global Justice*. Rowman & Littlefield.

Flood Wall St. West Welcoming Committee. 2015. Press release on the one-year anniversary of Flood Wall Street actions. September 22.

Foster, John Bellamy. 2000. *Marx's Ecology: Materialism and Nature*. Monthly Review Press.

Foster, John Bellamy, Brett Clark, and Richard York. 2010. *The Ecological Rift: Capitalism's War on the Earth*. Monthly Review Press.

Fothergill, Alice, and Lori Peek. 2004. Poverty and disasters in the United States: a review of recent sociological findings. *Natural Hazards* 32: 89–110

Fothergill, Alice, E. Maestas, and J. Darlington. 1999. "Race, Ethnicity, and Disasters in the United States: A Review of the Literature." *Disasters* 23(2): 156–173.

Foucault, Michel. 1995. *Discipline and Punish: The Birth of the Prison*. Vintage Books.

Fox, Steve. 1991. *Toxic Work: Women Workers at GTE Lenkurt*. Temple University Press.

Freeman, A. M. III. 1972. "The Distribution of Environmental Quality." Pp. 243–278 in *Environmental Quality Analysis: Theory and Method in the Social Sciences*. A.V. Kneese and B. T. Bower (eds.). Johns Hopkins University Press.

Freudenburg, William, Scott Frickel, and Robert Gramling. 1995. "Beyond the Society/Nature Divide: Learning to Think About a Mountain." *Sociological Forum* 10: 361–392.

Friedersdorf, Conor. 2015. "The Brutality of Police Culture in Baltimore." *The Atlantic*. April 22.

Fuentes, Annette and Barbara Ehrenreich. 1983. *Women in the Global Factory*. South End Press.

Bibliography

Fuller, Thomas. 2016. "San Francisco Police Chief Releases Officers Racist Texts." *New York Times*. April 30.

Fusté, José. 2010. "Containing Bordered 'Others' in La Frontera and Gaza: Comparative Lessons on Racializing Discourses and State Violence." *American Quarterly* 62(4): 811–819.

Gaard, Greta. 1993. *Ecofeminism: Women, Animals, and Nature*. Temple University Press.

Gaard, Greta. 2004. "Toward a Queer Ecofeminism." Pp. 21–44 in Rachel Stein (ed.), *New Perspectives on Environmental Justice: Gender, Sexuality, and Activism*. Rutgers University Press.

Gaard, Greta. 2017. *Critical Ecofeminism*. Lexington Books.

Galarza, Daniela. 2015. "Vegan Advocacy Group Compares 'Black Lives' to 'Chickens' and 'Cows.'" Eater.com. April 30.

Garfinkle, Adam M. 1991. "On the Origin, Meaning, Use, and Abuse of a Phrase." *Middle East Studies* 27(Oct.): 539–50.

Garza, Alicia. 2014. "A Herstory of the #BlackLivesMatter Movement." December 6. www.blacklivesmatter.com, accessed on August 12, 2015.

Garza, Alicia. 2015. Interview on Democracy Now! July 24.

Gedicks, Al. 1993. *The New Resource Wars: Native and Environmental Struggles Against Multinational Corporations*. South End Press.

Gedicks, Al. 2001. *Resource Rebels: Native Challenges to Mining and Oil Corporations*. South End Press.

Geneva Convention. 1949. Convention Relative to the Protection of Civilian Persons in Time of War. Article 33, 6 U.S.T. 3516, 75 U.N.T.S. 287. August 12.

Giddings, Paula. 2007. *When and Where I Enter: The Impact of Black Women on Race and Sex in America*. William Morrow, second edition.

Gilmore, Ruth Wilson. 2007. *Golden Gulag: Prisons, Surplus, Crisis, and Opposition in Globalizing California*. University of California Press.

Gilmore, Ruth Wilson. 2014. "Foreword: Sam Boat." Pp. vii–xi in Dan Berger. *The Struggle Within: Prisons, Political Prisoners, and Mass Movements in the United States*. PM Press.

Goldberg, David Theo. 2002. *The Racial State*. Blackwell Publishers.

Goldman, Michael and Rachel Schurman. 2000. "Closing the 'Great Divide': New Social Theory on Society and Nature." *Annual Review of Sociology* 26: 563–584.

Gordon, Uri. 2013. "Olive Green: Environment, Militarism, and the Israeli Defense Forces." Pp. 242–261 in Daniel E. Orenstein, Alon Tal, and Char Miller (eds.), *Between Ruin and Restoration: An Environmental History of Israel*. University of Pittsburgh Press.

Gottlieb, Barbara, Steven G. Gilbert, and Lisa Gollin Evans. 2010. *Coal Ash: The Toxic Threat to Our Health and Environment*. Physicians for Social Responsibility and Earth Justice.

Bibliography

Gottlieb, Robert. 1994. *Forcing the Spring: The Transformation of the American Environmental Movement*. Island Press.

Gottlieb, Robert and Anupama Joshi. 2013. *Food Justice*. MIT Press.

Graeber, David. 2002. "The New Anarchists." *New Left Review*. January/February. Pp. 61–73.

Green, Emma. 2016. "Why Does the United States Give So Much Money to Israel?" *The Atlantic*. September 15.

Greene, Jamal and Jennifer Mason McAward. N.D. "The Thirteenth Amendment." http://constitutioncenter.org/interactive-constitution/amendments/amendment-xiii, accessed July 2, 2016.

Greenpeace USA. 2014. "Why Ferguson matters to all of us (and really matters to Greenpeace)." August 18. http://www.greenpeace.org/usa/ferguson-matters-us-really-matters-greenpeace/, accessed on July 30, 2015.

Griswold, Alex. 2015. "CNN Guest: Black Men 'Hunted Down Like Deer and Like Dogs.'" April 14. Dailycaller.com.

Gutiérrez, Gabriel. 1994. "Mothers of East Los Angeles Strike Back." Pp. 220–233 in Robert Bullard (ed.), *Unequal Protection: Environmental Justice and Communities of Color*. Sierra Club Books.

Haddad, Carol. 1983. "Anti-Arab-ism." *Off Our Backs* 13(3): 21–22.

Hadid, Diaa. 2016. "As Attacks Surge, Boys and Girls Fill Israeli Jails." *New York Times*. April 30.

Ha-Levi, Havah. 1981. "The Taste of Mulberries." Pp. 56–61 in Fouzi el-Asmar, Uri Davis and Naim Khader (eds.), *Debate on Palestine*. Ithaca Press.

Haddad, Toufic. 2004. "Iraq, Palestine, and U.S. Imperialism," *International Socialist Review* 36. Web. 10 Nov. 2012. http://www.isreview.org/.

Hague, The. 1907a. Hague Regulations Respecting the Laws and Customs of War on Land, Article 50, 36, Statute 2295. October 18.

Hague, The. 1907b. Annex to the Convention: Regulations respecting the laws and customs of war on land – Section III : Military authority over the territory of the hostile state – Regulations: Article 42. October 18.

Hall, Jacquelyn Dowd. 2005. "The Long Civil Rights Movement and the Political Uses of the Past." *Journal of American History* (March): 1233–1263.

Hamilton, Cynthia. 1993. "Coping with Industrial Exploitation." In Robert D. Bullard (ed.), *Confronting Environmental Racism: Voices from the Grassroots*. South End Press.

Hamilton, Cynthia. 1995. "Toward a New Industrial Policy." In Bunyan Bryant (ed.), *Environmental Justice: Issues, Policies, and Solutions*. Island Press.

Haraway, Donna J. 1991. *Simians, Cyborgs, and Women: The Reinvention of Nature*. Routledge.

Hari, Johann. 2010. "The Wrong Kind of Green." *The Nation*. March 22.

Harlan, Sharon, David N. Pellow, and J. Timmons Roberts, with Shannon Elizabeth Bell, William G. Holt, and Joane Nagel. 2015. "Climate Justice and

Bibliography

Inequality." Pp. 127–163 in Riley Dunlap and Robert J. Brulle (eds.), *Climate Change and Society: Sociological Perspectives*. Oxford University Press.

Harlan, Sharon L., A. J. Brazel, L. Prashad, W. L. Stefanov, and L. Larsen. 2006. "Neighborhood Microclimates and Vulnerability to Heat Stress." *Social Science & Medicine* 63: 2847–2863.

Harris, Angela P. 2011. "Heteropatriarchy Kills: Challenging Gender Violence in a Prison Nation." *Washington University Journal of Law & Policy* 37(3): 13–65.

Harrison, Jill. 2008. "Abandoned Bodies and Spaces of Sacrifice: Pesticide Drift Activism and the Contestation of Neoliberal Environmental Politics in California." *Geoforum* 39(3): 1197–1214.

Harrison, Jill Lindsey. 2011. *Pesticide Drift and the Pursuit of Environmental Justice*. MIT Press.

Hartmann, Betsy. 2003. "Conserving Racism: The Greening of Hate at Home and Abroad." *Znet*. December 10. http://www.zmag.org.

Harvey, David. 1996. *Justice, Nature, and the Geography of Difference*. Blackwell.

Henterly, Lael. 2015. "The Disaster Waiting to Happen at the Northwest Detention Center." *The Seattle Globalist*. March 18. http://www.seattleglobalist.com/2015/03/18/northwest-detention-center-tsunami-disaster-evacuation-tacoma/34981, accessed June 28, 2016

Herod, Andrew. 2011. *Scale*. London: Routledge.

Heynen, Nik, Maria Kaika, and Erik Swyngedouw (eds.). 2006. *In the Nature of Cities: Urban Political Ecology and the Politics of Urban Metabolism*. Routledge.

Higgins, Robert. 1994. "Race, Pollution and the Mastery of Nature." *Environmental Ethics* 16: 251–263.

Holifield, Ryan. 2001. "Defining Environmental Justice and Environmental Racism." *Urban Geography* 22(1): 78–90.

Holifield, Ryan, Michael Porter, and Gordon Walker. 2010. "Introduction— Spaces of Environmental Justice—Frameworks for Critical Engagement." In Ryan Holifield, Michael Porter, and Gordon Walker (eds.), *Spaces of Environmental Justice*. Wiley-Blackwell.

Homefacts.com. N.D. "Victorville, San Bernardino County, CA Environmental Hazards Report – Superfund Sites." http://www.homefacts.com/environmental hazards/superfunds/California/San-Bernardino-County/Victorville.html, accessed June 28, 2016.

Hong, Grace Kyungwon. 2006. *Ruptures of American Capital: Women of Color Feminism and the Culture of Immigrant Labor*. University of Minnesota Press.

Hooks, Greg and C. Smith. 2004. "The Treadmill of Destruction: National Sacrifice Areas and Native Americans." *American Sociological Review* 69: 558–575.

Hossfeld, Karen. 1990. "'Their Logic Against Them': Contradictions in Sex, Race, and Class in Silicon Valley." In Kathryn Ward (ed.), *Women Workers and Global Restructuring*. Institute for Labor Relations Press.

Bibliography

Human Rights Watch. 1996. *All Too Familiar: Sexual Abuse of Women in U.S. State Prisons.* New York. December.

Human Rights Watch. 2015. *Callous and Cruel: Use of Force against Inmates with Mental Disabilities in U.S. Jails and Prisons.* New York. May.

Hunter, Floyd and Robert Dahl. 1962. "Who Governs: Democracy and Power in an American City." *Administrative Science Quarterly* 6(4): 517–519.

Hunter, Lori. 2000. "The Spatial Association Between U.S. Immigrant Residential Concentration and Environmental Hazards." *International Migration Review* 34(2): 460–488.

Human Rights Clinic. 2015. *Reckless Indifference: Deadly Heat in Texas Prisons.* University of Texas School of Law. Austin, Texas. March.

Hurley, Andrew. 1995. *Environmental Inequalities: Class, Race, and Industrial Pollution in Gary, Indiana, 1945–1980.* University of North Carolina Press.

Hurwitz, Jon and Mark Peffley. 2005. "Explaining the Great Racial Divide: Perceptions of Fairness in the U.S. Criminal Justice System." *The Journal of Politics* 67(3): 762–783.

Imarisha, Walidah. 2015. "Introduction." Pp. 3–5 in Walidah Imarisha and adrienne mare brown (eds.), *Octavia's Brood: Science Fiction Stories from Social Justice Movements.* AK Press.

INCITE! Women of Color against Violence and Critical Resistance. 2008. "The Critical Resistance Incite! Statement on Gender Violence and the Prison Industrial Complex." Pp. 15–29 in CR10 Publications Collective 2008. *Abolition Now! Ten Years of Strategy and Struggle against the Prison Industrial Complex.* AK Press.

INCITE! Women of Color Against Violence. 2009. *The Revolution Will Not Be Funded: Beyond the Non-Profit Industrial Complex.* South End Press.

Institute of Medicine. 1999. *Toward Environmental Justice: Research, Education, and Health Policy Needs.* Committee on Environmental Justice. National Academies Press.

International Committee of the Red Cross. 2014. "Gaza: Damaged Water and Sewage Systems Pose Health Danger." October 13. www.icrc.org, accessed on January 15, 2016.

International Committee of the Red Cross. 2015. "Israel and the occupied Palestinian territory: Planned house demolitions are illegal." October 17. www.icrc.org, accessed on March 15, 2016.

International Court of Justice. 2004. "Legal Consequences of the Construction of a Wall in the Occupied Palestinian Territory." Summary Document. The Hague, Netherlands.

International Jewish Anti-Zionist Network (IJAN). 2012. *Israel's Worldwide Role in Repression.* IJAN.

James, Joy. 1996. *Resisting State Violence: Radicalism, Gender, and Race in U.S. Culture.* University of Minnesota Press.

Bibliography

James, Joy (ed.). 2003. *Imprisoned Intellectuals: America's Political Prisoners Write on Life, Liberation, and Rebellion.* Rowman & Littlefield.

James, Joy (ed.). 2005. *The New Abolitionists: (Neo) Slave Narratives and Contemporary Writings.* SUNY Press.

James, Joy (ed.). 2007. *Warfare in the American Homeland: Policing and Prisons in a Penal Democracy.* Duke University Press.

Jamjoun, Hazem. 2010. "Challenging the Jewish National Fund." *The Electronic Intifada.* July 20.

James F. Jarboe. 2002. "The Threat of Eco-terrorism." Congressional Testimony. February 12. http://www.fbi.gov/congress/congress02/jarboe 021202.htm.

Jerusalem Media and Communications Center. 1994. *Israeli Obstacles to Economic Development in the Occupied Palestinian Territories.* JMCC, second edition.

Johnson, Corey G. 2013. "Female Inmates Sterilized in California Prisons Without Approval." Center for Investigative Reporting. July 7.

jones, pattrice. 2009. "Free as a Bird: Natural Anarchism in Action." Pp. 236–246 in Amster, Randall, Abraham DeLeon, Luis A. Fernandez, Anthony J. Nocella II, and Deric Shannon (eds.), *Contemporary Anarchist Studies: An Introductory Anthology of Anarchy in the Academy.* Routledge.

Jordan, June. 1989. "Finding the Way Home." In *Life as Activism: June Jordan's Writings from "The Progressive."* Litwin.

Kalof, Linda and Amy Fitzgerald. 2007. *The Animals Reader: The Essential Classic and Contemporary Writings.* Bloomsbury Academic.

Kamb, Lewis. 2012. "A Rare Look Inside Tacoma's Northwest Detention Center." *InvestigateWest,* Seattle, WA. September 9, http://invw.org/2012/09/09/ mainbar-1-1303/, accessed June 28, 2016

Kang, Jerry. 2005. "Trojan Horses of Race." *Harvard Law Review* 118: 1489–1593.

Kershner, Isabel. 2015. "Israeli Forces Arrest Palestinian in Drive-By Shooting in West Bank." *New York Times.* November 15.

Khalek, Rania. 2015. "Israeli Arms Fuel Atrocities in Africa." *Electronic Intifada.* September 16.

Khalidi, Walid. 1992. *All that Remains: The Palestinian Villages Occupied and Depopulated by Israel in 1948.* Institute for Palestine Studies.

King, Martin Luther, Jr. 1963. "Letter from Birmingham Jail."

King, Ynestra. 1989. "The Ecology of Feminism and the Feminism of Ecology." In Judith Plant (ed.), *Healing the Wounds: The Promise of Ecofeminism.* New Society Publishers.

Kim, Catherine, Daniel Losen, and Damon Hewitt. 2012. *The School-to-Prison Pipeline: Structuring Legal Reform.* New York University Press.

Kimmerling, Baruch and Joel Migdal. 1993. *Palestinians: The Making of a People.* Free Press.

Bibliography

Klein, Naomi. 2015. *This Changes Everything: Capitalism vs. the Climate.* Simon & Schuster.

Klein, Naomi. 2014. "Why #BlackLivesMatter Should Transform the Climate Debate." *The Nation.* December 12.

Klinenberg, Eric. 2002. *Heat Wave: A Social Autopsy of Disaster in Chicago.* University of Chicago Press.

Komorosky, Dawna, Dianne Rush Woods, and Kristine Empie. 2015. "Considering Companion Animals: An Examination of Companion Animal Policies in California Domestic Violence Shelters." *Society & Animals* 23: 298–315.

Krakoff, Sara. 2002. "Tribal Sovereignty and Environmental Justice." In Mutz, Kathryn, Gary Bryner, and Douglass Kenney (eds.), *Justice and Natural Resources: Concepts, Strategies, and Applications.* Island Press.

Krauss, Celene. 1993. "Blue Collar Women and Toxic Waste Protests: The Process of Politicization." In Hofrichter, Richard (ed.), *Toxic Struggles: The Theory and Practice of Environmental Justice.* New Society Publishers.

Kruvant, W. J. 1975. "People, Energy, and Pollution." Pp. 125–167 in D. K. Newman and D. Day (eds.), *The American Energy Consumer.* Ballinger Publishing.

Kuipers, Dean. 2009. *Operation Bite Back: Rod Coronado's War to Save American Wilderness.* New York: Bloomsbury.

Kurtz, Hilda. 2003. "Scales, Frames, and Counter-Scale Frames: Constructing the Problem of Environmental Injustice." *Political Geography* 22: 887–916.

Kurtz, Hilda. 2010. "Acknowledging the Racial State: An Agenda for Environmental Justice Research." In Ryan Holifield, Michael Porter, and Gordon Walker (eds.), *Spaces of Environmental Justice.* Wiley-Blackwell.

LaDuke, Winona. 1999. *All Our Relations: Native Struggles for Land and Life.* South End Press.

LaDuke, Winona and Sean Aaron Cruz. 2013. *The Militarization of Indian Country.* Makwa Enewed, second edition.

Lamothe, Dan. 2014. "Pentagon Defends Program Supplying Military Gear to Ferguson Police." *Washington Post.* August 19.

Lavelle, Marianne and Marcia Coyle. 1992. "Unequal Protection: The Racial Divide in Environmental Law." *National Law Journal* 15: SI-SI2.

LaViest, Thomas. 1989. "Linking Residential Segregation to the Infant-Mortality Race Disparity in U.S. Cities." *Sociology and Social Research* 73: 90–94.

Lee, Alexander. 2008. "Prickly Coalitions: Moving Prison Abolition Forward." Pp.103–112 in CR10 Publications Collective, *Abolition Now! Ten Years of Strategy and Struggle against the Prison Industrial Complex.* AK Press.

Lee, Hedwig, Christopher Wildeman, Emily A. Wang, Niki Matusko, and James S. Jackson. 2014. "A Heavy Burden: The Cardiovascular Health Consequences of Having a Family Member Incarcerated." *American Journal of Public Health* 104(3): 421–427.

Bibliography

Lehn, Walter and Uri Davis. 1988. *The Jewish National Fund*. Kegan Paul International.

Lentin, Ronit. 2001. *Israel and the Daughters of the Shoah: Reoccupying the Territories of Silence*. Berghahn Books.

Lerner, Michael. 2012. *Embracing Israel/Palestine: A Strategy to Heal and Transform the Middle East*. North Atlantic Books.

Lerner, Steve. 2006. *Diamond: A Struggle for Environmental Justice in Louisiana's Chemical Corridor*. MIT Press.

Levin, Kelly, Benjamin Cashore, Steven Bernstein, and Graeme Auld. 2012. "Overcoming the Tragedy of Super Wicked Problems: Constraining Our Future Selves to Ameliorate Global Climate Change." *Policy Sciences* 45(2): 123–152.

Lipsitz, George. 2006. *The Possessive Investment in Whiteness: How White People Profit from Identity Politics*. Temple University Press.

Lockwood, Randall and Frank Ascione (eds.). 1999. *Cruelty to Animals and Interpersonal Violence: Readings in Research and in Application*. Purdue University Press.

Lombardi, Kristen, Talia Buford, and Ronnie Greene. 2015. "Environmental Justice, Denied." Center for Public Integrity. August 3.

Lorber, Benjamin. 2013. "Keren Kayemet Le Yisrael and Environmental Racism in Palestine." earthfirstjournal.org. January 11.

Lyiscott, Jamila. 2014. "Stop Hitting Yourself." theglamsavvylife.com. September 17, accessed on August 26, 2015.

McCarthy, John D. and Mayer Zald. 1977. "Resource Mobilization: A Partial Theory." *American Journal of Sociology* 82(6): 1212–41.

McClintock, Anne. 1995. *Imperial Leather: Race, Gender, and Sexuality in the Colonial Conquest*. New York: Routledge.

McDavid, Eric. 2016. Comments on Panel "Defending the Earth & Abolishing Prisons: Voices from the Struggle" at Fight Toxic Prisons convergence. June 11. University of District Columbia David Clark Law School, Washington, D.C.

McGowan, Daniel. 2016. Comments on Panel "Defending the Earth & Abolishing Prisons: Voices from the Struggle" at Fight Toxic Prisons convergence. June 11. University of District Columbia David Clark Law School, Washington, D.C.

McGreal, Chris. 2006a. "Israel: Worlds Apart." *The Guardian*. February 6.

McGreal, Chris. 2006b. "Brothers in Arms: Israel's Secret Pact with Pretoria." *The Guardian*. February 7.

MacDonald, Alex. 2012. "The Trouble with Veolia and Palestine." *Huffington Post*. November 26.

MacGregor, Sherilyn. 2006. *Beyond Mothering Earth: Ecological Citizenship and the Politics of Care*. UBC Press.

Mann, Barry, Cynthia Weil, and Brenda Russell. N.D. "None of Us Are Free" (later recorded by various artists such as Ray Charles, Lynyrd Skynyrd, and Solomon Burke).

Bibliography

Manza, Jeff and Chris Uggen. 2008. *Locked Out: Felon Disenfranchisement and American Democracy*. Oxford University Press.

Marbury, Hugh. 1995. "Hazardous Waste Exportation: The Global Manifestation of Environmental Racism." *Vanderbilt Journal of Transnational Law* 28.

Margulis, Charles. 2015. "Black Lives Matter and Environmental Justice." January 26. http://www.ceh.org/news-events/blog/black-lives-matter-environmental-justice/, accessed on July 31, 2015.

Marlowe, Jen. 2015. "Parting the Brown Sea: Sewage Crisis Threatens Gaza's Access to Water." Al Jazeera America. April 18.

Márquez, John. 2014. *Black-Brown Solidarity: Racial Politics in the New Gulf South*. University of Texas Press.

Martin, Marc. 2004. "Critics Say New State Prison Defies Logic." *SF Gate.* January 5. http://www.sfgate.com/news/article/Critics-Say-New-State-Prison-defies-logic-They-2816998.php, accessed June 24, 2016

Masalha, Nur. 2012. *The Palestine Nakba: Decolonising History, Narrating the Subaltern, Reclaiming Memory*. Zed Books.

Massad, Joseph. 2004. "The Persistence of the Palestinian Question." In Begoña Aretxaga (ed.), *Empire and Terror: Nationalism/Postnationalism in the New Millennium*. University of Nevada Press and Reno Center for Basque Studies: 57–70.

Massey, Douglas and Nancy Denton. 1998. *American Apartheid: Segregation and the Making of the Underclass*. Harvard University Press.

Mauer, Marc and Ryan S. King 2007. *A 25-Year Quagmire: The War on Drugs and its Impact on Society*. The Sentencing Project: Washington, D.C. September.

Melamed, Jodi. 2011. *Represent and Destroy: Rationalizing Violence in the New Racial Capitalism*. University of Minnesota Press.

Melman, Yossi. 2008. "Sources: Israeli Businesswoman Brokering E. Guinea Arms Sales." *Haaretz*. November 12.

Mendieta, Eduardo. 2005. "Introduction." In Angela Davis, *Abolition Democracy: Beyond Empire, Prisons, and Torture*. Seven Stories Press.

Mennis, Jeremy and Lisa Jordan. 2005. The distribution of environmental equity: exploring spatial nonstationarity in multivariate models of air toxic releases. *Annals of the Association of American Geographers* 95: 249–268.

Mills, Charles. 1999. *The Racial Contract*. Cornell University Press.

Mills, Charles. 2001. "Black Trash." Pp. 73–93 in Laura Westra and Bill E. Lawson (eds.), *Faces of Environmental Racism: Confronting Issues of Global Justice*. Rowman & Littlefield.

Mock, Brentin. 2014. "Why Environmentalists Should Support the Black Lives Matter Protests." Grist.org. December 8.

Mogul, Joey L., Andrea J. Ritchie, and Kay Whitlock. 2011. *Queer (In)justice: The Criminalization of LGBT People in the United States*. Beacon Press.

Mohai, Paul, David N. Pellow, and J. Timmons Roberts. (2009) "Environmental Justice." *The Annual Review of Environment and Resources* 34: 405–430.

Bibliography

Mohai, Paul and Robin Saha 2007. "Racial Inequality in the Distribution of Hazardous Waste: A National-Level Reassessment." *Social Problems* 54(3): 343–370.

Mohanty, Chandra Talpade. 2004. *Feminism Without Borders: Decolonizing Theory, Practicing Solidarity.* Duke University Press.

Moore, Bethany. 2014. "Marlin: Prison Unit Experiences Plumbing, Sewage Problems." September 30. http://www.kwtx.com/ourtown/home/headlines/Marlin-Hobby-Unit-Experiences-Plumbing-Sewage-Problems-277694721. html, accessed July 1, 2016.

Moore, Darnell and Patrisse Cullors. 2014. "Five Ways to Never Forget Ferguson – and Deliver Real Justice for Michael Brown." *The Guardian.* September 4.

Moore, Donald, Jake Kosek, and Anand Pandian (eds.). 2003. *Race, Nature, and the Politics of Difference.* Duke University Press.

Moraga, Cherríe. 1993. *The Last Generation: Prose and Poetry.* Canadian Scholars Press.

Morris, Aldon. 1984. *Origins of the Civil Rights Movement.* Free Press.

Mortenson, Tessa. 2012. "Interview with Malo." Pp. 105–108 in Save the Kids, *Let me Live: Voices of Youth Incarcerated.* Arissa Media Group.

Mountain, Michael. 2014. "In Israel-Gaza War, Animals Pay Price." Earthintransition.org. July.

Mucchetti, Anthony. 2005. "Driving While Brown: A Proposal for Ending Racial Profiling in Emerging Latino Communities." *Harvard Latino Law Review* 8: 1–10.

Muir, Diana 2008. "A Land out with a People for a People without a Land." *Middle East Quarterly* 15(2): 55–62.

Muntaqim, Jalil A. 2010. *We Are Our Own Liberators: Selected Prison Writings.* Arissa Media Group.

Myers, Meghann. 2008. "Sentenced to Rap: LBGT Inmates Face Unusually High Risk of Sexual Assault in Prison." *San Francisco Bay Guardian.* December 23.

Nathan, Susan. 2007. *The Other Side of Israel: My Journey Across the Jewish/Arab Divide.* Nan A. Talese Publishers.

Nazaryan, Alexander. 2014. "The U.S. Department of Defense is one of the World's Biggest Polluters." *Newsweek*, July 17. http://www.newsweek. com/2014/07/25/usdepartment-defence-one-worlds-biggest-polluters-259456. html, accessed March 1, 2016.

New York City Police Department. 2012. *Annual Firearms Discharge Report.* New York. Ray Kelly, Commissioner.

Newell, Peter. 2005. "Race, Class, and the Global Politics of Environmental Inequality." *Global Environmental Politics* 5(3): 70–94.

Nibert, David. 2011. *Animal Oppression and Human Violence: Domesecration, Capitalism, and Global Conflict.* Columbia University Press.

Bibliography

Nibert, David and Michael W. Fox. 2002. *Animal Rights/Human Rights: Entanglements of Oppression and Liberation.* Rowman and Littlefield.

Nichols, Jason. 2015. "Black Baltimore Residents Aren't 'Animals.' We Punish People for Killing Animals." *The Guardian.* April 28.

Nocella, Anthony J. II, K. Animashaun Ducre, and John Lupinacci (eds.). 2016. *Addressing Environmental and Food Justice toward Dismantling the School-to-Prison Pipeline.* Palgrave MacMillan.

Nocella, Anthony J. II, Steven Best, and Peter McLaren (eds.). 2010. *Academic Repression: Reflections from the Academic Industrial Complex.* AK Press.

Norgaard, Kari Marie. 2011. *Living in Denial: Climate Change, Emotions, and Everyday Life.* MIT Press.

Nixon, Rob. 2011. *Slow Violence and the Environmentalism of the Poor.* Harvard University Press.

Nocella, Anthony, Priya Parmar, and David Stovall (eds.). 2014. *From Education to Incarceration: Dismantling the School-to-Prison Pipeline.* Peter Lang.

Novotny, Patrick. 2000. *Where We Live, Work and Play: The Environmental Justice Movement and the Struggle for a New Environmentalism.* Praeger.

O'Connor, James. 1994. "Is Sustainable Capitalism Possible?" In M. O'Connor (ed.), *Is Capitalism Sustainable? Political Economy and the Politics of Ecology.* Guilford Press.

Omi, Michael and Howard Winant. 1994. *Racial Formation in the United States: From the 1960s to the 1990s.* Routledge.

Opall, Barbara 2009. "Israel 3rd among World Arms Suppliers: MoD Numbers Conflict with U.S. Report." *Defense News.* October 5.

Orenstein, Daniel E. 2013. "Zionist and Israeli Perspectives on Population Growth and Environmental Impact in Palestine and Israel." Pp. 82–105 in Daniel E. Orenstein, Alon Tal, and Char Miller (eds.), *Between Ruin and Restoration: An Environmental History of Israel.* University of Pittsburgh Press.

Oreskes, Naomi and Erik M. Conway. 2010. *Merchants of Doubt: How a Handful of Scientists Obscured the Truth on Issues from Tobacco Smoke to Global Warming.* New York: Bloomsbury Press.

Pappé, Ilan. 2001. "The Tantura Case in Israel: The Katz Research and Trial." *Journal of Palestine Studies* 30(3): 19–39.

Pappé, Ilan. 2007. *The Ethnic Cleansing of Palestine.* Oxford: Oneworld Publications.

Parenti, Christian. 1999. *Lockdown America: Police and Prisons in the Age of Crisis.* New York: Verso.

Parenti, Christian. 2003. *The Soft Cage: Surveillance in America from Slavery to the War on Terror.* Basic Books.

Park, Lisa Sun-Hee. 2011. *Entitled to Nothing: The Struggle for Immigrant Health Care in the Age of Welfare Reform.* New York University Press.

Park, Lisa Sun-Hee and David N. Pellow. 2011. *The Slums of Aspen: Immigrants vs. the Environment in America's Eden.* New York University Press.

Bibliography

Parsons, Talcott. 1954. *Essays in Sociological Theory*. New York: The Free Press.

Pearson, Michael, John Murgatroyd, and Ed Lavandera. 2014. "'Complete destruction': 2 die, dozens hurt as explosion shatters Florida jail." CNN.com. May 1. http://www.cnn.com/2014/05/01/justice/florida-jail-gas-explosion/index.html, accessed June 28, 2016.

Pellow, David N. 1998. "Bodies on the Line: Environmental Inequalities and Hazardous Work in the U.S. Recycling Industry." *Race, Gender & Class* 6: 124–151.

Pellow, David N. 1999a. "Negotiation and Confrontation: Environmental Policy-Making Through Consensus." *Society and Natural Resources* 12: 189–203.

Pellow, David N. 1999b. "Framing Emerging Environmental Movement Tactics: Mobilizing Consensus, De-mobilizing Conflict." *Sociological Forum* 14: 659–683.

Pellow, David N. 2000. "Environmental Inequality Formation: Toward a Theory of Environmental Injustice." *American Behavioral Scientist* 43: 581–601.

Pellow, David N. 2002. *Garbage Wars: The Struggle for Environmental Justice in Chicago*. MIT Press.

Pellow, David N. 2007. *Resisting Global Toxics: Transnational Movements for Environmental Justice*. MIT Press

Pellow, David N. 2014. *Total Liberation: The Power and Promise of Animal Rights and the Radical Earth Movement*. University of Minnesota Press.

Pellow, David N. 2016. "Toward a Critical Environmental Justice Studies: Black Lives Matter as an Environmental Justice Challenge." *DuBois Review* 13(2): 221–236.

Pellow, David N. and Robert J. Brulle (eds.). 2005. *Power, Justice, and the Environment: A Critical Appraisal of the Environmental Justice Movement*. MIT Press.

Pellow, David N. and Lisa Sun-Hee Park. 2002. *The Silicon Valley of Dreams: Environmental Injustice, Immigrant Workers, and the High-Tech Global Economy*. New York University Press.

Penniman, Leah. 2015. "Radical Farmers Use Fresh Food to Fight Racial Injustice and the New Jim Crow." *Yes! Magazine*. January 28.

Perrow, Charles. 1999. *Normal Accidents: Living High-Risk Technologies*. Princeton University Press.

Perrow, Charles and Simone Pulver. 2015. "Organizations and Markets." Pp. 61–92 in Riley Dunlap and Robert J. Brulle (eds.), *Climate Change and Society: Sociological Perspectives*. Oxford University Press.

Petrikin, Jonathan (ed.). 1995. *Environmental Justice*. Greenhaven Press.

Pew Charitable Trusts. 2010. *Collateral Costs: Incarceration's Effect on Economic Mobility*. Washington, D.C.

Phelps, Michelle. 2013. "The Paradox of Probation: Community Supervision in the Age of Mass Incarceration." *Law & Policy* 35 (1–2): 51–80.

Bibliography

Piven, Frances Fox and Richard Cloward. 1978. *Poor People's Movements: Why They Succeed, How They Fail.* Vintage.

Piven, Frances Fox and Richard Cloward. 1993. *Regulating the Poor: The Functions of Public Welfare.* Vintage.

Portugese, Jacqueline. 1998. *Fertility Policy in Israel: The Politics of Religion, Gender and Nation.* Praeger Publishers.

Principles of Working Together. 2002. Adopted at the Second People of Color Environmental Leadership Summit. Washington, D.C. October.

Prison Ecology Project. 2016. "Examples of Prison Pollution and Environmental Justice Issues in U.S. Prisons." PEP, Lake Worth, Florida.

Pulido, Laura. 1996. "A Critical Review of the Methodology of Environmental Racism Research." *Antipode* 28(2): 142–159.

Redden, Molly. 2015. "The Pentagon just realized it gave too much military equipment to the Ferguson Police." *Mother Jones.* August 12.

Ringquist, Evan J. 2005. "Assessing Evidence of Environmental Inequities: A Meta-Analysis." *Journal of Policy Analysis and Management* 24(2): 223–247.

Rios, Victor. 2011. *Punished: Policing the Lives of Black and Latino Boys.* New York University Press.

Richie, Beth. 2002. "The Social Impact of Mass Incarceration on Women." In Marc Mauer and Meda Chesney-Lind (eds.), *Invisible Punishment: The Collateral Consequences of Mass Imprisonment.* New York: New Press.

Richie, Beth. 2012. *Arrested Justice: Black Women, Violence, and America's Prison Nation.* New York University Press.

Riley-Smith. Jonathan. 1991. *The First Crusade and the Idea of Crusading.* University of Pennsylvania Press.

Robbins, Paul. 2007. *Lawn People: How Grasses, Weeds, and Chemicals Make Us Who We Are.* Temple University Press.

Roberts, Dorothy. 1998. *Killing the Black Body: Race, Reproduction, and the Meaning of Liberty.* Vintage.

Roberts, Dorothy. 1999. "Race, Vagueness, and the Social Meaning of Order-Maintenance Policing." *Journal of Criminal Law and Criminology* 89(3): 775–836.

Roberts, J. Timmons and Bradley Parks. 2006. *A Climate of Injustice: Global Inequality, North-South Politics, and Climate Policy.* MIT Press.

Roberts, J. Timmons and Melissa Toffolon-Weiss. 2001. *Chronicles from the Environmental Justice Frontline.* Cambridge University Press.

Robinson, James. 1991. *Toil and Toxics: Workplace Struggles and Political Strategies for Occupational Health.* University of California Press.

Rodriguez, Dylan. 2006. *Forced Passages: Imprisoned Radical Intellectuals and the U.S. Prison Regime.* University of Minnesota Press.

Rosenfeld, Maya. 2004. *Confronting the Occupation: Work, Education, and Political Activism of Palestinian Families in a Refugee Camp.* Stanford University Press.

Bibliography

Rudolf, John. 2012. "Alabama Women's Prison Inmates Sexually Abused By Guards, Report Says." *Huffington Post*. May 22.

Rudoren, Jodi. 2014. "Israel Struggles with Its Identity." *New York Times*. December 8.

Sachar, Howard M. 2007. *A History of Israel: From the Rise of Zionism to Our Time*. Alfred Knopf, third edition.

Said, Edward. 1999a. *After the Last Sky: Palestinian Lives*. Columbia University Press.

Said, Edward. 1999b. "Palestine: Memory, Invention, and Space." Pp. 3–10 in Ibrahim Abu-Lughod, Roger Heacock, and Khaled Nashef (eds.), *The Landscape of Palestine: Equivocal Poetry*. Birzeit University Publications.

Sakala, Leah. 2014. "Breaking Down Mass Incarceration in the 2010 Census: State-by-State Incarceration Rates by Race/Ethnicity." Prison Policy Initiative. May 28. http://www.prisonpolicy.org/reports/rates.html, accessed June 25, 2016.

Sandilands, Catriona. 2016. "Queer Ecology." Pp. 169–171 in Joni Adamson, William A. Gleason, and David N. Pellow (eds.) *Keywords for Environmental Studies*. New York University Press.

Santa Ana, Otto. 2002. *Brown Tide Rising: Metaphors of Latinos in Contemporary American Public Discourse*. University of Texas Press.

Sayre, Nathan. 2005. "Ecological and Geographical Scale: Parallels and Potential for Integration." *Progress in Human Geography* 29(3): 276–290.

Schelling, T. C. 1971. "Dynamic Models of Segregation." *Journal of Mathematical Sociology* 1: 143–186.

Shlaim, Avi. 1999. *The Iron Wall: Israel and the Arab World since 1948*. W.W. Norton & Company.

Schlosberg, David. 2004. "Reconceiving Environmental Justice: Global Movements and Political Theories." *Environmental Politics* 13: 517–540.

Schlosberg, David. 2007. *Defining Environmental Justice: Theories, Movements, and Nature*. Oxford University Press.

Schlosberg, David and David Carruthers. 2010. "Indigenous Struggles, Environmental Justice, and Community Capabilities." *Global Environmental Politics* 10(4): 12–35.

Schnaiberg, Allan. 1980. *The Environment: From Surplus to Scarcity*. Oxford University Press.

Schnaiberg, Allan and Kenneth Gould. 1994/2000. *Environment and Society: The Enduring Conflict*. The Blackburn Press.

Shrader-Frechette, Kristin. 2007. *Taking Action, Saving Lives: Our Duty to Protect Environmental and Public Health*. Oxford University Press.

Schroeder, Richard, Kevin Martin, Bradley Wilson, and Debarati Sen. (2008). "Third World Environmental Justice." *Society & Natural Resources* 21(7): 547–555.

Bibliography

Schwab, James. 1994. *Deeper Shades of Green: The Rise of Blue-Collar and Minority Environmentalism in America.* Sierra Club.

Scott, James. 1999. *Seeing Like a State: How Certain Schemes to Improve the Human Condition Have Failed.* Yale University Press.

Scott, James. 2010. *The Art of Not Being Governed: An Anarchist History of Upland Southeast Asia.* Yale University Press.

Scott, James. 2014. *Two Cheers for Anarchism: Six Easy Pieces on Autonomy, Dignity, Meaningful Work, and Play.* Princeton University Press.

Scott, Rebecca. 2010. *Removing Mountains: Extracting Nature and Identity in the Appalachian Coalfields.* University of Minnesota Press.

Seager, Joni. 1994. *Earth Follies: Coming to Feminist Terms with the Global Environmental Crisis.* Routledge.

Selznick, Philip. 1949. *TVA and the Grass Roots: A Study in the Sociology of Formal Organization.* University of California Press.

Sentencing Project. 2013. *Report of The Sentencing Project to the United Nations Human Rights Committee Regarding Racial Disparities in the United States Criminal Justice System.* Washington, D.C. August.

Sentencing Project. 2016. *The Color of Justice: Racial and Ethnic Disparity in State Prisons.* Washington, D.C.

Shabecoff, Philip. 2003. *A Fierce Green Fire: The American Environmental Movement.* Island Press.

Shakur, Assata. 1987. *Assata: An Autobiography.* Lawrence Hill Books.

Shakur, Assata. 2005 [1978]. "Women in Prison: How We Are." Pp. 79–89 in Joy James (ed.), *The New Abolitionists: (Neo) Slave Narratives and Contemporary Writings.* SUNY Press.

Shrader-Frechette, Kristin. 2002. *Environmental Justice: Creating Equality, Reclaiming Democracy.* Oxford University Press.

Sierra Club. 2014. Statements posted to facebook in support of #BlackLivesMatter. December.

Silliman, Jael and Annanya Bhattacharjee (eds.). 2002. *Policing the National Body: Race, Gender, and Criminalization.* South End Press.

Simmons, Skyler. 2016. "Welcome to Appalachia's Gulag Archipelago." *Earth First! News Wire.* March 16.

Smith, Andrea. 2005. *Conquest: Sexual Violence and American Indian Genocide.* South End Press.

Smith, Barbara. 1983. "A Rock and a Hard Place: Relationships Between Black and Jewish Women." *Women's Studies Quarterly* 11(3): 7–9.

Smith, Mick. 2011. *Against Ecological Sovereignty: Ethics, Biopolitics, and Saving the Natural World.* University of Minnesota Press.

Smits, David. 1994. "The Frontier Army and the Destruction of the Buffalo: 1865–1883." *The Western Historical Quarterly* 25(3): 312–338.

Smith, Ted, David Sonnenfeld, and David N. Pellow (eds.). 2006. *Challenging*

Bibliography

the Chip: Labor Rights and Environmental Justice in the Global Electronics Industry. Temple University Press.

Stein, Rachel (ed.). 2004. New Perspectives on Environmental Justice: Gender, Sexuality, and Activism. Rutgers University Press.

Stolberg, Sheryl Gay and Jess Bidgood. 2016. "Baltimore Police Fostered a Bias against Women." New York Times. August 12.

Sturgeon, Noel. 1997. "The Nature of Race: Discourses of Racial Difference in Ecofeminism." In Karen J. Warren (ed.), Ecofeminism: Women, Culture, Nature. Indiana University Press.

Sudbury, Julia (ed.). 2005. Global Lockdown: Race, Gender, and the Prison-Industrial Complex. New York: Routledge.

Sudbury, Julia. 2009. "Challenging Penal Dependency: Activist Scholars and the Antiprison Movement." Pp. 17–35 in Julia Sudbury & Margo Okazawa-Rey (eds.), Activist Scholarship: Anti-Racism, Feminism, and Social Change. Paradigm Publishers.

Superville, Darlene. 2015. "Obama Defends Black Lives Matter Movement." Associated Press. October 23.

Swyngedouw, Erik and Nik Heynen. 2003. "Urban Political Ecology, Justice, and the Politics of Scale." Antipode 35: 898–918.

Szasz, Andrew. 1994. Ecopopulism: Toxic Waste and the Movement for Environmental Justice. University of Minnesota Press.

Szasz, Andrew and Michael Meuser. 1997. "Environmental Inequalities: Literature Review and Proposals for New Directions in Research and Theory." Current Sociology 45: 99–120.

Sze, Julie. 2006. "Boundaries and Border Wars: DES, Technology, and Environmental Justice." American Quarterly 58(3): 791–814.

Sze, Julie. 2007. Noxious New York: The Racial Politics of Urban Health and Environmental Justice. MIT Press.

Sze, Julie. 2016. "Scale." Pp. 178–180 in Joni Adamson, William Gleason, and David N. Pellow (eds.), Keywords for Environmental Studies. New York University Press.

Tal, Alon. 2002. Pollution in a Promised Land: An Environmental History of Israel. University of California Press.

Tarabeih, Hussein. 2013. "Environmental Challenges Facing Arab Society in Israel." Pp. 190–208 in Daniel E. Orenstein, Alon Tal, and Char Miller (eds.), Between Ruin and Restoration: An Environmental History of Israel. University of Pittsburgh Press.

Taslitz, Andrew E. 2008. "Wrongly Accused Redux: How Race Contributes to Convicting the Innocent—The Informants Example." Southwestern University Law Review 37: 101–157.

Taylor, Dorceta. 1997. "American Environmentalism: The Role of Race, Class and Gender in Shaping Activism, 1820–1995." Race, Gender and Class 5: 16–62.

Taylor, Dorceta. 1997. "Women of Color, Environmental Justice, and

Bibliography

Ecofeminism." In Karen J. Warren (ed.), *Ecofeminism: Women, Culture, Nature*. Indiana University Press.

Taylor, Dorceta. 2000. "The Rise of the Environmental Justice Paradigm: Injustice Framing and the Social Construction of Environmental Discourses." *American Behavioral Scientist* 43: 508–80.

Taylor, Dorceta. 2009. *The Environment and the People in American Cities, 1600s-1900s: Disorder, Inequality, and Social Change*. Duke University Press.

Thomas, William Isaac and D. S. Thomas. 1928. *The Child in America: Behavior Problems and Programs*. Knopf.

Tometi, Opal. 2015. Interview on Democracy Now! July 24.

Torres, Bob. 2007. *Making a Killing: The Political Economy of Animal Rights*. AK Press.

Travis, Jeremy, Bruce Western, and Steve Redburn (eds.). 2014. *The Growth of Incarceration in the United States: Exploring Causes and Consequences*. The National Academies Press.

Tsolkas, Panagioti. 2015. "Mass Incarceration vs. Rural Appalachia." *Earth Island Journal*. August 24. http://www.earthisland.org/journal/index.php/elist/eListRead/mass_incarceration_vs._rural_appalachia/, accessed July 1, 2016.

Tsolkas, Panagioti. 2016. "Incarceration, Justice, and the Planet: How the Fight Against Toxic Prisons May Shape the Future of Environmentalism." *Prison Legal News* 27(6): 1–14.

Twine, Richard, 2012. "Revealing the 'Animal-Industrial Complex' – A Concept and Method for Critical Animal Studies?" *Journal for Critical Animal Studies* 10(1): 12–39.

United Church of Christ. 1987. *Toxic Wastes and Race in the United States*. UCC Commission for Racial Justice.

United Church of Christ. 2007. *Toxic Wastes and Race Revisited*. Commission for Racial Justice.

United Nations. 2012. *Gaza in 2020: A Livable Place?* August. United Nations Country Team in the Occupied Palestinian Territory. August.

United Nations Security Council. 2015. "Letter dated 21 August 2015 from the Panel of Experts on South Sudan established pursuant to Security Council resolution 2206 (2015) addressed to the President of the Security Council." p. 21.

United States Environmental Protection Agency, Region III Office. 2000. "Graterford State Prison Cited for Alleged Violations of Environmental Laws—EPA Launches Compliance Improvement at All Prisons throughout Mid-Atlantic Region." News Release. Philadelphia. October 19. https://yosemite.epa.gov/r3/press.nsf/7f3f954af9cce39b882563fd0063a09c/2901aa875415d8b185256983004e37b5?OpenDocument, accessed June 25, 2016.

United States Environmental Protection Agency, Region III Office. 2003. "Maryland to Improve Environmental Management at 34 Prisons as Part of Jessup Prison Settlement—EPA Also Cites Mt. Olive Prison in West Virginia As Part of Ongoing Compliance Initiative." News Release. Philadelphia. June 10.

Bibliography

United States Environmental Protection Agency, Region III Office. 2007. "Federal Prisons to Get Environmental Checks." News Release. Philadelphia. July 25.

United States General Accounting Office (GAO). (1983) *Siting Hazardous Waste Landfills and Their Correlation with Racial and Economic Status of Surrounding Communities*. Washington, D.C.

United States Environmental Protection Agency, Region III Office. 2011. "EPA Settlement Will Reduce Air Pollution from Four Pennsylvania Prisons." News Release. Philadelphia. January 4.

United States Sentencing Commission. 2007. *Report to Congress: Cocaine and Federal Sentencing Policy*. May.

Upadhya, Vivek. 2014. "The Abuse of Animals as a Method of Domestic Violence." *Emory Law Journal* 63: 1163–1209.

Urbina, Ian. 2013. "Blacks Are Singled Out for Marijuana Arrests, Federal Data Suggests." *New York Times*. June 3.

Valentine, Katie. 2014. "Why Supporting the Fight Against Racist Police Killings Could Mean a New Chapter In Environmentalism Climate Progress." December 19. www.thinkprogress.org.

Vargas, Joao H. Costa. 2010. *Never Meant to Survive: Genocide and Utopias in Black Diaspora Communities*. Rowman & Littlefield.

Vera III, Frank. 2016. "Re: George AFB's Atmospheric Nuclear Weapons Testing Radiological Decontamination Centers." Letter addressed to Mary Aycock, EPA Site Manager for George Air Force Base. February 28.

Voyles, Traci Brynne. 2015. *Wastelanding: Legacies of Uranium Mining in Navajo Country*. University of Minnesota Press.

Walker, Gordon. 2009. "Globalizing Environmental Justice: The Geography and Politics of Frame Contextualization and Evolution." *Global Social Policy* 9(3): 355–392.

Walker, Gordon. 2010. "Beyond Distribution and Proximity: Exploring the Multiple Spatialities of Environmental Justice." In Ryan Holifield, Michael Porter, and Gordon Walker (eds.), *Spaces of Environmental Justice*. Wiley-Blackwell.

Walker, Gordon. 2012. *Environmental Justice: Concepts, Evidence, and Politics*. Routledge.

Walmsley, Roy. 2015. *World Prison Population List*. Institute for Criminal Policy Research, eleventh edition.

Warren, Karen J. 1994. "Introduction." In Karen J. Warren (ed.), *Ecological Feminism*. Routledge.

Warren, Karen J. 1997. "Taking Empirical Data Seriously: An Ecofeminist Philosophical Perspective." In Karen J. Warren (ed.), *Ecofeminism: Women, Culture, Nature*. Indiana University Press.

Washington, Sylvia Hood. 2003. *Packing Them In: An Archeology of Environmental Racism in Chicago, 1865–1954*. Lexington Books

Bibliography

Weber, Max, David S. Owen, Tracy B. Strong, and Rodney Livingstone. 2004. *The Vocation Lectures: Science as a Vocation, Politics as a Vocation.* Hackett.

Wegman, Jesse. 2014. "The Injustice of Marijuana Arrests." *New York Times.* July 28.

Weitz, Yosef. 1940. *Diary,* A246/7. Central Zionist Archives.

Welsome, Eileen. 2010. *The Plutonium Files: America's Secret Medical Experiments in the Cold War.* Random House.

Western, Bruce. 2007. *Punishment and Inequality in America.* Russell Sage Foundation.

White, Richard. 1993. *"It's Your Misfortune and None of My Own": A New History of the American West.* University of Oklahoma Press.

White, Rob. 2008. *Crimes against Nature: Environmental Criminology and Ecological Justice.* Willan.

Whitehorn, Laura (with Marilyn Buck). 2005 [2001]. "Cruel But Not Unusual: The Punishment of Women in U.S. Prisons." Pp. 259–273 in Joy James (ed.), *The New Abolitionists: (Neo) Slave Narratives and Contemporary Writings.* SUNY Press.

Williams, David R. and Chiquita Collins. 1995. "U.S. Socioeconomic and Racial Differences in Health: Patterns and Explanations." *Annual Review of Sociology* 21: 349–386.

Williams, David R. and Chiquita Collins. 2001. "Racial Residential Segregation: A Fundamental Cause of Racial Disparities in Health." *Public Health Reports* 16: 404–416.

Williams, Kale. 2015. "SFPD Probes Racist, Homophobic Texts among Officers." *SF Gate.* March 16.

Williams, Kristian. 2015. *Our Enemies in Blue: Police and Power in America.* AK Press.

Williams, Patricia. 1992. *Alchemy of Race and Rights.* Harvard University Press.

Wilson, James Q. and George L. Kelling. 1982. "Broken Windows: The Police and Neighborhood Safety." *Atlantic Monthly,* March: 29–38.

Wilson, Sacoby. 2016. "Environmental Justice and Health Disparities: Passion, Partnerships, and Progress." Presentation at University of California, Santa Barbara. May 24.

Wing, Adrien Katherine (ed.). 2003 *Critical Race Feminism: A Reader.* New York University Press, second edition.

Women Against Imperialism. 1982. "Feminism, Anti-Semitism, and Racism . . . Taking Our Stand against Zionism and White Supremacy." *Off Our Backs* 12(7): 20.

World Bank. 1993. *Developing the Occupied Territories: An Investment in Peace.* Volume 5. Infrastructure. Washington, D.C.: World Bank.

Wright, Beverly and Robert Bullard. 1993. "The effects of occupational injury, illness, and disease on the health status of Black Americans: A Review."

Bibliography

In Hofrichter, Richard (ed.), *Toxic Struggles: The Theory and Practice of Environmental Justice*. New Society Publishers.

Wright, Paul. 2015a. Letter to the Bureau of Prisons regarding Proposed USP/ FPC Letcher County Draft Environmental Impact Statement. Human Rights Defense Center. March 30.

Wright, Paul. 2015b. "Comment on the Inclusion of Prisoner Populations in EPA's Draft Framework for EJ 2020 Action Agenda." Letter addressed to Charles Lee, Deputy Associate Assistant Administrator for Environmental Justice, USEPA Office on Environmental Justice. Human Rights Defense Center. July 14.

Wright, Paul. 2016. "From the Editor." *Prison Legal News*. June 3, p. 16.

Yang, Tseming. 2002. "International Environmental Protection: Human Rights and the North-South Divide." Chapter 4 in Kathryn Mutz, Gary Bryner, and Douglas Kenney (eds.), *Justice and Natural Resources: Concepts, Strategies, and Applications*. Island Press.

Young, Iris Marion. 2001. "Activist Challenges to Deliberative Democracy." *Political Theory* 29(5): 670–690.

Yusoff, Kathryn. 2013. "Geologic Life: Prehistory, Climate, Futures in the Anthropocene." *Environment and Planning D* 31(5): 779–795.

Yuval-Davis, Nira. 1985. "Front and Rear: The Sexual Division of Labor in the Israeli Army." *Feminist Studies* 11: 649–676.

Index

Index

Index

Index

Index

Index

Index

Index